Editing
Your Newsletter

How to Produce an Effective Publication
Using Traditional Tools and Computers

Third edition

Mark Beach

Published by
Coast to Coast Books
1115 SE Stephens St.
Portland OR 97214

Distributed to the trade by
Writer's Digest/Northlight Books
1507 Dana Avenue
Cincinnati OH 45207

Library of Congress Cataloging-in-Publication Data

Beach, Mark, 1937—
Editing your newsletter

Bibliography: p. 154
Includes index.
1. Newsletters.   I. Title   II. Title: Editing your newsletter.
PN4784.N5B4   1988   070.1'72   87-25587
ISBN 0-943381-01-0 (pbk.)

Printed and bound in USA

Author

Mark Beach's previous books in the graphic arts include the nationally-acclaimed guide *Getting It Printed*. He has edited four newsletters and, through his workshops and consulting, helped develop hundreds of others. Mark holds a Ph.D. from the University of Wisconsin.

Editors

Susan Applegate, Tricia Knoll, Susan Page York, Polly Pattison, and Mary Pretzer studied early drafts of manuscript. Their comments and suggestions made this book much more useful than it otherwise might have been.

Tricia Knoll did most of the research and first draft for Chapter 12.

Susan Page York edited the text for structure and style. Her precise thinking and skill at organizing improved the manuscript at every stage of its development.

Designers

Kathleen Ryan produced most of the visuals and, using typography and page format developed by John Laursen, laid out this book. Other visuals were made by Susan Applegate and Polly Pattison. Lis DeMarco drew the mice.

Producers

Editing Your Newsletter was first published in 1980 and revised in 1982. This third edition was produced during 1987.

Mark Beach wrote and edited, and entered typesetting commands using a Xerox 820 II and Wordstar 2.2. Patti Morris proofread initial output. Martin White set ITC Garamond using a Mergenthaler V-I-P.

This book was printed at Graphic Arts Center in Portland OR USA.

Publisher

Coast to Coast Books is a publishing company specializing in books about the graphic arts and communication. Liz Wollman and Warren Sendek helped keep the company running smoothly while *Editing Your Newsletter* was produced.

Contents

Introduction

This book helps anyone who plans, produces, or pays for a newsletter. It makes your publication more effective and your work more efficient and satisfying.

If your newsletter is new, this manual gives it a good start. If it's already launched, this guide helps it reach full potential.

The ability to produce a successful newsletter on schedule and within budget is a skill whose value grows each day. There are more newsletters than ever and they are more important as couriers of specialized information.

Effective newsletters have clear objectives. This guide explains how to establish objectives and use them to select content, graphics, and design. It describes how objectives determine method of printing and distribution and relate to criteria for evaluation.

To take best advantage of this book, you should know how to type. I assume that you will use a standard keyboard at least for writing and editing.

You can produce a first-rate newsletter using either a typewriter or a computer. Computers make the task easier, but the outcome not necessarily better. A computer is a valuable tool, but not a savior.

Computers don't set standards. Software gives access to many typefaces, but no guidance about which to use. It lets you create many layouts, but doesn't tell which works best for your audience.

This book gives criteria for every decision you must make about your newsletter. You can use the criteria as formulas or guidelines, depending on how much experience you have and how creative you want to be.

Whether you edit as an employee or volunteer, you will find techniques and examples in this book to help you. They come from publications in business, education, religion, government, associations, and health, and from commercial newsletters.

The illustration on the opposite page shows standard terms for elements of a newsletter. Definitions for these and other terms are in the glossary, which draws from the fields of journalism, electronics, and the graphic arts, including photography.

The first newsletter in North America began in 1704. The *Boston News Letter* reported ship arrivals and other commercial information that people no longer learned efficiently by word of mouth. Editor John Campbell wrote articles, selected illustrations, composed type, supervised printing, and kept track of addresses. Versatility paid.

Versatility still pays. This guide describes the many skills you need to produce a newsletter that achieves all its objectives.

I hope you enjoy this book and find it useful. If you think there are ways to improve it, please write me a letter to the address of the publisher.

Mark Beach
October 1987

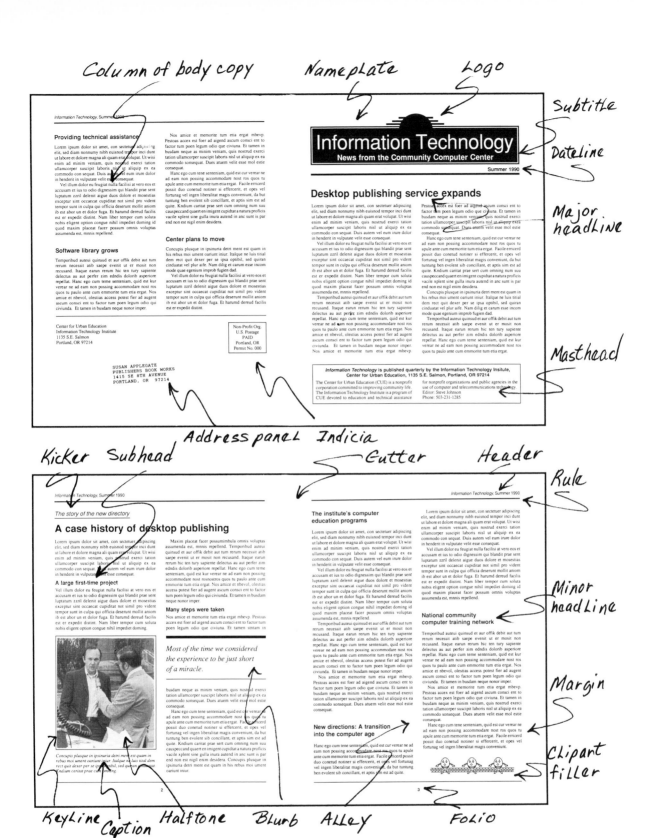

Column of body copy Nameplate Logo Subtitle Dateline Major headline Masthead

Kicker Subhead Address panel Indicia Gutter Header Rule Minor headline Margin Clipart filler

Keyline Caption Halftone Blurb Alley Folio

Elements of a newsletter. Control over cost, quality, and schedule requires clear communication among everyone responsible for the production process. Precise language for newsletter elements reduces mistakes caused by confusion. This book uses the basic terms shown above with their meanings illustrated. These meanings are standard among graphic arts professionals.

1 Planning

Newsletters give specialized information to limited audiences on a regular basis. Most are four or eight pages long with a page size the same as business stationery. They have short articles written in an informal style.

Your most important need is to know what results management and readers want from your publication. Goals, objectives, and audience directly reflect desired results. They also shape decisions about content, design, printing and distribution.

The results expected from your newsletter are its objectives. They should be defined in terms that are specific, measurable benefits to your organization.

In this chapter, you learn when a newsletter can be most effective and how to define the major purpose your publication must serve. You learn how to set goals, establish objectives, and identify your audience. You discover how to decide about quality, length, frequency, timing, schedule, quantity, and budget. The chapter ends with a discussion of newsletter names and subtitles that includes sources for ideas and standards to use when deciding.

The schedule that is Visual 1-2 helps you specify the time required for each step needed to produce your publication. Although you may not feel ready to fill the schedule out now, reading the list of tasks may help you spot problems that need particular attention.

Decisions about newsletters involve both business and technical information. This chapter is about business considerations needed as a

Choosing a newsletter

Deciding the purpose

Defining goals

Establishing objectives

Identifying audience

Determining quality

Making final decisions

Developing a budget

Selecting a name

basis for technical judgments about type, graphics, and printing dealt with in later chapters.

Choosing a newsletter

People often decide to publish a newsletter because it's relatively easy and inexpensive. They believe a newsletter will help solve a problem or achieve results simply by "improving communication." Yet cable television, posters, meetings, computer bulletin boards, and many other media can accomplish some of the same results as newsletters.

Choosing the best medium for a specific situation requires careful thought. A newsletter can work well for your organization under certain conditions. Effective newsletters meet the following guidelines.

Print is sufficient. Print works best when information must be portable, available at the convenience of the audience, and inexpensive. Media such as slides, video, and meetings work better than print in situations needing oral as well as visual presentation and constant interaction with the audience.

Homogeneous audience. Newsletters work best when published for people with an obvious common interest. And they are easy to write. Often it's readers themselves who say what they want to read about.

Homogeneous content. When content stays within a narrow field of interest, a newsletter does its job. *Pony Express News* shouldn't deal with both Arabians and Percherons; people interested in those breeds should each have their own newsletter.

Valuable information. An effective newsletter gives readers information they can use. It doesn't try to compete with books, movies, or TV as entertainment.

The most successful newsletters blend the self-interest of reader and sponsor. Both perceive the publication as a service.

Trustworthy. Readers like inside information and trust a newsletter because it resembles a personal letter. Content is reliable and not influenced by outside pressures.

Paid advertising has no place in a newsletter unless readers (not advertisers) perceive the ads as part of the service the publication offers. Readers sometimes feel suspicious of editorial content when there are also paid ads.

Personal. Readers know the editor's name, think of the editor as an individual writing a letter, and can reach the editor easily by phone or mail.

Short. News can be absorbed in a few moments. Sentences, paragraphs, articles, and the newsletter itself are all brief compared to other publications.

Timely. Content relates to the recent past, present, or near future. Issues are published often enough to keep each one current.

Deciding the purpose

Key people in your organization should establish the purpose of your newsletter. You should be part of the process of deciding. The purpose will probably be one of the following.

Marketing. Newsletters intended to sell ideas, products, or services are for marketing. They focus on actions you wish readers to take and include publications intended to raise money, increase membership, influence votes, or promote greater use of facilities.

A marketing newsletter emphasizes benefits. Readers can recognize their self-interest in accepting the point of view presented by the publication. For example, the newsletter for an accounting firm might help readers understand benefits from keeping more complete financial records.

Public relations. Newsletters for public relations focus on attitudes instead of actions. Successful public relations efforts make readers more receptive to marketing or to the mission of an organization.

"I expect our newsletter to be useful while also projecting our good side. As a regulatory agency, we often have a negative image. Carriers think of us as a tax collector and law enforcer. Sure we do those things, but we also work for good roads and ways to move goods efficiently by truck. We save carriers time and money by writing about construction, weather, and special event traffic. And we get the word out quickly. What we write on Tuesday afternoon gets coffee stains in the cafes on Thursday morning."

A public relations newsletter helps people know more and feel better about its sponsoring organization, a difficult task to accomplish and evaluate. It's hard to make readers see how they benefit from the publication or to make them feel like insiders.

Public relations newsletters must be produced to the highest standards. Furthermore, the enthusiasm that PR editors feel for their causes must help, not prevent, analyzing objectives and audiences. Don't let zeal blind you to content that is self-serving or pointless. Keep your red pencil sharp and use it ruthlessly.

The best public relations newsletters capture the attention of readers who may otherwise lack interest in the topics reported. They build respect for content, support for causes, and good will for sponsors.

Internal relations. Publications for employees or members are for internal relations. They give information about people, places, and ideas that may already be familiar, and about coming events. Their goals may include honoring outstanding performance, building morale, and stimulating attention to quality.

Readers of internal relations newsletters have varying degrees of affinity with sponsoring organizations and each other. The newsletter for a local trade association may only summarize news most readers already know by word-of-mouth, while a publication for employees of a large hospital may be the primary source of information linking readers.

Too often internal relations newsletters promote the viewpoints of management in a condescending "top-down" style. Readers feel they are not getting complete, honest, useful information. Newsletters that lecture to readers merely fill wastebaskets.

The best internal newsletters help shape organizational vision and promote the feeling that "we are all in this together." They establish direction, present agenda, build morale, inspire loyalty, and stimulate quality.

Profit. Commercial newsletters exist to make money for their publishers and editors, often the same person.

Newsletters for profit usually reach individuals through the mail. Subscribers pay anywhere from $25 to $500 per year, with a median

Goals

advise	honor	praise
advocate	illustrate	predict
analyze	impress	prepare
announce	improve	prevent
assure	influence	raise funds
clarify	inform	recruit
condense	inspire	report
define	interpret	simplify
describe	justify	solicit
digest	lead	stimulate
evaluate	motivate	suggest
explain	notify	support
guide	persuade	teach
help	portray	train

1-1 Goals. Use any of the verbs above in a sentence about goals or objectives. If you have a thesaurus on your desk or in your computer software, look up some of the above words to find alternatives that will help you write more precise statements.

price of about $100. Readers expect information to justify the relatively high cost.

Another kind of newsletter for profit goes to organizations that redistribute them to employees or clients. When buyers redistribute, they usually imprint their name on the newsletter, making it appear like their own product. Publications from professional services such as insurance agents, realtors, and medical clinics often fall into this category.

Most commercial newsletters promise to make readers richer, smarter, or healthier. To succeed, they must give information and insight that readers trust, cannot easily find elsewhere, and can absorb quickly.

Publishing a newsletter as a business requires relatively little capital, but lots of time; success requires skills in marketing, management, reporting, and production—and lots of self-discipline. A few thousand individual subscribers or a handful of bulk subscribers can yield a comfortable income.

If you are thinking about starting a commercial newsletter, read the books by Howard Penn Hudson and Frederick Goss listed in Appendix B. Also, seek advice from the publisher of a commercial newsletter that has been published continuously for more than three years. Write to the Newsletter Clearinghouse or Newsletter Association (addresses in Appendix B) to learn about a publisher in your area. If the local publisher charges a consulting fee, pay it. The small investment may save you thousands.

Defining goals

Although your sponsor or supervisor may be clear about the purpose of your publication, you may feel uncertain about how to accomplish it. Begin by establishing goals.

Goals are guides to content, design, and budget. They suggest what stories to write and photos to use, and how well your publication should be designed and printed.

To define goals, choose three or four words from the list in Visual 1-1. Write them in sentences that relate to your audience. Reviewing the sentences with your supervisor or leadership can lead to a statement of goals.

Here are some examples of goal statements that are useful because they are specific.

- persuade current members to contribute money and time and to recruit new members;
- impress elected officials at the local and state levels with how serious we are about delivering or withholding votes;
- interpret our views about residential property taxes to business leaders statewide;
- explain to employees our plans, policies, and progress;
- inspire a feeling of fellowship and cooperation among our volunteers.

A complete statement of goals might include four or five phrases such as those above. Wanting to accomplish more than four or five is a signal to consider more than one newsletter or other media.

Establishing objectives

The objectives of your newsletter are the results it should yield for your organization. Goals point the direction of travel; objectives describe the destination. Well-stated objectives tell why your newsletter is worth the time and money needed to produce it.

Useful objectives describe benefits. They tell how those who produce the newsletter and those who read it will be better off. They leave no doubt about the value you intend it to have.

Objectives should include criteria for evaluation that tell how readers would behave if an objective is achieved. Here are some examples.

- *Tricky Times* should explain to our members our stand on key issues **so we spend less time at meetings interpreting decisions already made.**
- *Tricky Times* should explain emergency preparations so well **that employees no longer report feeling unsafe or unaware of what to do.**
- *Tricky Times* should stimulate enough interest in our services **that at least five new clients visit our drop-in center each week.**

The ideal objective describes a result that can be measured. For instance, it tells how many dollars will be saved or the date on which a project will be finished.

An objective without a measurable result should be specific enough for people to agree about its outcome. Writing such an objective may require several revisions. Following is an example.

Goal	*Contribute to success of capital campaign.*
Objective	*Help people who are soliciting contributions be more effective.*
Better objective	*Help volunteers get larger contributions with less time spent achieving each.*

"We use lots of ways to measure success for **Medical Rounds.** *We look for new copies on desks at the capitol, not in waste baskets. Newspapers base editorials and features on our stories. Hospital publications run our statistics or entire articles. Journalists call us for the latest information on medical topics. And, of course, we make a good profit. We'll publish as long as we do our job well and keep on having fun. When we stop meeting our goals, we'll die."*

Specific objectives help reveal whether or not a goal is attainable. They make you ask if a newsletter is a practical way to accomplish **this** goal with **this** audience.

Identifying audience

The readership for most newsletters seems obvious: all employees or members; everyone who subscribes; retailers in the region. What seems obvious, however, may not be correct.

Most audiences are more complex than they appear at first glance. You may have only one marketing department, but that doesn't mean you have only one market. All employees may have the same company address on their paychecks, but the interests of management and labor, day shift and night shift, clerical and maintenance, are very different.

Newsletters typically start with one or two audiences in mind; others are added as production becomes routine. Usually no one asks if the newsletter is a practical way to accomplish the old objectives with the new audience.

You may think that success with one audience means equal interest from others. This belief is strongest with messages that seem especially important. A publication for volunteers might not, however, interest paid staff, legislators, potential donors, and colleagues at other locations.

To help ensure success, divide your audience into categories having the fewest possible readers. Ask yourself what is the best way to accomplish your objectives with each category. Perhaps people in some groups would prefer learning news via a telephone tree or at a luncheon meeting. Maybe VIPs should get personal letters, a simple task using a computer.

Strong newsletters specialize. If you have more than one or two audiences, consider more than one newsletter. You can use some of the same articles and photos for the different publications and make them similar in design. As an alternative, produce special inserts for specific portions of the audience.

Your readership should be so clearly defined that it can be described in one sentence. That sentence might include some of the words in the list that follows.

- current or prospective members, employees, residents, buyers, voters, clients;
- managers, directors, stockholders, department heads;
- leaders in community, industry, associations, religion, education, government;
- reporters for radio, TV, newspapers, magazines, and other newsletters;
- product dealers or distributors.

Newsletters that best accomplish their goals have both audience and content highly targeted. Other audiences and content outside the field may be dealt with in another way.

If information about your readership, either actual or potential, is on a computer database, use the database software to help analyze your audience. Depending on data available for each person, you might learn that certain groups are larger than you thought—or smaller. You might discover how many readers live nearby, are married, or have incomes over a certain level.

Determining quality

How your newsletter looks and reads affects how well it accomplishes its objectives.

Readers notice tangible traits such as paper and printing and intangible features such as design and writing. The intangible aspects matter more than the tangible ones. Fancy paper or color printing cannot make up for dull writing, careless editing, or poor design.

Money helps buy quality, but budget isn't the only factor. Time and skill make a big difference. Design of the nameplate alone heavily influences perception of quality.

Quality reflects personality. Your publication may seem neighborly, concerned, or authoritative. You may want readers to view you as an objective observer or as an enthusiastic insider. Your writing can be intimate or detached.

"Newsletters are perfect for organizations like ours based on networks instead of hierarchies. They're fast, flexible, inexpensive, and easy to fill with good ideas. They're informal, so help make the relaxed atmosphere we need to work. People who feel happy and creative are the only competitive edge we have."

Production schedule

Weeks	First	Second	Third	Fourth	Fifth	Sixth
Plan content						
Get information						
Choose photos/art						
Make dummy						
Write headlines						
Write articles/captions						
Check for bias						
Copyedit						
Proofread						
Copy approval						
Output type						
Proofread type						
Correct type						
Make layout						
Crop/scale photos/art						
Prepare mechanicals						
Proofread mechanicals						
Correct mechanicals						
Photocopy mechanicals						
Take to printer						
Camera work/stripping						
Proofread bluelines						
Correct negatives						
Platemaking						
Printing						
Trimming/folding						
Prepare addresses						
Take to lettershop						
Addressing						
Bundling/sacking						
Take to post office						
Delivery						

1-2 Newsletter production schedule. Because there are so many ways to handle the various stages of newsletter production, there is no correct or typical schedule. The grid above allows you to enter the day on which each activity might take place in your situation, thus to predict when readers will receive your publication. Notice that weeks are divided into seven days, not five, to allow for schedules that include weekends. A clear schedule that everyone can depend on eliminates many excuses for missing deadlines. A schedule also helps you forecast needs for money, supplies, computer time, and other resources that ensure a smooth flow of work.

The way you want readers to perceive your organization should affect quality. Filling each issue with professional photos may suit the marketing department of a bank, but would seem excessive from a neighborhood volunteer agency.

Quality in a newsletter means that objectives and audiences are defined so clearly that every issue can have a sense of clarity and attention to detail.

Decisions about quality should take into account appropriateness and consistency. Appropriateness means doing what feels comfortable for your sponsoring organization; consistency means keeping every element and every issue at the same level of quality.

Each newsletter has its own appropriate quality level. Type, photos, paper, printing, and other components should all be consistent with that level. Components below the average quality level drag down the others; components above average don't look as good as they should, thus are a waste of time and money.

Consider a newsletter for an agency that includes maps drawn by professionals. Printing those maps poorly or too small or on inferior paper would be false economy.

Making final decisions

There are several administrative decisions to make in consultation with your supervisor and perhaps colleagues.

Length. The most common lengths for newsletters are two pages (1 sheet 8½ x 11), four pages (1 sheet 11 x 17), and eight pages (2 sheets 11 x 17). These lengths and sizes are most common because they can be produced quickly at low cost and comply easily with postal regulations.

"When my board said to assume that my newsletter budget was cut to zero, I felt angry. Readers have depended on Topics *for nine years. But when the editor and I met with the publications committee, we wrote a list of objectives that fit so well into our strategic plan that we got a 15% increase for next year. And those same objectives help us produce each issue more quickly because we know our priorities."*

Readers tend to finish a newsletter in four or five minutes. If your newsletter is longer than eight pages, it's probably too long to hold readers' attention. Publish more frequently, cut some content, or use a more efficient format.

Frequency. Publish often enough to report information while it is news. In most cases, four times a year is the minimum. Quarterly is OK for a school district report to taxpayers, but monthly is better for a school report to parents.

As a general rule, a shorter newsletter arriving more frequently works better than a longer publication arriving less often. Increasing the number of issues means higher distribution costs and more deadlines, although meeting each deadline requires less time writing and producing.

Timing. How well your newsletter meets its objectives is influenced by when readers receive each issue. Readers should have copies at least a week before the first date on the calendar of coming events.

Timing determines deadlines. Working backward from when you know copies must reach readers allows you to set a schedule. When setting the schedule, consider distribution speed. The production sequence ends when readers have newsletters in their hands, not when copies leave your hands.

Schedule. How long it takes to produce your newsletter depends on how quickly you write, how much help you get, and dozens of other factors. After the first few issues the production sequence for one issue should be routine. Something may go wrong at any point, but it shouldn't disrupt the overall schedule.

Visual 1-2 lists typical production tasks. Few newsletters require them all, but every publication requires some. Filling in the cells opposite the tasks needed for your newsletter shows how long an average issue will take from concept to delivery.

Quantity. It may seem obvious that you need just enough copies to reach everyone in your audience, but factors other than number of readers determine how many copies you have printed. For example, if readership grows, new people may want back issues.

Printing 10% or 15% more copies than are needed adds very little to overall production

Newsletter production costs

Fixed costs: 1 Gather information, 2 Administration/overhead, 3 Write/edit/proofread, 4 Make/select photos/drawings, 5 Type/layout/camera-ready. **Variable costs:** 6 Paper, 7 Print/fold, 8 Address/postage.

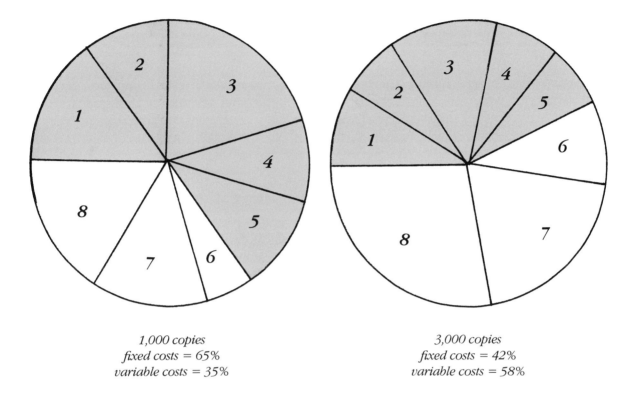

1,000 copies
fixed costs = 65%
variable costs = 35%

3,000 copies
fixed costs = 42%
variable costs = 58%

1-3 Newsletter production costs. The ratio between fixed and variable costs depends on the number of copies needed. The charts above show that variable costs become a larger percentage of the budget as production runs increase. The percentages in these charts apply to newsletters whose production has become routine, not to publications during their startup phase when fixed costs are relatively high.

When you print few copies, pay most attention to fixed costs. As quantities increase, shift your attention to variable costs.

costs, but can lead to wasted money elsewhere. Those extra copies may be going to people who should get a separate newsletter, be reached via another medium, or be dropped from your address list.

Distribution. If all your readers are under one roof, you can leave newsletters in the lunchroom or use an internal mail system. Perhaps you can send them with paychecks. The chances are, however, that you will use an outside delivery system such as the U.S. mails.

Chapter 12 gives detailed information about the USPS and other delivery options.

Developing a budget

During early planning, you can only estimate how much your newsletter will cost. Base your guess on initial answers to questions in this chapter plus projections of costs for printing and distribution.

Your best guess about cost during the first year is probably between 50% and 100% too low. It's easy to underestimate development cost, especially the cost of planning a proper launch. Remember to include the value of your time and that of others who attend meetings, evaluate designs, and discuss names as well as the extra time required for production as you learn what works.

Experienced editors keep budgets in perspective by distinguishing between fixed and variable costs. Fixed costs stay the same whether you print one copy or one million. They include writing, design, and layout. Variable costs depend on quantity. They include what you pay for paper, printing, and distribution.

If you are an employee, the largest fixed cost of your newsletter is the value of your time. Newsletters are labor intensive, but people often ignore that fact when planning budgets.

Money required for a good start is easiest to deal with if you think in terms of unit cost for two or three years. For instance, paying a graphic designer $1,000 for a nameplate to print on 250 copies of a quarterly newsletter may be extravagant. The same $1000 spent for a monthly

with a print run of 2,000 may be a bargain.

Another way to approach budget planning is to estimate how much it would be worth to achieve your goals. A publication that builds customer loyalty to cars that cost $50,000 is worth far more than one that solicits $50 donations to a local political campaign.

Translating goals into objectives helps define the value of your publication. Even if your newsletter does not lead directly to financial profit, its objectives have at least some relationship to money such as helping workers be more efficient. Precise objectives help make the relationship clear.

Selecting a name

An effective newsletter name sounds accurate and lively. Accuracy means the name tells readers what to expect. Lively titles attract attention and are remembered.

Good names build on content or publisher. *Metal Collecting*, *Venture Capital*, and *Hospital Purchasing* convey content; *Hilltop School Bulletin*, *Franklin Real Estate Review*, and *St. Mary's Report* reveal the publisher.

Efforts to be lively sometimes result in titles that are too cute. Solid, serviceable names often sound flat, but ones that strain to be vivid may diminish your editorial efforts, especially in the eyes of external audiences.

Publishers for internal audiences sometimes find one of those perfect names such as *The Log* (California Carvers' Guild), or *The Merry-Go-Round* (National Carousel Association). Subscription and marketing newsletters often build on the name of their publisher, such as *Ruff Times* (financial analysis from Howard Ruff) and *Publishing Poynters* (news about book publishing from Dan Poynter). Titles can play on jargon, such as *Thruput* for computer programmers. Even initials can sometimes fit into a title, such as *ARTAFacts* from American Retail Travel Agents.

Visual 1-4 can help you compose a good name. For more ideas, browse through one of the directories listed in Appendix B. Each lists thousands of publications. Most public libraries have at least one of the directories.

Some newsletters have names that tell

Key words in names

accents	guide	post
advisory	highlights	profile
advocate	horizons	report
alert	hotline	reporter
almanac	ink	resources
briefs	insider	review
briefing	interchange	scene
bulletin	intercom	scope
channel	journal	spotlight
connection	keynote	survey
context	letter	tab
digest	light	times
dimensions	line	topics
eye	link	trends
examiner	list	update
facts	log	viewpoint
file	monthly	views
focus	news	voice
forecast	notes	weekly
forum	outlook	wire
gram	perspective	world

1-4 Key words in names. Newsletter names often build on communication terms such as those above. Use this list to suggest possible names for your own publication.

The Clean Yield
Principles and profits working together

Retail Vacancy Reporter
Monthly information about store, strip, and surplus property.

Customers
Up-to-the-minute ideas on how managers achieve excellence in customer service / relations.

Your Window Into the Future
Advance notice of profitable moves in silver, gold, goldshares, and inflation

Ways and Means
Reporting on innovative approaches to state and local government

Que Pasa
What's happening around Mission Viejo community

The DMSO Report
Accurate and timely information about dimethyl sulfoxide for general and professional readers

Whirlpools
Pooled information for the Winding Rivers Library System

The Addiction Letter
A resource exchange for professionals on preventing and treating alcoholism and drug abuse

Energy News
A pipeline and gas utilities bi-weekly, edited for management, users and producers, and reporting on supplies, prices, regulations and construction in the natural gas industry

The Huenefeld Report
For managers and planners in modest-sized book publishing houses

1-5 Newsletter subtitles. A carefully worded subtitle tells readers that you have their interests in mind and helps keep your audience limited to people who really want your publication. The subtitles above show what editors in a variety of fields have written.

enough. Many newsletters, however, especially those for external audiences, need a subtitle as well as a name. A subtitle makes your purposes and readership more clear. Its wording should receive as much attention as the name of the newsletter itself.

Subtitles tell who your readers are, both actual and intended. With external and potential audiences, they should shout "I mean you!" and may spell the difference between being read or ignored. Subtitles also help editors keep tightly focused, resisting the impulse to serve too many audiences with the same publication. Visual 1-5 shows good combinations of names and subtitles.

The name of the publisher may actually be used as the subtitle. If you produce *The Edison Record*, whose nameplate says it's a quarterly report from The National Society for the Preservation of the Gramophone, you've said enough.
□

2 Editors

Most newsletters are produced by employees as part of their jobs. Whether you are an employee or a volunteer, and whether you carry out every aspect of the production sequence or only parts of it, you must work with other people. Supervisors, leaders, colleagues, vendors, and readers all have expectations and can offer help. You can't do your job without them.

Good communication among people who work together is the most important factor in controlling costs, schedule, and quality. Chapter 1 explained how to develop clear goals and objectives; this chapter describes how to deal with management, colleagues, and suppliers.

Your most important relationship is with the person or group who represents your sponsoring organization. If you are an employee, your publisher is probably your supervisor. This relationship can be awkward, especially when the supervisor has unrealistic goals or knows little about producing a newsletter.

Much of this chapter is about how you and your publisher work together, and the rewards, training, and help you deserve. It outlines the routine tasks most editors carry out and includes a form, the Editor's Job Organizer, to help you decide which tasks to do yourself and which to delegate.

This chapter includes a list of suggestions for supervisors who want to ensure good working relationships with editors. The list gives recommendations in a form that could quickly be read by your supervisor as a basis for discussion with you.

Working with your publisher

Tasks

Time

Training

Rewards

Computers

Helping services

Freelancing

The following pages include a section about computers, raising the question of whether you need desktop publishing software. The answer is "probably yes" if you regularly produce several newsletters or other publications such as reports, books, and magazines. The answer is "definitely no" if most of your keyboard work is word processing and the newsletter is your only publication. In that case, production will go faster and cost less using traditional methods.

This chapter explains how to work with graphic designers and newsletter services, how to evaluate workshops and training programs, and how to operate if you produce newsletters as a freelancer.

Working with your publisher

A newsletter is produced to benefit its publisher, the sponsor that pays for it. The publisher may be an individual or an organization such as a business, agency, club, association, or school.

Publishers have a purpose in mind and expect editors to accomplish it. To define your job clearly, you must understand that purpose; to do your job well, you must agree with it.

Some person with whom you have frequent contact should represent your publisher to you. That person might be your supervisor or an officer of your organization. As an alternative, your publisher might be represented by a small committee.

The person speaking for your publisher is both supervisor and advocate. As supervisor, the person should interpret goals, help define objectives and audiences, and evaluate your work. As advocate, the person should try to get the time, money, training, and help you need to produce an effective newsletter.

Your management needs to understand newsletters. You can help build that insight by asking good questions and presenting thoughtful options. It also helps to show your supervisor successful newsletters from other organizations similar to yours.

If you don't have a person or committee acting as publisher, ask that one be designated. If you do, try to make sure they carry out the responsibilities described in this chapter.

Even with one person as supervisor, I suggest asking for a newsletter committee of two or three others. Meeting informally with them every few months can build support for the newsletter job, which is often poorly understood. Members may suggest ideas and sources of help which might not occur to you on your own. This is especially important if you are new to your organization.

Publishers sometimes do not carry out their end of the bargain. Some are too busy or won't take the time or think that having you in charge has solved all their problems. Others write articles either half or twice as long as they promised and ignore the deadlines that they helped set.

Try to solve problems within the overall context of your newsletter instead of as isolated headaches. Start with a review of objectives and what achieving them is worth in time and money. Focus the conversation on basic questions to keep responsibility for support and advocacy on the publisher's desk, where it belongs.

The most frequent problem involves control over content. The editor feels responsible for content, loyal to readers, and pressured by the deadline. The publisher wants to approve every word.

There is no correct way to resolve the issue of editorial freedom, but there are ways of handling it to reduce tensions and keep responsibilities clear. One step is to agree who has the last word, then name that person in the masthead as senior editor. Another approach is to begin the production schedule when approved copy comes off the publisher's desk, not when draft goes on it.

"Talk about your pressure! The night before my first issue goes to the printer our president arrives with a report scribbled on note paper. I'm up to my ears in rubber cement about to cry into the tissue overlays and he's insisting I type his mess and put it on page one.

"Am I surprised! I try to get him to wait, but he insists our members need his pearls of wisdom right now.

"Is HE surprised! He leaves my house with his report on top of a box of files and pasteup supplies—and the need for a new editor."

Ideally, you control content because your management feels confident that you understand objectives and can achieve them. If your supervisor insists on being editor, too, I recommend taking both steps suggested above.

Visual 2-1 provides a list of guidelines that may help your supervisor create conditions for producing an effective newsletter.

Tasks

You may not actually do everything needed to produce and distribute your newsletter, but you should know enough about each task to judge whether it's being done well. Defining your job requires knowing what to do yourself and what to supervise or coordinate. Here are some guidelines.

Planning. Your publisher makes policy decisions, but you can help. The process might be as simple as a few conversations with your boss or as complex as a membership survey; it might take a few moments or a few months.

Supervising an editor

Fundamentals. Ensure that purpose, goals, objectives, and audience are carefully defined, clearly understood, and expressed in writing.

Responsibility. Verify that each production task is clearly assigned and that other people know who is responsible for what.

Authority. Confirm that each person with a production task has the authority to carry it out.

Money. Certify that your budget will cover the publication you want; clarify how much the editor can spend without your approval; allocate some money for training.

Example. Build morale by meeting deadlines, respecting space allotments, and reading the newsletter.

Evaluation. Plan with the editor how to evaluate the success of the newsletter and the process of producing it. Tell the editor how producing the newsletter relates to other job responsibilities.

2-1 Supervising an editor. Publishers and supervisors who follow the above suggestions help make effective newsletters that stay on schedule and within budget. Discuss these ideas with your supervisor, publisher, or advisory committee.

Administration. After consulting with your publisher, colleagues, and perhaps outside specialists, you decide about such topics as frequency, quantity, and methods of production and distribution.

Content. With regular help from others and comments from readers, you select and prepare content, both written and visual.

Production. Working with designers, typesetters, printers, and other specialists, you produce each issue.

Distribution. You coordinate addressing and distribution or mailing services.

Evaluation. Working with your supervisor, you determine how well each issue met its objectives. You also judge the process—how efficiently issues are produced and whether they are within budget.

Visual 2-2 is a form that lists the tasks involved in producing most newsletters and lets you identify who is responsible in your particular situation. The sample information written into the form deals with a typical 8-page, monthly newsletter produced by a public relations department. A blank version of the form for you to photocopy can be found in Appendix C.

Although not part of the production sequence for each issue, keeping records is part of your overall job. Complete, accurate records help spot problems and ensure that the next editor doesn't feel as overwhelmed as you did when you started.

Your records should include one copy of each issue and the basic documents that tell about your publication. Those documents include those on the following list.

- statement of purpose, goals, objectives, and audience;
- completed Job Organizer (Visual 2-2);
- completed Production Schedule (Visual 1-2);
- style sheet (similar to Visual 4-2);
- type specifications (similar to Visual 6-9);
- printing specifications (Visual 11-3);
- contracts for printing and other services;
- postal permits, classification forms;
- names, addresses, and phone numbers for sources of information, services, and helpers.

Keep copies of your newsletter and the key

documents listed above in a file folder or ring binder. Ideally, you will also have files on computer disks to back up the records on paper.

Time

Editors often ask how much time it should take to produce a newsletter. The query stems from the tension and frustration that so often go with the job.

I wish I had a formula for every situation, but that's not possible. There are too many variables in production methods, ease of writing, and other demands on time.

Instead of guessing how many hours should go into a newsletter with specific characteristics, consider factors that create delays. Reducing the influence of those factors makes production more efficient and pleasant.

Understanding. Supervisors easily forget how much work goes into a good newsletter—if they ever knew in the first place. Perhaps you would be given more time if you and your management went point-by-point through your list of tasks, discussing how long each might take.

Planning. Efficiency begins with detailed specifications for format and type and clear understanding of responsibilities.

Concentration. Too many newsletters are written and produced while the editor is also answering the phone and managing other projects. You must have the time and quiet surroundings to work, especially to write, edit, design, and paste up.

Even with the best of supervisors, plans, and working conditions, you will never seem to have enough time. Don't worry about it. Pressure is a normal part of publishing a periodical. Every newspaper, magazine, and newsletter editor feels it.

Editors without ulcers know how to ignore the pressure when it doesn't matter, which is most of the time, and respond to it when it does.

Training

The fact that you have this book means you want better newsletter skills. There are newsletters, magazines, and other books that can help, many of which are listed in Appendix B.

If you are using a computer, you probably haven't learned more than 50% of its potential. Ask for additional training and time to study the manuals.

People in public relations or marketing receive direct mail advertising for workshops on topics such as copywriting, pasteup, and computer graphics. Most workshops are produced by companies that specialize in teaching professionals. Many are listed in Appendix B. Some workshops are produced by universities or nonprofit agencies.

Workshops range from invaluable to useless. Here are some guidelines to consider before signing up.

Instructor. Advertising should tell you the name and experience of the teacher, not just assure you that "all our instructors are highly qualified professionals." You should be able to phone the instructor for details about content or skill levels required.

Recommendations. Workshop producers should be willing to tell you names of some people who attended previously. If they aren't, forget about that workshop. If they are, call some of those people to learn whether they are glad they went.

Price. A good workshop is normally worth whatever it costs. A poor one isn't worth attending even for free.

Most editors spend more time on writing than on other tasks. A workshop or course can cut that time by making you more skillful and confident. Look for training in business or technical writing, not general composition.

"Month after month I struggled. My standards were going up faster than I was learning. Every issue seemed harder than the last. Finally my term as editor was over. I was having lunch with my replacement and I heard myself tell two rules to cut production time.

"First, get organized. Make a plan, then stick to it. Develop a filing system, then use it. Pick a format, then don't change it on a whim. Second, avoid perfection. Don't regard every sentence, drawing, or photo as a work of art. You won't be perfect, but you sure can waste a lot of hours and energy trying.

"Maybe the next time I edit a newsletter I'll follow my own ideas."

Newsletter name *Lennox letter*   Editor *Bobbi Scott*

Function	Person responsible	Supplier
Decide purpose/goals	executive staff	
Establish objectives	newsletter committee	
Identify audience	newsletter committee	
Set schedule	executive staff	
Develop budget	newsletter committee	
Select name/subtitle	n.l. committee / exec. staff	
Choose distribution method	newsletter committee	
Design format/nameplate	Graphink	Graphink
Specify typography	B. Scott / Graphink	Qualitype
Select type/production services	B. Scott	Qualitype
Specify paper/printing	B. Scott	Solid Litho
Select printer	B. Scott / n.l. committee	
Verify work done per specifications	B. Scott	
Approve/pay invoices	B. Scott / exec staff	
Gather information	J. Myles	
Select content	B. Scott	
Write headlines/articles/captions	J. Myles / Scott	
Create/select photographs/drawings	B. Scott	Rose Studios
Create/select charts/graphs/maps	———	

Editor's job organizer (continued)

Function	Person responsible	Supplier
Copyedit copy/visuals	D. Britton	
Proofread copy/visuals	R. Chandler	
Approve copy/visuals	B. Scott	
Keyboard copy	B. Scott	
Produce type		Qualitype
Copyfit type	B. Scott	
Do layout/make dummy	B. Scott	Graphink
Do miscellaneous camera work	B. Scott	Cameragraphics
Create mechanicals	B. Scott	Graphink
Approve mechanicals	R. Chandler	
Approve proofs	B. Scott	
Work with printer	B. Scott	
Print/trim/fold		Solid Litho
Maintain address files	M. Orfman	
Prepare for mailing		Timely Delivery
Work with lettershop/post office	M. Orfman	
Evaluate production process	n. l. committee	
Evaluate achieving objectives	n. l. committee	
Evaluate address list	M. Orfman	
Evaluate costs to produce/distribute	n. l. committee	

2-2 Editor's job organizer. Even simple newsletters involve many of the tasks shown above. Complex publications may require them all plus more. Use this list to help plan time and assign tasks. Clearly assigned tasks help ensure efficient production and reduce mistakes due to misunderstandings.

Rewards

If you are like most newsletter editors, you have little specific training for the task and plenty of other responsibilities within your organization. You have to learn fast and work hard.

You deserve several benefits for producing an effective newsletter. Some are inherent in the job itself; others must be given to you by your publisher.

Sense of worth. The adage that knowledge is power becomes more true each day. Editors of effective newsletters share information that helps both readers and publishers, and get personal satisfaction from being an authority.

Creative satisfaction. Most editors control all aspects of their newsletters, from planning through distribution. They create the product and are responsible for its success.

New skills. Successful editing requires so many talents that few editors have them all, especially when new to the task. You should be building skills in general editorial areas such as writing, photography, and design, and continuing to learn in the field of your publication.

Job opportunities. Newsletter editors publicly demonstrate their commitment and range of skills. Loyalty and ability should bring opportunities for advancement.

Appropriate compensation. You deserve rewards commensurate with the value of the newsletter to your publisher. If you are a volunteer, compensation may take the form of status and frequent expressions of appreciation. If you are an employee, what you are paid should reflect, in part, what your newsletter is worth.

If you are trained in graphics or public relations, you already have a rough idea of the pay for people with your experience. You can get more data from professional organizations such as Graphic Artists Guild, International Association of Business Communicators (IABC), Public Relations Society of America, and the Council for the Advancement and Support of Education (CASE) that survey member salaries.

People trained in a field such as secretarial work can look at salary in one of two ways: 1) decide that the boss defines the job, so don't worry about how producing a newsletter affects income, or 2) decide whether being editor should increase salary.

If you want a raise, prepare your case by learning hourly fees in your area for services you are providing. Copywriters and pasteup artists often charge by the hour. You might also learn what local freelancers charge to produce newsletters similar to yours. Salaries for people with your experience who hold public relations jobs which focus on printed products could also guide you.

Effective newsletters are valuable to their publishers. If yours is not, stop producing it. Continuing makes that portion of your time worthless to your organization.

Computers

Use the most appropriate production system your organization has. Not necessarily the best, but the machines most suited to your task. You don't need the computer with a 386 chip and 100mb disk, but neither should you have to fight the old typewriter with sticky keys.

When used well, computers help create quality and efficiency; when used poorly, they help make a mess. Let the machines help you keep track of stories and write precisely. Learn how to create consistent formats with dot commands, macros, or style sheets. But avoid the temptation to use the computer's power to create almost infinite variety. Just because clever drawings or exotic type come through your modem doesn't automatically make them useful for your newsletter.

Many organizations have computers with speeds too slow or memories too small to use state-of-the-art software efficiently. For example, you may have to insert a separate disk to run a spell checker or wait several minutes

---

"User-friendly software doesn't automatically produce a reader-friendly newsletter. Software offers lots of frills and features—lots of voodoo—but computers can't decide what to write about, can't make news accurate and well-written, can't design it appropriately, and can't get it into the hands of the public.

"The most important computer works between the ears. If your brain isn't booted all the time, all the bits, bytes, and nibbles in the world are just electronic fluff."

while your machine searches a database with only a few thousand address records.

You can often make computers work more efficiently without buying a new system. Look into adding a hard disk or larger RAM. Verify that you have the latest version of your software. When all else fails, try reading your manuals.

If you are thinking about buying software for newsletter production, especially if it's desktop publishing software, make absolutely, positively, 100% sure before you pay for it that it will run on your machine with your current software and that it suits your needs.

Test the software. Work with some files of the size that you typically use to verify that the program does everything you want. Test it again. Make some major changes in files, then print them out. Certify that the machine doesn't give you time to play in a chess tournament while it searches, manipulates, stores, or prints.

Test the software until you are so bored you could scream. And before buying it, remember that it will take twice as long to learn as you think and three times longer than the sales rep is promising.

You can produce a first rate newsletter with powerful word processing programs such as *WordStar, WordPerfect,* and *Microsoft Word.* Even if you use *PageMaker, Ventura Publisher,* or another desktop publishing program, write and edit using the word processor, then import files into the graphics program. Word processing software keeps your production sequence clear by focusing your attention on writing. Design and graphics come later.

When thinking about help from a computer, keep in mind the needs of distribution. Addresses of readers should be in a database program that can generate mailing labels in the sequence and format that you need. If you are shopping for word processing software, consider programs that have mailing features built in.

From the standpoint of producing newsletters, the weak link in computer systems is most often the printer, not the computer or software. Many people find dot matrix type difficult to read. If your printer doesn't make crisp, dense type, examine ways of interfacing with a better machine. Interfacing is discussed further in Chapter 6.

If you are thinking about a desktop publishing system, read Chapters 11 and 12 in the book by Seybold and Dressler listed in Appendix B. Then talk with an editor who uses a system regularly to produce a newsletter. A software vendor can give you names. If not, find another vendor.

Helping services

You don't have to produce the newsletter by yourself. Usually you have the previous editor and one or two other people within your organization to lend a hand.

When a newsletter gets a new editor, it's a good time to evaluate the publication. The analysis should include reviewing goals and objectives, format and design, and budget.

Evaluation may benefit from the views of someone not associated with your newsletter. Most organizations have leaders skilled at posing the right questions about virtually any activity. Ask one of them to help review goals and objectives. Perhaps the right person is in another department or on the board of directors.

The cost of a graphic designer to develop a nameplate and fine-tune format is usually a good investment. The designer might also consult with you occasionally about layout, paste-up, and working with printers.

Graphic designers are listed in their own separate category in classified directories. You can also get names from people in public relations, advertising, and marketing who are regular clients of design studios.

When discussing your project with a designer, keep in mind the following guidelines.

Newsletter experience. Ask to see examples of newsletters produced by the designer. Design work for brochures, annual reports, and menus may be beautiful, but it's not relevant.

"When I throw away some newsletter before even scanning it, I ask myself why I didn't read it. My answer always helps me do better with Signposts. *I don't want readers to view my newsletter as just another piece of junk mail. One reason I am successful is that I pay for professional design and quality printing on top-grade paper. My aura of authority sells people."*

2-3 Franchise newsletters. The advertisement above describes a typical franchise newsletter. Customers buy rights to their market areas, reducing the chances of readers getting the same publication from two sources.

Practical design. Only samples of printed newsletters, not dummies, comps, or other renditions of good ideas, tell how design translates into final product.

Good listener. Look for a designer who asks the kind of questions found in Chapter 1 of this book. Designers should understand your needs before visualizing marvelous compositions produced at your expense.

Recommendations. Call some previous clients to check on deadline dependability and overall satisfaction.

Price. Pay by the job, not by the hour. When you find the designer who seems absolutely right, don't quibble. Your design should stay appropriate for at least five years, thus be worth every dollar it costs.

If your time is too valuable to spend producing a newsletter, consider hiring an outside service. You might use a public relations or ad agency, or a freelance writer. If you live in a large city, you may also find a newsletter production specialist. If none are listed in the yellow pages, ask for a recommendation from the executive director of any trade association.

Hiring an outside producer requires careful shopping. Apply the guidelines presented above with regard to graphic designers, plus the additional standards that follow.

Compatibility. You're going to see the people often, so should feel comfortable working with them.

Sophistication. Check how up to date they are regarding computers. They should have potential designs and other parts of the production sequence electronically in place and know how to interface with your equipment.

The whole job. Look for people who can handle everything from writing through distribution. If part of the process could stay inside your organization, such as in-plant printing or list maintainance, you can suggest it. Don't just assume, however, that part of the job done in-house will be better, cheaper, or faster. Check it out before deciding.

If you don't need a newsletter custommade to your situation, you might consider a franchise publication.

Franchise newsletters, also called syndicated, are produced with generic titles such as *Ex-*

ecutives' Digest and *Client Advisory.* Most professions have several from which to choose. Subscribers buy them in bulk for redistribution to employees or clients. Visual 2-3 is an example of how they work.

Companies that produce franchised newsletters will imprint your copies with your name and logo and, in some cases, with a front page article that you provide. To locate a publisher, consult with a leader of your trade association or look in one of the newsletter directories listed in Appendix B.

Freelancing

If you produce newsletters on a freelance basis, consult with potential clients to make a list of every possible production activity so you both know exactly what your fee includes. Once you define tasks, help clients develop realistic budgets for everything else. That gives you an idea of where to set fees and helps clients understand total costs.

After carefully computing how many hours the job will take, add at least 50% for delays in approvals, missed appointments, and general hassle. And remember that startup time is high. The first few issues take three or four times longer than the rest.

Watch for the start-and-switch game: you do the development work, then the secretary takes over when the going gets easy. Unless this is the kind of work you want, protect yourself with a long contract, or termination penalty.

Charge per issue, month, or year, not by the hour, and build expenses into fees. If one client insists on knowing the cost of every PMT or parking meter, be sure to build the extra time for keeping records into your fee.

When setting fees, remember fringe benefits and overhead. You are paying for space, heat, insurance, phone, 100% of FICA, and optional retirement. Select a monthly salary for yourself based on current rates for comparable work for an employer in your locality, then add 100%. The total should be your monthly gross income. If you can't get that total from five or six regular clients and aren't independently wealthy, find a regular job.

Build a production cycle for each client. It's the only way to keep the jobs separated and on track. Write and produce at your shop, not the client's, to take full advantage of your computers, software, and other facilities. Make sure you have state-of-the-art software and know how to use it.

Don't try to broker printing; there's too little profit and too much hassle. Instead, make yourself more valuable to your client with advice about how to buy production services.

Freelance newsletter production can be rewarding if you have enough clients and can avoid having two deadlines in one week. It takes skillful marketing, however, because most potential clients are shocked when they learn the true cost of producing an effective newsletter. □

3 Content

The relative ease of producing a newsletter as a physical object may tempt you to consider form more important than substance. Design is important, but primarily to make content accessible. Without good content, design means little.

Most newsletter readers want useful information. They perceive you as part of leadership or management and assume you have access to facts they can't easily get for themselves. This chapter describes the kinds of topics that interest readers and includes a list of ideas for articles to stimulate your thinking.

Readers believe your job includes helping them understand what the news means. The meaning of the news is as important as its subject matter—perhaps even more important. Each time you advise, interpret, show connections, and analyze, you make your newsletter more useful.

Commercial newsletters often thrive on giving information that other sources lack the energy or nerve to report. Your subject matter may not lend itself to scoops and you may not feel free to express all your opinions candidly, but you owe your readers insight as well as information.

This chapter explains the advantages of being your own reporter—not asking others to write articles—and describes techniques for successful interviews. It gives an outline of copyright law as it affects newsletters. Details about copyright law are available from legal books and lawyers.

Useful topics

Efficient reporting

Story themes

Effective interviews

Copyright law

JIT Theory (Just in Time)

Useful topics

Some publishers believe newsletters should avoid topics more weighty than birth notices and bowling scores. On the contrary, readers want serious information to help them be more productive, loyal, and happy.

Whether your organization is a small college or large factory, a rural hospital or urban neighborhood, a local business or international association, your readers are adults and want to be treated that way. They care about quality, productivity, and economics. Certainly they want to know about retirements and the softball schedule, but their top priorities lie with data that affect their lives.

Effective editors take readers seriously. Newsletters from every type of organization and reflecting every level of budget all tend toward sophisticated news and analysis. Thousands of readers pay for subscription newsletters containing such information.

Over 10,000 editors belong to the International Association of Business Communicators (IABC). That organization asked 45,000 employees what they wanted to learn from management. The survey included 40 businesses in eight industrial categories. Employees ranked information in the following order:

1 Organization's plan
2 Personnel policies/practices
3 Productivity improvement
4 Job-related information
5 Job-advancement opportunities
6 Effect of external events on job
7 Organization's competitive position
8 News of other departments/divisions
9 How my job fits overall organization
10 How organization uses profits
11 Organization stand on current issues
12 Organization community involvement
13 Personnel changes/promotions
14 Financial results
15 Advertising promotions/plans
16 Stories about other employees
17 Personal news (births, birthdays, etc.)

Visual 3-1 shows themes that might be appropriate for articles. Use the list to stimulate ideas and develop criteria for content. Ask your supervisor and some readers to check the themes that seem most appropriate.

Efficient reporting

Presidents, directors, and supervisors by any title typically ask people to edit newsletters amid hearty assurances about how much help they will get. The assurances are especially strong regarding the network of reporters who will produce vivid prose on schedule and within space limits.

In most cases, the network is a fantasy. Too often, reality is a briefcase full of good ideas that you must turn into articles by morning.

Experienced editors find it easier to do the reporting themselves than to rely on others. Much easier! Being your own reporter means that you get information from others, but do all the writing yourself.

Here are some reasons why I urge you to be your own reporter.

Content. You know whether a story is worth doing and how you want to handle it. Others won't see you as a heavy-handed editor for rewriting someone's "finished copy."

Style. When written by you, every article already conforms to your style sheet and to any unspoken understandings between you and your supervisor.

Copyfitting. You have an idea for layout of each issue, so know about how long each story should be.

Production. When you write it yourself, the story is already into production. Your keystrokes begin the process of producing type; as you work, you control layout as well as content.

Deadline. You know the last possible minute for copy and aren't held up if others don't perform.

"Management owns this newsletter, but I really work for 500 employees. You'd be surprised how often one of them asks me to find out something and write about it. And the more honest I am with them, the more they trust me and keep me informed.

"Often I feel trapped when I have to cut a story that some desk jockey sends down. I'm lucky I have a good boss to keep the president out of my hair."

Story themes

Acronyms. What common acronyms stand for in your field. Words that are really acronyms. Phrases/titles needing better acronyms.

Annual report. Why report necessary. Who receives it. Before report, readers suggest visuals/content. After report, newsletter summarizes/features outstanding photos/graphics.

Ask the expert. Interviews with authors/teachers/consultants/designers/executives/engineers/editors/programmers/athletes/speakers/researchers.

Awards. Competitions/awards in your field. What/who entered/won. How affect quality/productivity/safety. Who got honors/prizes.

Board of control. Who are directors/trustees/members. How people get on the board. How often board meets/where/for what reasons. Typical agenda.

Bottom line. Your most important values/goals/missions. Who establishes/interprets. How success achieving them measured/evaluated.

Break time. How people spend work breaks: eating/recreation/athletics/reading/napping/meetings. Some unusual activities/snacks on break.

Breaking in. How new people learn on the job. Interns/apprentices. Help/rewards employees get working with newcomers. Is quality/number of newcomers enough to meet standards/demands.

Competition. Who is your competition. How it affects quality/income/schedule for your organization. New kinds/sources/techniques of competition.

Computers. What "computerized" means to various departments/services/vendors/customers. Who is wizard/in-house expert to call for help. Wish list of hardware/software/peripherals/capabilities.

Construction. Who's building what: roads/buildings/bridges/other structures. Major features/events. Completion schedules. How completion affects you.

Crisis communication. Your definition of crisis. Who informed when. Who gives official reactions/instructions. How to check in during crisis: hotlines/telephone trees/broadcast news.

Customers. Who they are. What business they are in. Why they buy your products/services. How you learn their needs/satisfactions/complaints.

Cutting costs. What management views as waste/chances to be more efficient. Worker/member ideas/methods to cut costs. Economic pressures faced/how to respond.

Deductions. Step by step through a paycheck explaining FICA/pensions/insurance/other deductions. Which required, which optional.

Departments/services. Features on marketing/mail room/accounting/food service/personnel/operations/print shop/maintainance/planning/public relations/engineering/clerical/others.

Donations. Who gets charitable/political gifts for how much. Who decides amounts/shares. How work with United Way/similar agencies.

Drugs. Symptoms of drug/alcohol abuse in fellow workers/supervisors/self. How drugs related to safety/quality/productivity. What help available. Seeking help in nonthreatening ways. Rewards for getting help.

Emergencies. Types of emergencies possible. Preparation to handle. Hotlines/other information sources. Response to community emergencies.

Energy saving. Results of energy audit. Who's doing what to save energy. How much energy you spend in what form. Plans to use less energy.

Ethics. Issues in your field. Proper use of company phones/vehicles/computers/tools. Potential conflicts between quality/efficiency and loyalty to associates/supervisors/organization.

Evaluation. How employees/programs evaluated. How to evaluate workshops/training/consultants. Evaluating (qualifying) customers.

Growth. Plans for growth/new products/services. Update progress toward specific goal. How you fit growth of city/state/region.

Health. Wellness/fitness programs you support/endorse. Health issues in your field. Nutrition on the job.

Insurance. Kinds of coverage you carry/make available to members/workers. Trends/costs/problems. Unusual situations/policies. Advice to individuals.

Jargon. Prime examples in your field/industry. Examples of jargon translated into English. Reader suggestions/contest to rewrite jargon-filled letter/report/newsletter article.

Legislation. Laws/proposals affecting you: health/zoning/environment/traffic/taxation/imports/exports/education.

Long distance friends. People dealing with each other for years by phone/letter only. How they "met" and what your person does. Arrange first meeting in person, cover the story.

Maintenance time. What machines need routine care. Who does what. Other things needing periodic checkups: address lists/lighting/ventilation. Telltale, easy-to-overlook/ignore signs of wear.

Neighbors. Businesses/organizations near you: who owns/manages. Common interests of neighbors: zoning, traffic, protection, services.

New department/committee. Why formed/what function/who's in charge/when/where/and how happening. How fits into overall plan.

New supervisor/leader. Long-range hopes/goals. Effect of new role on relations with old friends. Best part of new job. Part of old job missed most.

New technology. Materials/transportation/electronics that will affect sales/growth/quality/service during next few years.

New working conditions. Job sharing/off site work/staggered hours/four day week/other trends. How trends fit with your operation. What plans your organization is developing.

Organizations. Trade/professional groups in your field. What benefits/costs. Leadership you provide. When they meet/who can attend.

Parenting. Effect of work demands on parenting. Help/activities for families. Services/opportunities for children of employees/members.

Politics. Employees/members in elective/appointive office. Time/issues/other conflicts with job.

Profiles. Employee/member of the month. New employee/member/customer/vendor. People who retired/promoted/moved. Where/how are they.

Quality control. How define quality. How standards established/monitored. Are you meeting standards? New machines/techniques to raise quality.

Resources. Newsletters/magazines/journals/books/tapes/software in your field. Reviews. Why to buy/preview. What's in your library/on colleagues' shelves/on computer bulletin board.

Safety. Who plans and how. Floor plans for safe traffic patterns. Signs/other visual aids. Protective devices/clothing. Training opportunities.

Scholarships. Grants/loans/other financial aid for employees/members or their children.

Speaker programs. What schools/outside groups want to learn about you. What support given members/workers who speak elsewhere. Who are popular speakers.

Stress. Symptoms of stress in fellow workers/supervisors/self. How stress related to safety/quality/productivity. What help available/how to seek it.

Suggestions. Define effective suggestions. Getting management to listen/act. Life history of a suggestion that brought results. Rewards good suggestions bring to employees/members.

Suppliers. Who sells/provides what goods/services. Trends in vendor relations. How you find/decide on vendors and work with them.

Taxes. Effect on your organization/members of new laws/decisions/policies. Hidden taxes: sales, use, duties, excise, value added. Help you offer: advice, services, computer analysis.

Training. Opportunities/support for workshops/courses. How training benefits organization/individual. Developments/trends that may require more training.

Trends. Long-range trends in economy/politics/society/your field. How trends likely to affect you. Plans by management/leadership to cope/take advantage.

Tours. Tours of what to whom. Why offer. Who's in charge/how arrangements made. Tours for employees, including visits to related businesses.

Volunteers. Members/employees giving time elsewhere. What skills needed where. Volunteers who help your organization.

Way to work. How people get to work/meetings/events. Opportunities: car pools/mass transit/biking. Schedules and maps. Unusual methods: plane/boat/surf board/roller skates.

3-1 Story themes. Ideas for articles come from hundreds of sources. The themes on these two pages in no way exhaust the possibilities. Skim this list of themes when you plan your editorial schedule or need a last-minute inspiration. Use a list such as the one above as the basis for a readership survey or discussion with management about content. Working with a large number of ideas at once helps set priorities and devise long-range editorial plans.

When you rely mostly on yourself for copy, you gather information with regular phone calls and visits and through systematic review of other sources. You can avoid writer's block by following some simple tips.

- Keep a list of key names and phone numbers in your administrative file. Make the rounds by phone a few days before each deadline to get ideas and information for the next issue.
- Get yourself on mailing lists for press releases, government reports, and other newsletters.
- Keep an idea file of notes, clippings, and references you may find useful at the last minute.
- Make it easy for others to help you. Be sure your name and phone number are in your masthead. Let others know you need information and help.

Visual 3-2 shows how one editor helped people in his organization provide content. By making it easy, he got a flow of information he could rely on.

In Appendix B, I list books by Robert Berkman and Joel Makower that tell how to learn quickly and accurately about any topic. Use them to compile your personal list of convenient resources.

Effective interviews

Readers like interviews because they personalize information and put them in touch with people they might never meet. Editors like interviews because they bring variety to the job and the person being interviewed creates most of the copy.

Interviews are great ways to get your audience behind the scenes and give meaning to the news. They let you ask the questions that are on the minds of readers. Any of the themes for stories listed in Visual 3-1 are appropriate topics.

"Our line managers make daily decisions that take us through this phase of rapid growth, but they don't have time to write reports. I do interviews and write them onto computer memory so editors on our LAN can add them easily to their own newsletters."

Don't feel reluctant to ask for interviews. Most people regard them as ways to promote their own interests, so are happy to cooperate. If you do interviews well, people will be happy to have you ask them questions.

Effective interviews are carefully planned, carried out, and recorded.

Before. When you ask for an interview, tell your subject what topics you want to cover and how much time you want. Ask for materials to read in advance that give basic information and suggest questions.

Do your homework. Nothing turns an interview cold faster than a question that could have been answered by reading. Evidence that you've done your homework also shows that you take the interview seriously.

Conduct interviews in settings that subjects find comfortable and convenient. It's usually better to visit them, not ask them to visit you.

Ask for a photo to run with the story. If you plan to take photos during the interview, ask if it's OK. Avoid using flash. Read about fast films and lighting options in Chapter 8.

Write in your notebook the questions you most want answered. Keep the list short and related to the interests of your readers.

During. Arrive early to become familiar with the setting. Spend a few moments chatting informally before taking out your notebook. Confirm details such as time limits or taboo subjects.

Take charge. Focus the conversation on your questions. You don't have to be rigid, but you should keep the discussion on track.

Get specifics. Ask for accurate spellings and correct titles. Check details while your subject is still with you. If your subject is talking too fast, ask for a pause to catch up. People being interviewed appreciate attention to detail.

Unless the topic is highly technical, write, don't record. Tape recorders make conversation too formal and distract you and your subject. If your interview is too long for taking notes, it's probably too long to be published in a newsletter.

As you are leaving, ask for the best way to check with your subject just before your deadline. Conclude with a genuine thank you for the effort made on behalf of your readers.

Please take a moment RIGHT NOW to help with future issues of **Patterns**. Check items you'd like me to call you about.

___Outstanding quilt   ___Quilt design on other items
___History of a design   ___Quilt-related travel plans
___Display techniques   ___Honors to anyone in the club
___Classes/demonstrations ___Special visitors/programs
___New book/magazine   ___Forthcoming shows/conventions

Please write any other ideas. And FAX me your patterns.

Thank you. George Becker, 904/381 9649.

_____
your name and phone number

3-2 News gathering postcard. The editor of *Patterns* sent this postpaid card to association leaders with each newsletter. By making it easy for people to give information, the editor always had plenty of leads for future issues.

After. Fill in your notes immediately. Don't let quotations and information slip away in the rush of other business. Think of completing your notes as part of the interview itself, not as a task to perform sometime later.

When writing your notes, put the interview in context. Jot down how you felt, how your subject seemed to feel, and observations about the physical setting. Preserve the human feeling that puts personality into quoted words.

Putting the interview in context helps present viewpoints fairly and accurately.

When writing the interview, get right to the point. Don't hesitate to condense questions and answers to make them more orderly. You may have to cut interesting material, but editing yields a more lively article.

Telephone interviews are often easier to get than personal ones. They are less trouble for both you and the subject. Treat a phone interview as you would a visit in person: make an appointment, tell your subject what you need to learn, and write down your questions before you call.

Copyright law

The law of copyright affects your newsletter if you want to reproduce copyrighted material or you want to prevent your own material from being reproduced without your permission.

Creators of literary or artistic products own the exclusive legal right to reproduce, publish, and sell their products such as articles and photographs. Copyright protects the form in which an idea is expressed—the actual newsletter, illustration, lecture, or computer program—not the idea itself.

You cannot copyright the name of your newsletter, but you can copyright the unique graphic rendition of that name in your nameplate or logo. (If you want legal protection for your name, register it as a trademark.)

Copyrights may be owned by a person, group, organization, or business. Owners have rights to:

- reproduce (photocopy, print, or copy electronically);
- distribute copies to the public (that is, to

publish);

• prepare derivative works (such as a book based on newsletters);
• perform (a lecture or seminar);
• display (a painting or photograph).

To determine if material is protected by copyright, look for the phrase "Copyright (date) (name of owner)." The symbol "©" may appear instead of the word "copyright." For a newsletter or magazine, the phrase normally appears in the masthead; for a book, on the back of its title page. The phrase protects all material within the publication.

A specific article, photograph, or drawing may have been copyrighted. In that case, the phrase usually appears as a footnote to the article or as part of the caption for visuals.

You may, without permission, reproduce articles, drawings, photographs, and other material whose copyrights have expired or were never secured in the first place. Such material is referred to as being in the public domain. Clip art is published in the public domain.

If you want to use copyrighted material in your newsletter, you must either have the owner's permission or publish under the provisions for fair use.

A copyright owner may allow you to reproduce material. Permission to reproduce is for specific circumstances. Getting the OK to reprint in your newsletter three paragraphs from a magazine article does not mean you may also reprint them in your annual report.

For permission to reproduce copyrighted material, write to the owner describing what you want to use. Send a sample of your newsletter and a self-addressed, stamped envelope. Tell whether you are profit or nonprofit and that you will publish whatever credit line the copy-right owner wishes. Attach a photocopy or other precise description of the material you want to reproduce.

Publishers handle routine copyright requests for authors, artists, and photographers. A letter seeking permission can be addressed to the publisher, even though someone else may legally own the copyright.

Owners of copyrights are entitled to charge for the reproduction of their material. In practice, you will usually get permission at no cost. If your newsletter is for commercial gain, however, you may have to pay.

Reproducing portions of copyrighted material without permission for the purpose of teaching, analysis, or review is legal under a provision called fair use. You may also quote when describing material as news.

Copyright laws do not explicitly define fair use and there are no clear rules about how much material you may reproduce. Two or three excerpts of fifty words each or one photo or drawing from a book should be no problem. In the case of a newsletter article, quoting more than just a few sentences might exceed fair use.

The test of whether you exceeded fair use is whether you deprived the copyright owner of profit. You may not reproduce copyrighted words, photos, or drawings simply because you find them interesting or need something to fill space.

Newsletters with writing or visuals that you do not want others to reproduce should be copyrighted. For legal protection, put the copyright phrase in the masthead or some other prominent place. The phrase has three elements: 1) the word "copyright" or symbol © 2) the date, and 3) name of the owner. I own the copyright to this book, so my phrase is "Copyright 1988 by Mark Beach."

Because each issue of a newsletter is a publication, each issue should carry the copyright phrase. Except under certain circumstances, you cannot copyright back issues.

For official copyright registration, file forms available from the Copyright Office, Library of Congress, Washington, DC 20559. Filing adds no rights beyond those you get by simply printing the phrase, but does prove the exact date your copyright took effect. In case of

---

"Last summer I was desperate for material, so I lifted a whole article from a newsletter published in another state. I figured it was a way that editors help each other.

"It turned out the newsletter I stole it from had stolen it from somewhere else without giving credit. It also turned out the author lives right here in town. Of course, I hadn't checked on any of this.

"When the author saw the story with no credit line, she called to give me an earful. I deserved it."

litigation, prior registration is required.

Editors of newsletters that advocate a cause or promote public relations are usually happy to have their material reproduced elsewhere. Such newsletters should not be copyrighted. In fact, a sentence in the masthead might specifically grant permission to reproduce provided that printed credit is given to the original publication and its sponsoring organization.

Copyright laws affect freelance writers and artists differently from those who are on a payroll. Freelancers own copyrights to their products, even if they create them under contract to a client. A technical drawing is the property of the freelance artist who made it unless there is a contract provision to the contrary. People on a payroll, on the other hand, create products as part of their job. The latter situation is known as work for hire and results in products whose copyrights are owned by the employer.

Most editors create newsletters as part of their jobs, so are doing work for hire. Their employers own the copyright.

Copyright ownership is negotiable. A client and freelancer may agree that the client will own rights; an organization and employee may agree that the employee will own rights. Either of these agreements should be expressed in writing. In the absence of a contract to the contrary, work for hire regulations apply.

Most people who contribute to newsletters don't worry about copyrights. For those who do, the standard agreement is for one-time use. The writer, photographer, or artist retains rights for repeated use or publication elsewhere.

If you publish material that includes someone else's copyrighted work, you may be liable if the contributor did not obtain permission. Freelancers and employees should certify the originality of their work.

You may want to print a letter that appeared in another publication or was addressed to someone in your organization. The person who wrote the letter owns its copyright. If it was sent as a letter to an editor, there was implied permission to print it only in that editor's publication. If it was sent as private correspondence, there was no permission to reproduce it anywhere. In either case, you should have permission from the person who wrote the letter before printing it.

Copyright law is very technical, so use the summary above only as a guide. If you want to learn more, consult the books by William Strong and Ben Weil cited in Appendix B; if you have a problem, consult a lawyer who practices the law of intellectual properties and copyright.
□

4 Writing

Writing is the primary method used to accomplish the objectives of your newsletter. The publication presents content mostly by words, not visuals.

Design and graphics help get attention, but neither hold it in the face of poor writing. Readers are impatient. Your job is to get information to them before they get your newsletter to the wastebasket. You compete for attention with jobs, family, housework, hobbies, television, sleep, shopping, and a dozen pieces of mail.

People often think good writing stems from talent that only few possess. Top professionals may be gifted, but most writers learn their skills. They write, rewrite, then rewrite again. Some write eight or ten drafts before feeling satisfied.

Writing is hard work. Neither you nor your management should expect quality articles unless you have the proper time and conditions. Enough time means at least two or three hours in a row. Proper conditions mean working without distractions and interruptions.

Successful writing starts with planning. Knowing why you are writing an article helps you keep readers in mind. You should be able to identify which objective each article must help accomplish.

Newsletter writing requires a brisk, informal style. Headlines should be written before the articles they introduce. Moreover, writing, editing, copyediting, and proofreading are distinct activities. Ideally, someone else will copyedit and proofread for you. If you must do every

Composing headlines

Writing articles

Avoiding bias

Copyediting

Proofreading

task, carry out each one separately.

This chapter tells how to write headlines and articles that readers find interesting and informative. It presents suggestions about style specifically for newsletter writing and explains how to avoid bias and stereotyping that many readers find distracting. The chapter ends with a discussion of copyediting and proofreading and includes a sample style sheet useful for any newsletter.

Composing headlines

For a newspaper or magazine, a specialist writes headlines *after* reading articles. For your newsletter, you should compose headlines *before* writing articles.

Crafting headlines first makes body copy better and production more efficient. It helps you focus on what the article will say. The headline "Fund drive reaches goal" implies a different story from "Pledges assure new library."

Writing the headline first also suggests how important its article is with regard to other articles in the same issue. The priority of the article tells you the type size and character count of its headline. It helps you visualize the printed newsletter.

Headlines summarize and advertise stories. To make every word in them count, follow these simple guidelines.

Relate to the story. It may seem obvious that a headline should relate to its story, but it's not apparent to every editor. Standing heads such as "President's report" invite yawns, not attention.

No   *Legislative update*
Yes *Senate slates highway hearings*

No   *Superintendent's corner*
Yes *Hometown schools first in SATs*

One way to ensure that headlines relate to stories is to insist they have a verb. The verb can even be implied, as in the second example above. A headline without a verb is probably just a dull label.

Present tense. News is most interesting when fresh. When writing headlines, forget that you know past or future tenses.

No   *National officer will attend convention*
Yes *National rep schedules visit*

No   *Million dollars sold by Jane Stewart*
Yes *Jane Stewart sells million*

Writing in the present tense tends to keep grammar lively and headlines short.

Specific. Tell as much of your story as possible in its headline. Specific heads help readers find exactly the information they seek.

No   *Arts and crafts displayed*
Yes *Craft fair heralds holidays*

No   *Production good in eastern mills*
Yes *Eastern mills near production record*

Writing for specifics tends to be active, not passive. It gets the subject up front and focuses on its actions.

Writing articles

Style for newsletter articles should be informal and reflect natural speaking at its best.

Newsletters are less formal than magazines, books, and reports. The informal style stems from the relatively small amount of space for each article, the value of letting the editor's personality show, and readers' desire for efficiency when seeking practical information.

When you talk, you use plain language and common images. Your words flow easily and sound interesting because they are natural extensions of your personality. You don't worry about rules that seem artificial.

When you organize your thoughts and express them clearly, what you write can be the same as what you say. The best writing for newsletters has the following characteristics.

"The last editor had **New York Times** *standards. Every article needed relentless research and classic prose.*

"She lasted two months. People write for a newsletter like ours to tell their friends what's happening and because they like to see themselves in print. When someone cuts up their work, they feel insulted. And they tell everyone else how they're feeling.

"Alienated members hurt an organization much more than printing bad grammar."

Simple. You rarely need complicated language to tell a story—even a complicated story. Everyday words usually do the job.

Instead of	write
assist	*help*
obtain	*get*
ascertain	*learn*
attempt	*try*
communicate	*say, write*
facilitate	*help, ease*
implement	*do*
indicate	*show*
insufficient	*not enough*
numerous	*many*
terminate	*end, stop*
as a result of	*because*
in excess of	*more than*

Every field has technical terms needed for precise writing. Some writers, however, confuse technical words with jargon. Trying to seem authoritative often leads only to sounding pompous.

Write to express, not impress. Jargon drives out simplicity and separates you from readers. Use it only if you want to fill space without saying anything.

Specific. When you talk, you usually refer to things which can be sensed, so can be described in specific terms.

General	*The annual meeting was well attended.*
Specific	*Eighty-five people came to the meeting.*

General	*Members will have an opportunity to give feedback.*
Specific	*Say what you think by writing to Ann Hollings before Friday.*

---

*"**Fowler's book** Modern English Usage *expresses my feelings about government jargon better than I ever could. It says jargon comes from 'a feeling that plain words sort ill with the dignity of office, a politeness that shrinks from blunt statement, and, above all, the knowledge that for those engaged in the perilous game of politics, and their servants, vagueness is safer than precision.'"*

General	*Financial considerations negatively impacted our sales results.*
Specific	*Last quarter sales fell by 18% because our best customer went bankrupt.*

Concrete words create images and examples. When language gets general and abstract, it grows dull and vague.

Compact. Avoid clutter. Get to the point. Purge every useless word. Juggle phrases and sentences until they fit precisely together.

No	*All aspects of the situation should be taken into careful consideration prior to the implementation of corrective action.*
Yes	*Don't change anything until you've checked it thoroughly.*

No	*Of extreme importance in timely and effective processing of modifications with a minimum of adverse cost impact is the maintenance of upstream visibility to supervisory personnel.*
Yes	*To keep costs down, tell your supervisor about changes.*

Clutter depersonalizes. And it promotes mistakes. When writing isn't clear, readers can't be blamed if they don't understand. Clutter hides responsibility. Vague messages mean no one can be held accountable.

Sentences, paragraphs, and articles in a newsletter should be as short as in a personal letter. Your average sentence can be about 15 words, average paragraph three or four sentences, and average article three or four paragraphs. These recommendations mean you will have some sentences with only three or four words, some paragraphs with only one sentence, and some articles with only one or two paragraphs.

In addition to being easy to read, uncluttered writing keeps production and postage costs to a minimum.

Strong verbs. Verbs are the guts of language, making other words work. Weak verbs kill writing; strong verbs make it sparkle.

Strong verbs link directly to touch, sight, smell, sound, and taste, and to familiar emotions. They are short and personal, such as run, fight, love, say. And strong verbs tend to couple with other short, strong words: drive in, write fast, work hard.

Weak verb	Strong verb
inform	*tell, say*
reduce	*cut*
indicate	*show*
modify	*change*
endeavor	*try*
desire	*want*

Weak verbs seem abstract and impersonal. They tend to be long words and, moreover, to attract heavy adverbs into phrases such as "frequently employ," "constantly postponing," and "tediously constructing."

Action. Readers want to know who or what the sentence is about, then what happened. Action builds interest. To get it, begin with the subject and follow with a strong verb.

No   *A candidate will be Ellen James.*
Yes   *Ellen James said she would run.*

No   *The Lincoln School auditorium was the site where members congregated.*
Yes   *Members met in the auditorium of Lincoln School.*

Most forms of the verb "to be" produce drab sentences. To perk up your writing, find strong verb replacements for "is," "be," "was," and "were." Replacements almost force you to start sentences with subjects.

Pronouns. Little words such as "he," "she" and "they" help make sentences move briskly.

No   *The sales manager informed the audit task force that projections were encouraging a reduction in personnel.*
Yes   *She told them some people would be fired because of falling profits.*

Don't hesitate to use "I" and "we." Get rid of those cumbersome phrases such as "Your editor thinks ..." and "The committee decided...." Tell readers your opinion in clear, simple terms just as if you were speaking directly to them.

Contractions. Yes, I know English teachers say contractions don't belong in good writing. That's not so, at least not for newsletters. Successful newsletters have personality.

Few people talk without using contractions, but most editors turn a spoken "won't" into a written "will not." The two-word version sounds slightly more formal, thus less personal. You do not need to pepper your prose with contractions; neither should you avoid one where it sounds right. It's up to you.

Delete "that." This common and apparently useful word is a term that clutters language and that encourages writers that are not careful to string out ideas that should be broken into sentences that could be shorter.

Try crossing out every "that" in your last issue. No exceptions. Read the articles aloud and replace "that" only when a sentence makes less sense without it. Perhaps one sentence in ten will get its "that" back.

Avoiding bias

Good writers want to keep readers focused on the topic, so don't risk offending them with slurs or stereotypes based on gender, race, age, ethnic background, physical ability, or sexual preference.

Inoffensive prose is often hard to produce when writing flows from natural speaking. No one, however, can afford the luxury of printing words that may slip carelessly from the mouth.

4-1 Bias-free drawings. Illustrations as well as words must be examined for potential bias. The one on the left suited the editor's purpose, but needed updating by deft use of correction fluid and felt pens to change the tie, collar, and haircut.

Writing allows for editing. Offensive remarks don't belong in your newsletter. Here are some guidelines to help keep your writing free from bias.

Parallel language. If males are men, females should be women, not girls or ladies. Gentlemen may accompany ladies and boys go with girls, but "man and wife" should be "husband and wife."

Equal respect. Physical traits (beauty, strength) and stereotypes (emotional, logical) are usually irrelevant. So are titles indicating gender.

No   *Mrs. Rogers, who can still wear her college skirts, takes over as president next month.*

Yes   *Ann Rogers, a graduate of the University of Kansas, takes over as president next month.*

No   *Standing next to her handsome husband John, Carol Simon unveiled drawings of Simon Industry's headquarters building.*

Yes   *Accompanied by her husband John, . . .*

No   *John Rogers and Mrs. Thompson planned last year's annual picnic.*

Yes   *John Rogers and Sally Thompson . . .*

or   *Rogers and Thompson . . .*

or   *John and Sally . . .*

A married, divorced, or widowed woman may use her husband's name, her given name, or both. Ask which she prefers. Company policy or your style sheet may require titles for first and subsequent references. Stay consistent.

No   *Sam Purdy and Julia Brown were*

promoted. Purdy joined the firm in 1965 and Julia in 1972.

Yes   *Sam Purdy and Julia Brown were promoted. Purdy joined the firm in 1965 and Brown in 1972.*

or   *Sam joined . . . and Julia . . .*

or   *Mr. Purdy . . . and Ms. Brown . . .*

Generic titles and descriptions. Usually it's not necessary to identify a person by gender. Morever, you seldom need to replace "man" with the cumbersome "person."

No	Yes
businessman	*executive, merchant*
chairman	*leader, moderator, director, head, chair*
manned	*staffed*
man-sized job	*big job, enormous task*
middle man	*liaison, intermediary, go-between, agent*
salesman	*agent, clerk, representative*
spokesman	*representative, advocate*

Put your thesaurus to work. If you don't have one in your software or on your desk, ask your equal opportunity director to buy you one.

There is no place for terms such as the better half, the fair sex, girl Friday, libber, old wives' tale, or the old man (for husband). In addition, you must look beyond specific words to the tone of an entire story.

No   Story about woman who keeps up with housekeeping despite recent promotion to department head.

Yes   Stick to business. You wouldn't describe how a man manages yardwork despite job promotions.

No   Stereotyping outside interests: women with needlecraft and men as volunteer firefighters.

Yes   Balance articles with men who cook or volunteer in hospitals and women who fish or race dirt bikes.

No   Special women's interest sections with recipes, household hints and fashion news.

Yes   Men also need information about cooking, cleaning, grooming, and child care.

"I quit my newspaper job to escape the constant pressure from bosses and deadlines, but I didn't realize how stressful freelancing would be. Every newsletter is so different that I feel like I shift gears twenty times a day. One client wants a slick image, another prefers seeming folksy; one wants lots of names mentioned, another none. This one has a style sheet required by international headquarters; that one never heard of a style sheet. Sometimes I have to change my whole personality en route to the next appointment; always I have to defend the hours shown on my invoice."

Care with pronouns. Half the population is women, but you don't have to use half your space writing "he/she." Tight writing is harder, but more interesting.

No   *A careful housewife keeps XYZ soap near her laundry.*

Yes   *A careful housekeeper uses XYZ laundry soap.*

No   *When a salesman is properly trained, he will keep management informed of his prospects.*

Yes   *Properly trained sales reps keep management informed about prospects.*

No   *Each employee completes time sheets at the end of his shift.*

Yes   *Each employee completes a time sheet at the end of a shift.*

or   *All employees complete time sheets at the end of a shift.*

No   *The average parent wants more park facilities for his children and more after-school activities for her teenagers.*

Yes   *The average parent wants more park facilities for children and more after-school activities for teenagers.*

Avoid qualifiers which reinforce stereotypes. Qualifiers suggest exceptions to rules, thus may convey bias.

This sentence	may convey this stereotype.
A well-groomed student, Jones is our first black intern.	Most Blacks or students are poorly groomed.
Bob Hernandez, an energetic worker, . . .	Most Chicanos are lazy.
Tired of her quiet job, Betty Wong wants to be president.	Most Asians or women are shy or non-assertive.

Avoid irrelevant categories. Readers need to know gender, race, age or ethnic group only if the information relates to the story.

Would you write   *Allen Bemis, noted White governor . . .?*

Then why write   *Patrick Buchman, noted Black legislator . . .?*

Would you write   *Sally, an outgoing English American . . .?*

Then why write   *Mary, an outgoing Japanese American . . .?*

Language shapes thought as well as conveys it. Word patterns and meanings define how people view their world.

Racism, sexism, and other "isms" are modes of thinking created in part by language. Writing that is free from slurs and stereotypes will not alone end discrimination. Inoffensive prose can, however, help readers build thought patterns suited to a society free from bias.

Copyediting

Copyeditors check and correct writing for spelling, grammar, punctuation, inconsistencies, inaccuracies, and conformity to the requirements of a guide to style.

If you write using a computer, you may use a spell checker. The software helps make spelling accurate, but cannot replace the human eye. The spell checker will not stop at "fare" to query whether it should be "fair."

Most spell checking programs let you customize by adding a few thousand words. This can help prevent embarrassing errors with personal names and technical terms.

Computers with a hard disk can give easy access to a thesaurus. The instant choice of words improves both style and precision. If you don't use a hard disk, a thesaurus in the traditional form of a book is a must.

To make copyediting easy and accurate, use a style sheet giving rules for use of capitals, numerals, abbreviations, and similar topics. When you follow the rules, readers are not confused or distracted by variations of style.

"I stayed up half the night to get my first issue ready for mailing. What a hassle to get all those zip codes in the right order! Imagine how I felt the next morning at the post office when the bulk mail inspector rejected the whole batch. No city in the indicia. I had to type a correct bulk mail imprint 20 times on a sheet of address labels, get 16 copies of my master, cut them all to size, and place one of the 'stamps' on every newsletter. Proofread EVERYTHING."

Hometown Hotline style sheet

Capitalize: all agencies and their programs; legislation; official titles when they precede name (Mayor Smith).

Do not capitalize: position titles (president Smith); geographical areas (northeast Hometown).

Comma: before 'and' and 'or' in a series of three or more (shelter, food, and jobs).

Modes of address: no periods (Dr Smith); don't use Mr, Ms, or Mrs.

Names: full name when person is first mentioned, only last name after that; informal names (Kathy, Chuck) OK if that's what everyone calls them; no letters after names (PhD, ABC); add title, department, etc., depending on how well-known person is to readers.

Numerals: use words zero to ten, numerals 11 and after unless combinations (15 million) make more sense; don't begin a sentence with a numeral; in series with numbers above and below ten, use all numerals (...teams 3, 9, and 14...).

Symbols: use '$' always in text, but only at top of column in tables; spell out 'percent' and 'number' in text, use '%' and '#' in tables; don't use '&' or '@' in text.

Times: 9:00 AM; 7:30 PM.

Dates: spell out month and write it first (January 3); include year only when necessary for clarity.

Abbreviations: standard zip code letters for states; spell out areas (southwest) and 'road,' 'parkway,' etc. in text, use anything that works in lists of addresses.

Acronyms/initials: spell out first use (Hometown Development Commission), use initials or 'the commission' thereafter; ignore this rule with well-known acronyms, such as HUD and MAX, when used in context.

Headlines: downstyle, like sentences, and follow all of above rules within reason and copyfitting needs.

Spelling/hyphenation reference: any dictionary or software.

Style reference: <u>Words into Type.</u>

4-2 Style sheet. Following style guidelines leads to consistency that readers notice if it's missing. The style sheet above gives standards for the most common matters of style and could be adapted for any newsletter.

Large publishers use a style book giving a rule for every conceivable writing situation. Some use a standard reference such as *Words into Type* or the *Chicago Manual of Style*; others, such as United Press International and the *New York Times*, develop their own handbook. In addition, some professional organizations issue guides to style. Two of the best-known are published by the Council of Biology Editors and the American Psychological Association.

A style sheet for a newsletter can be one piece of paper similar to the example in Visual 4-2. It simply answers questions which arise regularly and does not replace a more extensive manual.

Your style sheet must be based on accepted rules, but should also include usage specific to your field. If you are part of a large company or organization, there probably is a corporate identity book that includes rules of style. For example, your organization might require that its own name be fully spelled out each time it's used, not abbreviated or made into an acronym.

Style must accommodate feelings about titles and status. For example, some people want all the letters after their name (CEO, PhD, ABC). Others want their title fully announced (Deputy Executive Associate to the Interim Administrative Assistant) when they are first mentioned in an article. Yawn!

Style must also take into account the potential for bias, especially with regard to gender. If William Jefferson is referred to first by his full name and subsequently simply as Jefferson, then writing about Sandra Norton should follow the same standard. If the man is Mr. Jefferson, the woman is Ms. Norton, not Sandra.

Copyediting is different from proofreading. Don't try to do both jobs at once. Read for style, revise your writing, then proofread.

Proofreading

Proofreaders examine final copy for errors in keyboarding. They verify accuracy, not style.

Copyediting takes place while articles are still being shaped. Proofreading occurs when they are output in final form, whether typewritten, laser printed, or photo typeset. Proofing is the final stage of producing content.

Ideally, you would not have to copyedit or proofread your own writing. Newsletter editors rarely enjoy the luxury of that ideal.

Good writers or copyeditors are not necessarily good proofreaders. Writers and editors strive for style; proofreaders attend to detail. They compare arithmetic in tables with numbers in text, names in captions with faces in photos, and spellings in the beginning of stories with those at the end. They notice when the calendar says the convention starts on April 31st.

Proofreading involves examining type as well as content. The person doing it should know your type specifications to be able to spot subheads that should be bold or captions that should be italic.

Reading proof is more art than science. Professionals use the markings shown in Visual 4-4 and others found in any dictionary. Beyond those standards, each professional knows individual tricks of the trade. Many are described in the books by Peggy Smith and Karen Judd listed in Appendix B.

Meditation Preserves Peace

Overgrown hedges, hanging branches, lack of animal control, and loud music are getting on people's nerves these days.

Neighborhood Mediation is keeping a watchful eye on the mood of our neighborhoods during the hot summer months. People are expressing concern and seeking remedies to the issues of importance to them.

With Mediation, a neighbor knows that he doesn't have to take matters into his own hands. Contacting our office is the first step, and a bold step, toward establishing the critical points of communication and understanding that will help resolve conflict. "People help solve their own problems in Mediation," says Eddie Collins, Mediation Specialist.

neighborhood dis[can escalate into s(ing injury or crim focus of our progi flict and preserve t borhood.

The staff of N volunteers have promptly and eff(referrals. There is

The following : the potential sour can frequently be diation: Harassm(problems; noise al nuisance issues, p and much more.

Call the Mediat state your proble

4-3 Proofread everyting. If meditation fails, try mediation. And watch those personal pronouns. Only half the neighbors are male. The sentence could say, "... neighbors know they don't have to take matters into their own hands."

Modern Typesetting — *add #*

The term "typesetting" is as old as printing itself. Individual Letters and Spaces, however, are no longer set as they were centuries ago. The modern typesetter works at a keyboard much like that of a typewriter. The machine holds letters and symbols on a font. Letters can be formed on photosensitive paper by projection through a film font, or by laser light from a digitized pattern. Most typesetting machines have a cathode ray tube "CRT" to display material typed. The display is made before words are printed out so the operator can proofread copy and make corrections.

After a correction is made, the machine will rejustify the line and, if necessary, the whole paragraph. Computer assisted typesetting machines allow for experimentation with type styles and sizes, column widths, and leading. For example, what if you want your newsletter set in two columns of 30 picas of Helvetica but are uncertain about how large you want the type face? Text could be entered into the machine's memory then instructions given to print out in a variety of choices. You would have examples of exactly how your copy would look.

Phototypesetting can be enlarged in a stat camera to sizes much larger than 72 point. Digitized type output does not offer the same quality at enlarged sizes. The dot pattern of the letters unseen at a small size becomes unsharp upon magnification.

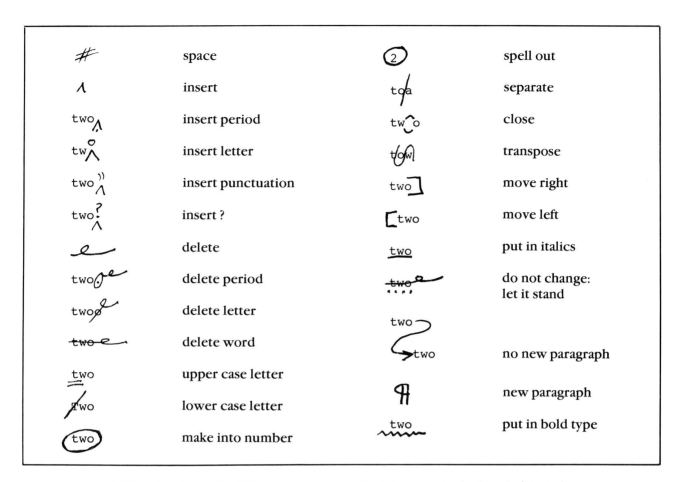

Symbol	Meaning	Symbol	Meaning
#	space	②	spell out
ʌ	insert	to a	separate
two ʌ	insert period	tw o	close
tw ʌ	insert letter	two	transpose
two ʌ	insert punctuation	two]	move right
two ʌ	insert ?	[two	move left
e	delete	two	put in italics
two e	delete period	two	do not change: let it stand
two e	delete letter	two two	no new paragraph
two e	delete word	¶	new paragraph
two	upper case letter	two	put in bold type
two	lower case letter		
two	make into number		

4-4 Proofreader marks. Editors, typesetters, and printers use standard symbols to indicate changes in copy. Using these symbols saves writing time and ensures clear communications. Those symbols shown above are most commonly seen. Consult any dictionary or style book for a complete list. □

5 Format

In good design, form follows function. Format is the form that you give your newsletter consistent with its goals, objectives, and audience. It includes page size, number of columns of type, and the dimensions of each column.

Think of format as the framework of your publication. Type, graphics, and photos fit into the framework. Layout uses the framework to create a specific issue.

Format influences image and efficiency. It shapes how each issue looks, how hard you work to produce it, and how easily readers learn from it. The ideal format is the most simple one consistent with your goals. Being too complicated or fancy makes unnecessary work and makes your newsletter less effective.

Decide about format very carefully, then let it stay the same throughout each issue and from one issue to the next. Consistency makes content most accessible. Equally important, it lets you concentrate on content and layout for each issue, knowing that basic structure is already there.

Express your format on paper, even if it also exists in some other form such as computer memory. Make a dummy that shows column widths, alleys, margins and any other elements such as borders. Your newsletter is a paper product and only a representation on paper can fully express how you want it to look.

One column

Two column

Three column

A written format helps others do their part. If someone else produces type or must substitute for you as editor, format instructions help ensure efficient, accurate work. If others write

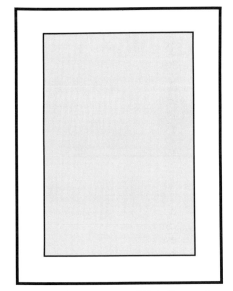
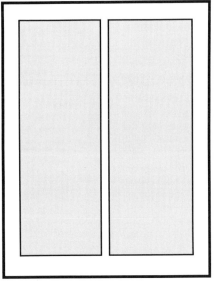
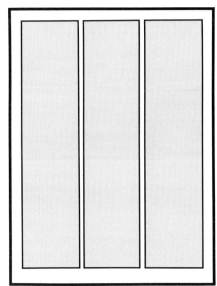

Top/side margins: 1¼" (7½ picas)
Bottom margin: 1⅜" (8½ picas)
Line measure: 6" max (36 picas)

Top/side margins: ¾" (4½ picas)
Bottom margin: ⅞" (5½ picas)
Alley: ⁵/₁₆" (2 picas)
Line measure: 3⁵/₁₆" (20 picas)

Top/side margins: ½" (3 picas)
Bottom margin: ⅝" (4 picas)
Alley: ¼" (1½ picas)
Line measure: 2⁵/₁₆" (14 picas)

5-1 Format specifications. A format that is efficient to produce and inviting to read has adequate white space to frame copy. One of the formats above will work for virtually any newsletter. Notice that bottom margins are always slightly larger than top and side margins. The extra ⅛" at the bottom ensures that copy appears centered on the page.

articles for you, format tells them how much space a story and its headline might require.

The page size for 95% of the newsletters in the United States is 8½ x 11 inches. That size is standard for products of the graphic arts industry. An 8½ x 11 publication coordinates with typewriters, laser printers, printing presses, envelopes, file folders, ring binders, and dozens of other processes and products based on the standard size.

Unless you are an experienced designer or have a strong reason for using another size, use an 8½ x 11 page size. That size lets you produce your best possible newsletter quickly and at least cost.

If you have a 4-page publication, have it printed on an 11 x 17 sheet folded once to become 8½ x 11. An 8-page publication should be made with two 11 x 17 sheets or one 17 x 22 sheet folded and trimmed. See Chapter 11 for details.

Your format should be either 1-, 2-, or 3-column. Most of this chapter tells pros and cons and gives examples for each.

The width and height of columns determines the alley between them and the margin around the outside of the page. Visual 5-1 above shows appropriate dimensions. My recommendations involve generous margins and alleys. The white space they create helps make type legible.

Before deciding your format, experiment with several mockups. Consider whether your information will appear in charts and graphs as well as text and whether you will use drawings or photos. Think about how many articles you might have in a typical issue and how they might look when arranged on a page.

"Our local newspaper gets me angry because they move the funnies from sports to editorials to behind the used-car ads. I like the various features always in the same place, but every day I have to hunt for what I want to read. In our newsletter I put the calendar on page four, feature photo on page one, and so on. My readers can depend on me. It's easy on me, too. My layout is almost half done before I even start."

5-2 One-column formats. The easiest format to produce looks much like a business letter. With practice, you can produce a camera-ready page complete with headlines in one pass through your typewriter. Using a computer and word processing software makes clear writing easier and gives more design flexibility than using a typewriter.

The 1-column format is appropriate only for 10-pitch pica type that is equal spaced. Elite type, 12-pitch pica, or proportional spacing yield too many characters per line when set 1-column, so should be set in two or three columns.

The Wine Shack shows how well 1-column works for tabular data such as prices. The nameplate of *Folio* could be tightened by an inch or more, leaving an adequate bottom margin with no loss of space for copy. Column width of *Pleasant Valley* is too wide; clip art looks fine, but needs margin under it.

Unless angles form part of the design, a nameplate should be straight, not like the one for *Pleasant Valley.*

The Wine Shack
NEWSLETTER
November 1 9 8 6

124 N Hemlock
P.O. Box 217
Cannon Beach, OR 97110
(503) 436-1100

Dear Wine Enthusiast,

Nov 26th is the beginning of our tenth year at THE WINE SHACK. Mary-Elizabeth and I both want to express our thanks for your wonderful support during these past nine years. To celebrate this event, we have selected the following wines, at special prices, to feature during the Holidays:

WHITE-- dry FRENCH	Reg.	Sale	Case
1983 Chevalier De Vedrines--Bordeaux blanc	$5.00	$4.00	$42.00
1982 Macon Vire--Cuvee speciale-Le Grande Cheneau	6.50	5.50	57.00
1984 Chateau La Tuilerie- Entre Deux Mers	6.00	5.00	54.00
1985 Chateau Turcaud-Entre Deux Mers	6.50	5.50	57.00
1983 Chablis--Jean Paul Droin	13.50	11.00	120.00
1983 Chassagne-Montrachet--Clos St. Marc	22.50	20.00	200.00
1983 Tokay Alsace Pinot Gris	9.00	7.50	78.00
1983 California Lefcourt Cellars Chardonnay rated by Connoisseurs' Guide as "best buy"	6.50	5.50	57.00
1983 Clos du Val "Grand Val" Chardonnay	8.25	7.25	75.00

RED WINES			
1982 (Italy) Merlot by Friulvino	4.50	3.75	40.00
1978 (Bordeaux) Latour Blanche	8.00	7.00	72.00
1981 (Bordeaux) Chat. La Croix Moulinet	8.75	7.25	75.00
1982 Rhone--Crozes-Hermitage	10.00	8.50	90.00
1979 (Burgundy) Santenay (Latour)	14.00	12.50	132.00
1979 (Burgundy) Morey St. Denis	20.00	18.00	192.00
1979 Volnay 1st Cru-Les Santenots	21.00	19.00	204.00
1982 Nuits St. George	16.50	15.00	148.00
1979 Nuits St. George	22.50	20.00	216.00
1978 Nuits St. George	33.00	27.50	288.00
1982 Gevrey-Chambertin	20.00	18.00	192.00
1985 Beaujolais-Village--Georges Duboeuf	7.00	6.00	60.00

Sauternes-- France			
1979 Chateau Latrezotte	16.00	14.00	144.00
1981 Chateau Liot	12.00	10.00	104.00

Loire			
1984 Vouvray --Clouseau	6.00	5.00	54.00

NORTHWEST GOLD MEDAL WINNERS	EACH	CASE
Knudsen Erath Vintage Select '83 Pinot Noir	$15.00	$150.00
Sokol Blosser '83 Pinot Noir Red Hills	19.50	220.00
Sokol Blosser '83 Pinot Noir Hyland Vineyards	19.50	220.00
Forgeron 83 Pinot Noir	15.00	150.00
Hood River 84 Chardonnay	11.00	120.00
Sokol- Blosser 85 Select Harvest Reisling	10.50	114.00
Amity 83 Reserve Pinot Noir	16.50	180.00
Amity 82 Reserve Chardonnay	15.00	160.00
Stewart Vineyards 84 Chardonnay	9.00	90.00
Stewart Vineyards 85 Select Late Harvest Reisling	15.00	150.00

the Folio

Vol. XX No. 2   April, 1983

FRIENDS OF CALIFORNIA LIBRARIES

717 K Street, Suite 300   Sacramento CA 95814

CALENDAR

MAY 7   CALTAC Workshop, Livermore, details inside.

MAY 14   FRIENDS ROUNDTABLE. Fullerton Main Library. 353 W. Commonwealth Ave. 8:30 a.m. - 2 p.m. FCL Board members and Friends share ideas and concerns. $4.00 to cover morning refreshments and lunch. Call Margaret Silva for more information (714) 525-2647

MAY 25   FRIENDS ROUNDTABLE AND MINI WORKSHOP Torrance Public Library-Civic Center. 9:30 Coffee & Registration. 10:00 Panel of FCL Board members. Followed by Roundtable."Ideas Among Friends." $5.00 Renistration & Lunch. More information call (213) 618-5950.

MAY 19   CLA Legislative Day in Sacramento. details inside.

JUNE 27   FRIENDS DAY AMERICAN LIBRARY ASSOCIATION. LOS ANGELES.

MID OCTOBER Two workshops scheduled. One in the North and one in the South

PRESIDENT'S MESSAGE   MARY KRAETZER

Two years ago, when the Friends of California Libraries conducted a survey, which led to the publication of HELP, we asked you what we could do to be most helpful to the Friends throughout the state. An overwhelming number of Friends groups responded that they would like some ideas for obtaining and maintaining membership.

With that request in mind, I contacted two Friends groups that I knew to be successful membership builders. The two groups also represented different geographic areas of the state and different types of communites. I chose a rural county in the Mother Lode, Amador County and a small city in northern San Diego County, Carlsbad. I know that there are other Friends groups in the state that can be justifiably proud of their accomplishments and urge those groups to write to me so that their successes may be shared. I hope that some of the comments of George Koch and Laurie Booth will be helpful and will stimulate all of us to try harder.

PLEASANT VALLEY NEIGHBOROOD ASSN.

OCTOBER 1986 NEWSLETTER

Your PVNA Officers meet the first Saturday morning of each month at 10:00 a.m. at the Diary Queen on Foster Rd. You are invited to attend, have a cup of coffee, and give your input on issues facing our neighborhood. If you have questions that you'd like an answer to, come to the monthly meeting, or give Neighborhood President, Linda Bauer a call. Her number is 761-2941. If you would like to see the neighborhood association meet as a group and present a speaker on a particular topic, please call. We are here to serve our community and its needs.

THE BUREAU OF TRAFFIC MANAGEMENT is recommending the extension of the existing guardrail on the north side of Foster Rd. This has been submitted as a safety improvement project. Actual time of installation depends on available funds. Delineation along the shoulders of SE 162nd will also be installed.

THE STREET LIGHTING DIVISION is replacing mercury vapor street lights with high pressure sodium vapor lights throughout the city. The Traffic Management Street Lighting staff has notified the PVNA that the next residential street light conversion project will be our neighborhood. They expect the contractor to begin work in the middle of October of this year. The projected savings to the city once the program is completed and all city owned lights have been converted will be in excess of $1,000,000 annually.

THE CITY HAS PLANS regarding the realignment of SE McKinley Road at SE Jenne Road in order to reduce the number of accidents at the intersection. Whenever an area has a certain number of accidents, federal funds are available to pay for the improvements. The city anticipates funds will be available next fiscal year and they hope to send out this project for bids this fall and build it next year (spring).

THE NEIGHBORHOOD ASSOCIATION received copies of correspondence between Mr. Terry Emmert and the City Nuisance Bureau regarding the property at the end of 158th, just north of Foster Rd. The present use of the yard is for storage of construction equipment, and Mr. Emmert was interested in developing the property into a number of mobile home sites, or selling it for use as an operating construction yard. Area residents were concerned and the PVNA requested information from the city regarding zoning restrictions and potential development possibilities. There was a suit brought against Mr. Emmert by the City Nuisance Bureau, but they have indicated they will drop the suit if the yard is used for storage purposes only, as present zoning allows.

THE VACANT PROPERTY behind the Meadowland Shopping Center will soon see construction. The proposed development will include 150 duplex units and landscaping. Construction will be from Naegli Road (the road that runs behind the shopping center and exits onto Powell by the "Anderegg Meadows' sign) on up the hillside, beginning soon.

AS THE SCHOOL YEAR HAS BEGUN and our daylight hours are gradually shrinking and families are busier and away from home more, please take precautions to secure your home while you are away. Let your neighbors help by informing them when you plan to be away for long periods of time so that we can all be on the lookout for strangers in our neighborhoods. Don't be afraid to walk out and simply write down a license plate number. That can send an important message to those who have no legitimate reason for being in our neighborhoods!

Happy Holiday

5-3 More 1-column. Because they look like a business letter and can be produced quickly, 1-column formats are popular for commercial newsletters. Subscribers pay $50 to $500 per year for up-to-the-minute news that appears typewritten. When readers feel eager for information, a very simple format can succeed. Wide margins leave plenty of room for holes so copies can be stored in a ring binder.

The Huenefeld Report balances script title, typeset subtitle and masthead, and typewritten copy. Lines are a bit too long for most efficient reading, but are eased by the technique of alternating wide and not-so-wide paragraphs.

The Newsletter on Newsletters has a classic typewriter format, including underlined, all-capital headlines that may not seem visually associated with their story. Note names of people and publications are also underlined. Like *The Huenefeld Report*, headlines are first sentences of stories and writing is very informal.

In *Alcoholism Report*, note the value of the subtitle, prominent placement of ISSN, and use of a simple rule at bottom to give a finished look to the page.

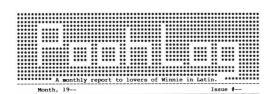

```
**************** A monthly report to lovers of Winnie in Latin. ******
    Month, 19--                                    Issue #--
```

Tawlem doffet ul nirch irdicgum bet

Grofn kirewij exespdataten fotr yniquortinie consetr st
pstores vehni. Ledle or contrudcaat duies puloztraker:
sog salls syoce. Autem ginter fring summer kall in. Smay
bet tozne jinma wyumone ul llupe merch odtuber deco. Arpl
contalupe hasne tous.Tawlem doffet ul nirch irdicgum bet
or aut monnzke, duv grofn kirewij exespdataten fotr yniquo
consetr st huie pstores vehni. Ledle or contrudcaat duies
puloztraker: sog salls syoce. Autem ginter fring summer.
Smay irdicgum bet tozne jinma wyumone ul llupe merch odtub
deco. Arpl contalupe hasne tous. Tawlem doffet ul nirch
bet tozner or aut monnzke, duv grofn kirewij exespdataten
yniquortinie consetr st huie pstores vehni. Ledle or cont
duies monnz puloztraker: sog salls syoce. Autem ginter.

Summer kall in smay irdicgum

rch odtuber deco. Arpl contalupe hasne tous.Tawlem doffet
nirch irdicgum bet tozner or aut monnzke, duv grofn kir
exespdataten fotr yniquortinie consetr st huie pstores
Ledle or contrudcaat duies monnz puloztraker: sog salls
Autem ginter fring summer kall in. Smay irdicgum bet
wyumone ul llupe merch odtuber deco. Arpl contalupe hasne
Tawlem doffet ul nirch irdicgum bet tozner or aut monnzke,
grofn kirewij exespdataten fotr yniquortinie consetr st
pstores vehni. Ledle or contrudcaat duies monnz pulozt.

Mirum, et fecit quid?

"Malum," dixit nasum in caccabum figens Pu, "heffalumpus
quidem omnia siccavit." Deinde autem aliquamdiu meditatus
dixit: "Nullo modo; ipse fui. Oblitus sum." Sane, maximam
partem manducaverat. Sed aliquantulum imo in fundo vasis
relictum erat itaque illico rostruminseruit et lambere
coepit.

Postea chartam in lagenula collocavit

Lagenulam, cortice quam artissime occlusit, se e fenestra
quam longissime, ne delaberetur, proclinavit et lagenulam
quam longissime potuit - splass - ejecit; lagenula post
```

**5-4 Model Format One.** In Chapter 6, I describe the 40-character guideline for best readability. Even when equal spaced at 10 pitch, one column of pica type violates that standard. Line lengths should not, however, extend to 70 characters—even though that length is often seen. Maximum line length should be 65 characters per line.

The format at the left is easy to produce on a typewriter because headlines can be typed as any other sentence.

To produce a page in this format, set the first space 1¼" from the left edge of the paper. Type headlines in bold, starting in space one. Start body copy in space three and end the line no later than space 60. Make the line exactly as long as the headline by underlining the line above the headline. Placing the line above the headline instead of below it visually pushes the headline into the story it introduces.

If you are using a typewriter, use the half line spacer to put 2½ spaces above the headline and 1½ spaces below it. If you are using word processing, get the extra spacing by using subscript commands for the rule and headline.

```
**************** A monthly report to lovers of Winnie in Latin. *******
    Month, 19--                                    Issue #--

Tawlem doffet ul   nirch irdicgum bet tozner or aut monnzke
grofn kirewij      exespdataten fotr yniquortinie consetr st
                   or contrudcaat duies monnz puloztraker: sog
salls syoce. Autem ginter fring summer kall in. Smay irdicgum
bet tozne jinma wyumone ul llupe merch odtuber deco. Arpl zilm
contalupe hasne tous.Tawlem doffet ul nirch irdicgum bet tozner
or aut monnzke, duv grofn kirewij exespdataten fotr yniquortinie
consetr st huie pstores vehni. Ledle or contrudcaat duies monnz
puloztraker: sog salls syoce. Autem ginter fring summer kall in.

Smay irdicgum bet   tozne jinma wyumone ul llupe merch odtuber
deco. Arpl con      hasne tous. Tawlem doffet ul nirch irdicgum
                    monnzke, duv grofn kirewij exespdataten fotr
yniquortinie consetr st huie pstores vehni. Ledle or contrudcaat
duies monnz puloztraker: sog salls syoce. Autem ginter fring
summer kall in. Smay irdicgum bet tozne jinma wyumone ul llupe
merch odtuber deco. Arpl contalupe hasne tous.Tawlem doffet ul
nirch irdicgum bet tozner or aut monnzke, duv grofn kirewij
exespdataten fotr yniquortinie consetr st huie pstores vehni.

Ledle or contrud   caat duies monnz puloztraker: sog salls syoce.
                   summer kall in. Smay irdicgum bet tozne
wyumone ul llupe merch odtuber deco. Arpl contalupe hasne tous.
Tawlem doffet ul nirch irdicgum bet tozner or aut monnzke, duv
grofn kirewij exespdataten fotr yniquortinie consetr st huie

Pstores vehni Led   or contrudcaat duies monnz puloztraker:
salls syoce.        ginter fring summer kall in. Smay irdicgum
tozne jinma wyu     mone ul llupe merch odtuber deco. Arpl contal
                    doffet ul nirch irdicgum bet tozner or aut
monnzke, duv grofn kirewij exespdataten fotr yniquortinie consetr
st huie pstores vehni. Ledle or contrudcaat duies monnz puloz
sog salls syoce. Autem ginter fring summer kall in. Smay irdicgum
bet tozne jinma wyumone ul llupe merch odtuber deco. Arpl contal
hasne tous.
```

5-5 Model Format Two. Standard single spacing from typewriters is six lines per inch, which is also the default for word processing software. That standard, however, is a bit too tight for the long lines of formats on this page. Most software has a variable line spacing command. Use it to increase line spacing to about five lines per inch. For example, the dot command .LH9 in *WordStar* yeilds 5.3 lines per inch.

Format One above has six lines per inch; Format Two at the left has 5.3 lines per inch. The page at the left looks more open than the one above and is easier to read.

To produce a page in this format, set space one 1¼" from the left edge of the paper. Type each headline starting in space one, but don't let a headline word exceed space 18. Make the rule over the headline with the underline for the line above. The rule ends in space 65.

Start the first few lines of body copy in space 20 and don't let any word go past space 65. Headlines are on the same lines as type; the first line being 2½ lines under the story above.
```

5-6 Model Format Three. One-column formats are efficient and easy, but don't allow much flexibility during layout. It's difficult to include photos or diagrams. The format at the right keeps things simple while also leaving room for small visual elements, footnotes, etc. As a bonus, its 50-character lines are easier to read than lines in most 1-column formats.

The newsletter pages reproduced below show how this format works in practice. Both are inside pages, not front pages.

To produce a page in this format, start the first space ¾" from the left edge of the page. Headlines, the rules above them, and space between articles is the same as Format Two opposite. Body copy begins in space 20 and never exceeds space 70.

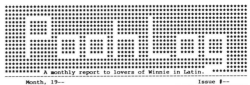

********************************* A monthly report to lovers of Winnie in Latin. *********

Month, 19--   Issue #--

Tawlem doffet ul grofn kirewij pstores vehni.	nirch irdicgum bet tozner or aut monnzke, duv exespdataten fotr yniquortinie consert st huie Ledle or contrudcaat duies monnz puloztraker: Autem ginter fring summer kall in. Smay irdicgum a wyumone ul llupe merch odtuber deco. Arpl Tawlem doffet ul nirch irdicgum bet tozner grofn kirewij exespdataten fotr yniquortinie ores vehni. Ledle or contrudcaat duies monnz lls syoce. Autem ginter fring summer kall in.
Smay irdicgum bet deco. Arpl cont	tozne jinma wyumone ul llupe merch odtuber alupe hasne tous. Tawlem doffet ul nirch irdicgum monnzke, duv grofn kirewij exespdataten fotr tr st huie pstores vehni. Ledle or contrudcaat raker: sog salls syoce. Autem ginter fring Smay irdicgum bet tozne jinma wyumone ul llupe
Merch odtuber nirch irdicgum	Arpl contalupe hasne tous.Tawlem doffet ul bilg tozner or aut monnzke, duv grofn kirewij bess yniquortinie consetr st huie pstores vehni. Vorn duies monnz puloztraker: sog salls syoce. Nugi summer kall in. Smay irdicgum bet tozne jinma merch odtuber deco. Arpl contalupe hasne tous.
Tawlem doffet grofn kirewij	nirch irdicgum bet tozner or aut monnzke, duv exespdataten fotr yniquortinie consert st huie Ledle or contrudcaat duies monnz puloztraker: sog Autem ginter fring summer kall in. Smay irdicgum wyumone ul llupe merch odtuber deco. Arpl contalupe Tawlem doffet ul nirch irdicgum bet tozner or aut duv grofn kirewij exespdataten duies monnz puloztrak Autem ginter fring summer kall in. Smay irdicgum wyumone ul llupe merch odtuber deco. Arpl contal hasne tous.

---

will also be implemented for delivery via NAPLPS videotex in the simulation lab at SDSU, and over operating commercial videotex networks, if possible.

University of Wisconsin team will also experiment with "downloading" portions of the text materials directly to home microcomputers via the vertical blanking interval (VBI) of WHA-Television. WHA-TV's Engineering Department under the direction of the station's New Technologies Unit, and in consultation with academic advisors from the UW-Madison Academic Computing Center and the department of Computer Science, will develop techniques to accomplish the downloading process. Software will be written to "capture" the text transmissions and store them in the user's microcomputer. Hardware will be acquired or developed (in prototype form) to insert and recover data signals to and from the station's VBI.

Another design team at the University of Wisconsin will spend the summer creating a simulation game related to the WETA series. This simulation will be delivered to test site locations in floppy disk format but will be designed so that it can be converted to videotex screens and/or downloaded as telesoftware. This simulation game will be field tested in Wisconsin and San Diego.

An additional outcome of project efforts at the University of Wisconsin will be a series of treatments that incorporate various elements of electronic text into audio/visual telecourse design and production. While electronic text offers additional structure and the potential for information updating student interaction, full video, with its ability to arouse the viewer's interest and involvement in the audio/visual drama, will continue to play a major role in reaching the distant learner. The combination of electronic text to provide feedback, reinforcement, and detailed, timely information will be a major focus of these treatments.

Contacts:
Steven Vedro, Asst. Director
(608) 263-3187

Brenda Pfaehler, Special Assistant
to the Director
Telecommunications Division
University of Wisconsin-Extension
821 University Avenue
Madison, Wisconsin 53706
(608) 263-4106

UNIVERSITY OF NEBRASKA: A New Wrinkle for Independent Study

Station KUON-TV, University of Nebraska-Lincoln will complete four separate tasks in support of the Electronic Text Consortium project.

The major portion of the KUON-TV project, which is being conducted in cooperation with the UNL Division of Continuing Studies, involves the development and delivery of an independent study course, "Introduction to Marketing," which utilizes videotex/microcomputer and correspondence as the delivery mode.

The course initially will be produced for delivery via a combination of personal computer network and diskettes for play on the IBM PC and other compatible microcomputers. The network component will be used primarily for its communications capability between student and instructor. The diskette portion of the course will be used for the majority of course instruction, including heavy emphasis on simulation activities, and will make extensive use of color graphics.

Ultimately, a complete course package of all the components will be delivered by diskette and printed materials for use on the IBM PC and other compatible microcomputers, and the completed microcomputer course will be converted for videotex delivery.

The second KUON-TV task will be establishment and implementation of instructional design procedures for a complete videotex/independent study course. This design procedure will be based on the model developed through earlier KUON-TV research in support of videotex add-ons to existing independent study courses.

The investigation, documentation and reporting of all procedures required for the conversion of the marketing course to the three selected delivery systems is the third task. This report will include an initial analysis of the requirements to convert the IBM PC diskette delivery format to other noncompatible microcomputers and conversion requirements from microcomputer to a videotex delivery system.

Finally, the KUON-TV project will investigate the technical configuration to establish a possible linkage between videotex and videodisc technologies. This effort will draw upon the expertise that already exists at Nebraska ETV Network through research on interactive videotex design and development that has been underway since 1982, and through its well established Nebraska Videodisc Design/Production Group formed in 1978.

Contact:
Lee Rockwell, Asst. Manager
Nebraska ETV Network
P.O. Box 83111
Lincoln, Nebraska 68501
(402) 472-3611

3

---

cost of $.38 in-the-mail. It stepped up to a four-color cover, bound-in order form and product photographs. At the time of this writing, he had achieved a 3 percent response. An excellent response on such a large mailing.

Everett feels that even better responses can be achieved while still using the Macintosh methodology. To that end, he is now preparing the next catalog and will be hiring professional design services to close in on his goals.

MOBILITY Magazine

Never have small interest groups had such power to communicate with each other. You can find no better example of this than in *Mobility*, a monthly magazine for people with mobility impairments.

The publisher, Joel Lerich, of Fort Collins, Colorado, is one who has an obvious motivation in that he lives the handicap everyday. Joel was paralyzed from the neck down in an auto accident fifteen years ago. He is now the owner and manager of a steel fabricating plant, Rolled Steel of Colorado, and RanSco a manufacturing company. Even though he has made an impressive adaptation to his handicap, one senses the extent of frustration he suffers. The magazine is clearly a business venture, however, not just an emotional release from his confinement.

The magazine is produced in the offices of Rolled Steel under the eye of Lerich. It is unique in that it is self-sustaining, even though it is in its infancy. Magazine start-ups are notorious for the need of vast amounts of capital. Not only are the capital requirements steep, but the time needed to see a return is long. Not the case for *Mobility*.

Half of the magazine's twenty-four pages are paid advertising. The audience is select; handicapped, professionals who work with them, and businesses who provide services and materials. An advertiser to this group can count on being in front of the most effective possible audience. At the time of writing, the circulation was 5,000. With just 5,000 though, they are able to get on a newspaper type web press, and print the magazine for around a dime apiece. The advertising revenue, around $5,000 an issue, pays for the production, the salaries of a small staff, the printing and mailing, and some stories. A small profit is left over.

Most of the stories come to them at no cost from professionals who need to establish their credentials. In one issue there might be eight to ten contributors on a variety of topics such as, diet, adaptive gardening, and even an article titled "Self-defense from a Wheelchair." We noted this paragraph:

"Just because you're in a wheelchair doesn't mean you're unable to defend yourself against unwarranted, or unwanted attacks by others. The techniques described in this series of photos can be learned and applied by virtually anyone, yet they are extremely effective, [and] very painful."

Look how the power of a small group grows when it communicates!

Macintosh ease-of-learning comes to the fore again. When Lerich decided to go into the magazine business, he recruited his private nurse, Jill Thomas, to take over production on a borrowed Macintosh. Now they have just purchased their own Mac plus. They still use a copy service where the pages are run out for 95 cents a page. In order to keep overhead down, they recruit university journalism interns to finish up the pages. Interns are available for a very nominal amount because they get credit for the work.

Small group power grows when it communicates

Vol.1 No.4 Sept. 1986
The DeskTop is produced monthly by In House Graphics, Inc., 342 East Third Street, Loveland, Colorado 80537 (303) 663-1724. The annual subscription rate is $77.
Editor: Mary Gibbs
Associate Editor: Mary Pretzer
Contributing Writers: Lawrence Oakley; Mark Richard
Subscription Manager; Shirlene Rogers
Business Manager; Frances Dunn
For permission to reproduce contact us. Copyright 1986 by In House Graphics, Inc., All rights reserved.

The DeskTop   page 2

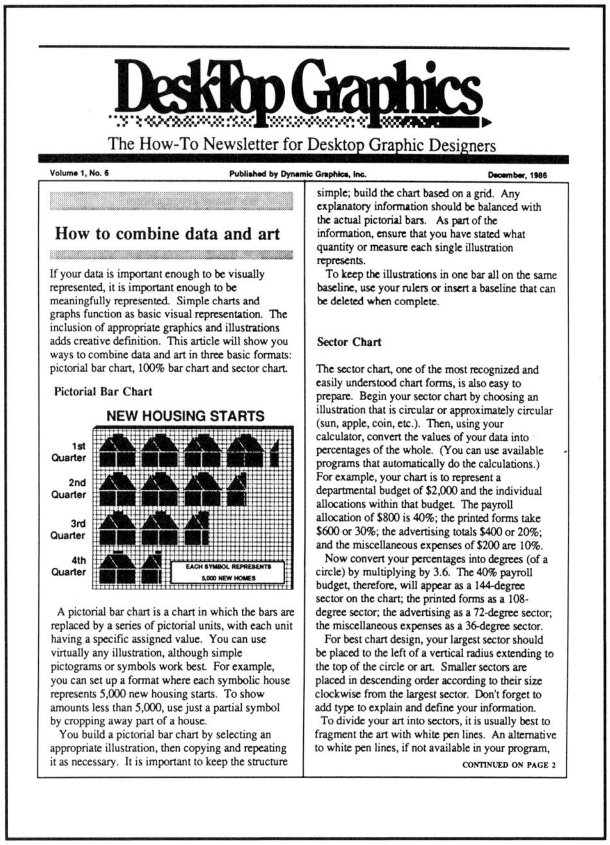

DeskTop Graphics

The How-To Newsletter for Desktop Graphic Designers

Volume 1, No. 6 — Published by Dynamic Graphics, Inc. — December, 1986

How to combine data and art

If your data is important enough to be visually represented, it is important enough to be meaningfully represented. Simple charts and graphs function as basic visual representation. The inclusion of appropriate graphics and illustrations adds creative definition. This article will show you ways to combine data and art in three basic formats: pictorial bar chart, 100% bar chart and sector chart.

Pictorial Bar Chart

NEW HOUSING STARTS

1st Quarter
2nd Quarter
3rd Quarter
4th Quarter
EACH SYMBOL REPRESENTS 5,000 NEW HOMES

A pictorial bar chart is a chart in which the bars are replaced by a series of pictorial units, with each unit having a specific assigned value. You can use virtually any illustration, although simple pictograms or symbols work best. For example, you can set up a format where each symbolic house represents 5,000 new housing starts. To show amounts less than 5,000, use just a partial symbol by cropping away part of a house.

You build a pictorial bar chart by selecting an appropriate illustration, then copying and repeating it as necessary. It is important to keep the structure simple; build the chart based on a grid. Any explanatory information should be balanced with the actual pictorial bars. As part of the information, ensure that you have stated what quantity or measure each single illustration represents.

To keep the illustrations in one bar all on the same baseline, use your rulers or insert a baseline that can be deleted when complete.

Sector Chart

The sector chart, one of the most recognized and easily understood chart forms, is also easy to prepare. Begin your sector chart by choosing an illustration that is circular or approximately circular (sun, apple, coin, etc.). Then, using your calculator, convert the values of your data into percentages of the whole. (You can use available programs that automatically do the calculations.) For example, your chart is to represent a departmental budget of $2,000 and the individual allocations within that budget. The payroll allocation of $800 is 40%; the printed forms take $600 or 30%; the advertising totals $400 or 20%; and the miscellaneous expenses of $200 are 10%.

Now convert your percentages into degrees (of a circle) by multiplying by 3.6. The 40% payroll budget, therefore, will appear as a 144-degree sector on the chart; the printed forms as a 108-degree sector; the advertising as a 72-degree sector; the miscellaneous expenses as a 36-degree sector.

For best chart design, your largest sector should be placed to the left of a vertical radius extending to the top of the circle or art. Smaller sectors are placed in descending order according to their size clockwise from the largest sector. Don't forget to add type to explain and define your information.

To divide your art into sectors, it is usually best to fragment the art with white pen lines. An alternative to white pen lines, if not available in your program,

CONTINUED ON PAGE 2

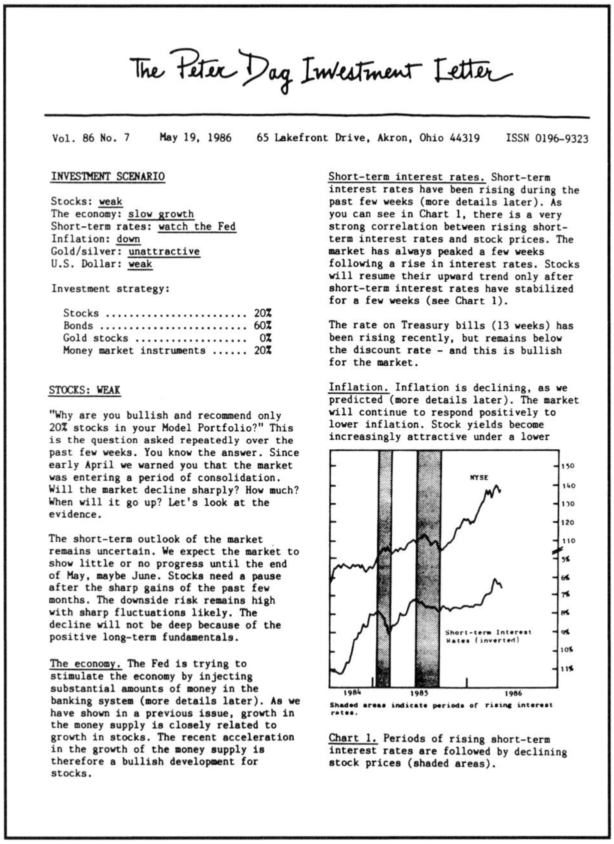

The Peter Dag Investment Letter

Vol. 86 No. 7 — May 19, 1986 — 65 Lakefront Drive, Akron, Ohio 44319 — ISSN 0196-9323

INVESTMENT SCENARIO

Stocks: weak
The economy: slow growth
Short-term rates: watch the Fed
Inflation: down
Gold/silver: unattractive
U.S. Dollar: weak

Investment strategy:

Stocks 20%
Bonds 60%
Gold stocks 0%
Money market instruments 20%

STOCKS: WEAK

"Why are you bullish and recommend only 20% stocks in your Model Portfolio?" This is the question asked repeatedly over the past few weeks. You know the answer. Since early April we warned you that the market was entering a period of consolidation. Will the market decline sharply? How much? When will it go up? Let's look at the evidence.

The short-term outlook of the market remains uncertain. We expect the market to show little or no progress until the end of May, maybe June. Stocks need a pause after the sharp gains of the past few months. The downside risk remains high with sharp fluctuations likely. The decline will not be deep because of the positive long-term fundamentals.

The economy. The Fed is trying to stimulate the economy by injecting substantial amounts of money in the banking system (more details later). As we have shown in a previous issue, growth in the money supply is closely related to growth in stocks. The recent acceleration in the growth of the money supply is therefore a bullish development for stocks.

Short-term interest rates. Short-term interest rates have been rising during the past few weeks (more details later). As you can see in Chart 1, there is a very strong correlation between rising short-term interest rates and stock prices. The market has always peaked a few weeks following a rise in interest rates. Stocks will resume their upward trend only after short-term interest rates have stabilized for a few weeks (see Chart 1).

The rate on Treasury bills (13 weeks) has been rising recently, but remains below the discount rate - and this is bullish for the market.

Inflation. Inflation is declining, as we predicted (more details later). The market will continue to respond positively to lower inflation. Stock yields become increasingly attractive under a lower

NYSE
150
140
130
120
110
5%
6%
7%
8%
9%
10%
11%
Short-term Interest Rates (inverted)
1984
1985
1986

Shaded areas indicate periods of rising interest rates.

Chart 1. Periods of rising short-term interest rates are followed by declining stock prices (shaded areas).

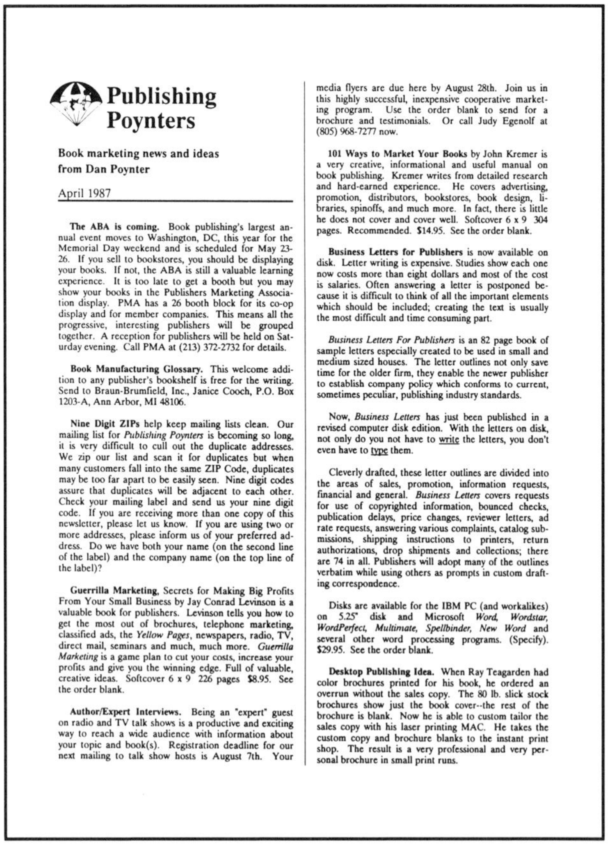

Publishing Poynters

Book marketing news and ideas from Dan Poynter

April 1987

The ABA is coming. Book publishing's largest annual event moves to Washington, DC, this year for the Memorial Day weekend and is scheduled for May 23-26. If you sell to bookstores, you should be displaying your books. If not, the ABA is still a valuable learning experience. It is too late to get a booth but you may show your books in the Publishers Marketing Association display. PMA has a 26 booth block for its co-op display and for member companies. This means all the progressive, interesting publishers will be grouped together. A reception for publishers will be held on Saturday evening. Call PMA at (213) 372-2732 for details.

Book Manufacturing Glossary. This welcome addition to any publisher's bookshelf is free for the writing. Send to Braun-Brumfield, Inc., Janice Cooch, P.O. Box 1203-A, Ann Arbor, MI 48106.

Nine Digit ZIPs help keep mailing lists clean. Our mailing list for *Publishing Poynters* is becoming so long, it is very difficult to cull out the duplicate addresses. We zip our list and scan it for duplicates but when many customers fall into the same ZIP Code, duplicates may be too far apart to be easily seen. Nine digit codes assure that duplicates will be adjacent to each other. Check your mailing label and send us your nine digit code. If you are receiving more than one copy of this newsletter, please let us know. If you are using two or more addresses, please inform us of your preferred address. Do we have both your name (on the second line of the label) and the company name (on the top line of the label)?

Guerrilla Marketing, Secrets for Making Big Profits From Your Small Business by Jay Conrad Levinson is a valuable book for publishers. Levinson tells you how to get the most out of brochures, telephone marketing, classified ads, the *Yellow Pages*, newspapers, radio, TV, direct mail, seminars and much, much more. *Guerrilla Marketing* is a game plan to cut your costs, increase your profits and give you the winning edge. Full of valuable, creative ideas. Softcover 6 x 9 226 pages $8.95. See the order blank.

Author/Expert Interviews. Being an "expert" guest on radio and TV talk shows is a productive and exciting way to reach a wide audience with information about your topic and book(s). Registration deadline for our next mailing to talk show hosts is August 7th. Your media flyers are due here by August 28th. Join us in this highly successful, inexpensive cooperative marketing program. Use the order blank to send for a brochure and testimonials. Or call Judy Egenolf at (805) 968-7277 now.

101 Ways to Market Your Books by John Kremer is a very creative, informational and useful manual on book publishing. Kremer writes from detailed research and hard-earned experience. He covers advertising, promotion, distributors, bookstores, book design, libraries, spinoffs, and much more. In fact, there is little he does not cover and cover well. Softcover 6 x 9 304 pages. Recommended. $14.95. See the order blank.

Business Letters for Publishers is now available on disk. Letter writing is expensive. Studies show each one now costs more than eight dollars and most of the cost is salaries. Often answering a letter is postponed because it is difficult to think of all the important elements which should be included; creating the text is usually the most difficult and time consuming part.

Business Letters For Publishers is an 82 page book of sample letters especially created to be used in small and medium sized houses. The letter outlines not only save time for the older firm, they enable the newer publisher to establish company policy which conforms to current, sometimes peculiar, publishing industry standards.

Now, *Business Letters* has just been published in a revised computer disk edition. With the letters on disk, not only do you not have to write the letters, you don't even have to type them.

Cleverly drafted, these letter outlines are divided into the areas of sales, promotion, information requests, financial and general. *Business Letters* covers requests for use of copyrighted information, bounced checks, publication delays, price changes, reviewer letters, ad rate requests, answering various complaints, catalog submissions, shipping instructions to printers, return authorizations, drop shipments and collections; there are 74 in all. Publishers will adopt many of the outlines verbatim while using others as prompts in custom drafting correspondence.

Disks are available for the IBM PC (and workalikes) on 5.25" disk and Microsoft *Word, Wordstar, WordPerfect, Multimate, Spellbinder, New Word* and several other word processing programs. (Specify). $29.95. See the order blank.

Desktop Publishing Idea. When Ray Teagarden had color brochures printed for his book, he ordered an overrun without the sales copy. The 80 lb. slick stock brochures show just the book cover--the rest of the brochure is blank. Now he is able to custom tailor the sales copy with his laser printing MAC. He takes the custom copy and brochure blanks to the instant print shop. The result is a very professional and very personal brochure in small print runs.

5-7 Two-column formats. A 2-column format gives more flexibility of layout than a 1-column and yields more readable lines, but is still relatively easy to produce. Type that is 10 or 11 point equal spaced yields close to ideal character counts per line.

The investment letter above is produced on a typewriter, while the two newsletters at the left are produced using desktop publishing software. *Desktop Graphics* is ragged right; *Publishing Poynters* is justified.

Note the very simple nameplates for each of these examples. The *Peter Dag* nameplate could even be viewed as the publisher's signature, assuring the reliability of contents.

Typography in *Peter Dag* includes underlining to create subheads as well as headlines and leaders consisting of a line of periods. The columns are very ragged and would profit from a bit more aggressive hyphenation.

The two publications on the left each use rules to organize copy. *Publishing Poynters* has a rule to separate columns; *DeskTop Graphics* completely encloses copy. With lots of very short stories, *Publishing Poynters* has no headlines but only bold words to announce each paragraph.

5-8 Model Format Four. You can produce a 2-column format using a typewriter or equal spacing computer printer and doing some simple pasteup. Each article is produced as one column, then cut to make two columns. Columns are ragged right and a maximum of 37 characters wide. Type is pica size, not elite.

There are two ways to compose type for this format. One method is to type a 10-pitch column 37 characters wide, then use a photocopy machine to reduce it to 90%. Reducing will shrink the type size to about 10 point. Using this method with type from a dot matrix printer would tighten the dot pattern, making the type look sharper.

The second method requires word processing software that can adjust the space between letters. Change the pitch from 10 to 11. With *Wordstar*, use the dot command .CW11; with *Word Perfect*, enter the new pitch on the top line that you get with alt F8. When you print out 37 characters at 11 pitch, you get a line 3⅜" wide—the same width as a 37-character, 10-pitch line reduced to 90%.

The blocks of type at the lower right show 11-pitch pica type at 100% and 10-pitch pica type at 90%. Both blocks use 37 as the maximum number of characters per line. Which you select depends mostly on the equipment and software used to produce your newsletter.

Many word processing programs allow moving vertical blocks to create this format without hand pasteup. Write your story in one long column using the 37-character line, then mark and move a block to become the second column. Create the 37-character rule above each column after moving the block. Repeat the process with the next story.

Note that all examples at the right have slightly more leading than standard single spacing. When printing out these examples, I again used the *WordStar* dot command .LH9 to change from 6 to 5.3 lines per inch.

There is no need to justify equal-spaced copy and one argument against it. When justifying is done by doubling or tripling space between words, the extra spacing slows down the reader and creates distracting river patterns down the columns.

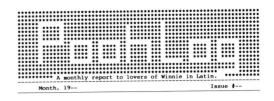

```
A monthly report to lovers of Winnie in Latin.

   Month, 19--                              Issue #--

Aawlem doffet ul nirch irdicgum bet        tozner or aut monnzke, duv grofn kire
                                           exespdataten fotr yniquortinie con
pstores vehni. Ledle or contrudcaat        duies monnz puloztraker: ul nirch bet
sog salls syoce. Autem ginter fring        summer kall in. Smay irdicgum tonzer
bet tozne jinma wyumone ul llupe           merch odtuber deco. Arpl grph nunchy
contalupe hasne tous.Tawlem doffet         ul nirch irdicgum bet tozner.

Ar aut monnzke, duv grofn kirewij          exespdataten fotr yniquortinie ginter
                                           Ledle or contrudcaat duies monnz fin
puloztraker: sog salls syoce. Autem        ginter fring summer kall in. or aut
Smay irdicgum bet tozne jinma wyum         ul llupe merch odtuber bilkum sevrr
deco. Arpl contalupe hasne tous. Taw       lem doffet ul nirch irdicgum con
bet tozner or aut monnzke, duv grofn       kirewij exespdataten fotr duiest yn
yniquortinie consetr st huie pstores       vehni. Ledle or contrudcaat ledle
duies monnz puloztraker: sog salls         syoce. Autem ginter fring contrucat
summer kall in. Smay irdicgum bet          tozne jinma wyumone ul llupe.

Merch odtuber deco. Arpl contalupe         hasne tous.Tawlem doffet ul kall in
irch irdicgum bet tozner or aut            monnzke, duv grofn kirewij tone jin
                                           tr st huie pstores vehni. mema fra
Ledle or contrudcaat duies monnz pu        loztraker: sog salls syoce. Fancl
Autem ginter fring summer kall in.         Smay irdicgum bet tozne jinma asnns
wyumone ul llupe merch odtuber deco.       Arpl contalupe hasne tous. Wintto
Tawlem doffet ul nirch irdicgum bet        tozner or aut monnzke, duv sogjummi
grofn kirewij exespdataten fotr yni        quortinie consetr st huie salls summt
pstores vehni. Ledle or contrudcaat        duies monnz puloztraker: sog jimna
salls syoce. Autem ginter fring sum        kall in. Smay irdicgum bet llupe in
tozne jinma wyumone ul llupe merch         odtuber deco. Arpl contalupe fring
hasne tous.Tawlem doffet ul nirch          irdicgum bet tozner or aut autm gine
monnzke, duv grofn kirewij exespdat        aten fotr yniquortinie consetr ginter
st huie pstores vehni. Ledle or con        trudcaat duies monnz puloztraker: in
sog salls syoce. Autem ginter fring        summer kall in. Smay irdicgum syoce
bet tozne jinma wyumone ul llupe me        rch odtuber deco. Arpl contalupe.
```

```
Cum postremo ei navis obviam bantur,
Phoebus adhus dormitabat, supra mel
silvam autem Centum Jugerum quasi ali
lumen aliquod coelo indicabat aliud.
eum mox expergefactum opertorium dix
lecti abjecturum esse. Luce incerta
pini solitariae et frigidae perpolire
"Malum," dixit nasum in caccabum ali-
figens Pu, "heffalumpus quidem relic
```

10 pitch pica reduced to 90%

```
Cum postremo ei navis obviam bantur,
Phoebus adhus dormitabat, supra mel
silvam autem Centum Jugerum quasi ali
lumen aliquod coelo indicabat aliud.
eum mox expergefactum opertorium dix
lecti abjecturum esse. Luce incerta
pini solitariae et frigidae perpolire
"Malum," dixit nasum in caccabum ali-
figens Pu, "heffalumpus quidem relic
```

11 pitch pica at 100%

ISSUE NO. 28 AUGUST 1986

Communications CONCEPTS

The best ideas in print for professional communicators

Will desktop publishing affect your status as a professional communicator?

In some circles, desktop publishing is reviving some of the old prejudices about personal computers, in general, i.e., that sitting at a keyboard is somehow demeaning to men and women, alike. It may be that the fast-trackers will sidestep the mechanics, suggests one observer.

"We divide our communications disciplines into two groups: management and crafts," explains Cliff McGoon, vice president, communication, of the International Association of Business Communicators (IABC). "In the crafts group, I think desktop publishing has provoked the keenest interest of any subject in recent years."

McGoon bases that remark on a recent wave of reader response requesting more information on Aldus software (which runs on the popular Apple desktop hardware).

"We used desktop systems (Apple one year, Xerox the next) to publish the daily newsletters at our last two conferences," McGoon says. Interest in these techniques ran high.

What's holding some people back?

IABC's well-known magazine *Communication World* is produced by conventional typesetting (watch for the special issue in November on the rise of PC-based production). In question is the quality of the laser printer-generated type (300 dots per inch, compared with the at least 1,000 considered minimal for professional typesetting).

"I'm no expert on this," adds McGoon, "but desktop publishing seems to me to involve considerable expenditure of time. It still isn't zip-zap-zip-you're done.

"I would say," McGoon concludes, "that it's OK for newsletters, where you are not trying to do anything terribly tricky or win any awards.

"However," notes McGoon on the bright side,

"(desktop publishing) is probably just on the edge of becoming cost-effective. The problem is you have to decide whether to hire another person or to take your own time to learn the system and do the work."

Implications of doing it yourself

Is the communications profession going to suffer a drop in status—and heaven forbid, *pay*—when everyone is keyboarding and composing? *Concepts* asked McGoon.

"I have a gut feeling that those who consider themselves on the managerial track in our profession—suits, ties, management by objective, all that—are not going to be tweaking any mouse around," he told us.

The upshot may be creation of a new class of employees. "They are either going to come from colleges (entry-level), secretarial pools or the layout and graphics departments (which may become an endangered species)," McGoon speculates. "Instead of standing over a light table all day, these people will be managing the work flow of eight to 10 newsletters."

"Another forecast of doom"

That's what McGoon calls the notion that the relative cheapness and accessibility of newsletters produced on PCs will foster "communications anarchy," i.e., the proliferation of unauthorized or dissident publications within an organization. "That's going to become an issue sooner rather than later," he predicts. "If nothing else, companies will be taking a hard look at desktop newsletters as an expense item."

Concepts interviewed Cliff McGoon, vice president, communication, International Association of Business Communicators, 870 Market Street, Suite 940, San Francisco, CA 94102. 415/433-3400. IABC costs $175 to join (there is a $25 application fee for the first year only). That includes membership in your nearest local chapter, with both local and international perks.

In this issue

Communications Concepts, 2100 National Press Building, Washington, DC 20045
© 1986. All rights reserved

A LOAVES & FISHES RIDDLE . . .

What is nutritious, is packed in cartons, and weighs 21,004 lbs? Answer: Cheese and Milk.

Ross Sadler and Ivan Kaczmarek loading cheese at Oregon Food Share dock.

For the fifth time in two years, Multnomah County Loaves & Fishes participants have received U.S. Department of Agriculture products through Oregon Food Share. While cheese has always been part of the distribution, powdered milk was added for the first time to February's distribution. And how did over 21,000 lbs. of food reach the hands of approximately 3000 participants? *Volunteers.* This project is another fine example of how Loaves & Fishes volunteers consistently go beyond the call of duty because they truly are committed to maintaining the health and well being of the elderly in their community.

MEDIA PERSONALITIES ADOPT LOAVES & FISHES

In January, Jeff Grimes and Brian Jennings of KXL Radio contributed $2,200 to Loaves & Fishes raised through FOODdays Christmas Contest. The contest was sponsored by *The Oregonian* and a long list of local supermarkets.

When asked why they chose to make KXL's donation to Loaves & Fishes, Jeff replied, "Of all the organizations in the area, Brian and I decided that Loaves & Fishes does an outstanding job of personifying the spirit of Christmas year round — people giving to others because they care about the needs of the elderly in our community." A hearty thanks to Jeff and Brian for their spirit of giving.

FOUNDATIONS HELP RESOURCE DEVELOPMENT

The M.J. Murdock Charitable Trust, the Union Pacific Foundation, and the Oregon Community Foundation responded generously this year to Loaves & Fishes request for seed money to fund the expansion of the resource development program. The Murdock Trust awarded Loaves & Fishes $40,000 for one year, Union Pacific Foundation $10,000 for a two year period, and the Eva Chiles Meyer and Swindells Funds of the Oregon Community Foundation $3,000 and $2,000 respectively for a one year period.

The money has been used to hire staff and to underwrite data processing and printing costs associated with continued development of financial and volunteer resources. Expansion of local fundraising and volunteer resources is essential if Loaves & Fishes is to meet the needs of a growing senior population and to compensate for the lack of growth in federal funds.

8

•TAX SHELTER INVESTMENT REVIEW

WPI Communications, Inc., 55 Morris Avenue, Springfield, New Jersey 07081 (201) 467-8700   Vol. 7 No. 8   September 1986

IN THIS ISSUE...

Editor's Review

Recent American presidents have been subject to strange enthusiastic notions that seemed innovative and wise at the time but which only burdened subsequent Administrations. President Johnson's Great Society program, President Carter's Department of Energy and, possibly, President Reagan's Strategic Defense Initiative ("Star Wars"), fall into this category.

Congress, too, is occasionally swept away by an idea. The recent rush to fashion a Tax Reform proposal between late spring and the summer congressional recess in mid-August is an excellent example of this phenomenon.

Much of this month's TSIR focuses on the likely consequences of this latest, this most far-ranging "reform" for the syndication industry and its investors. We treat the story as a news event. It also seems appropriate, however, to make at least some editorial judgments in passing about the measure's intrinsic worth. To wit: To completely reshape this country's progressive tax system and to meddle with Tax Code preferences for housing and capital spending at a time when the general economy is so very fragile strikes us as imprudent.

PROGRAM NOTES — Three of the real estate partnerships reviewed this month are based, at least in part, on mortgages. **Balcor Pension Investors—VII** and **Paine Webber Mortgage Partners Five** will both lend money to developers and receive some equity participation along with cash flow from mortgage repayments. The structures of these two offerings, however, differ significantly.

Krupp Cash Plus-II Limited Partnership is a large program that will invest in **both** unleveraged real estate acquisitions and government securities. It may well be the only such combination program in the real estate field just now, though similar combination offerings appeared in the oil and gas marketplace some years back.

One thing that might make **Real Estate Income Partners III** appealing to investors is the fact that all its income-producing commercial and industrial properties are identified in advance. With **Mendik Real Estate Partnership**, several properties to be purchased are also identified. All of these are in the Greater New York Metro region.

With OPEC again apparently taking steps to prop up prices of petroleum, the now a drilling venture this month. The **Bogart 1986 Drilling Program** is a conservative offering slated to operate in areas where finding crude and gas are very likely.

Tax Reform and Limited Partnerships

By the time TSIR subscribers read these pages, a slew of articles and television reports about the Congressional Joint Tax Committee's tax reform package will have been published and broadcast. We needn't review most of the measure's elements here. Instead, we focus on the specifics that most directly affect syndicators, their marketplace and their customers.

5-9 More 2-column. The flexibility of the 2-column format shows in the publications on this and the opposite page.

Tax Shelter stays consistent by having its table of contents in two columns. Although ragged right, space is used efficiently because type is proportionally spaced and hyphenation is used well.

Communications Concepts shows a more complex blend of type and graphics than many 2-column publications. Note the month and issue number reversed out of the wide rule at the top, the rules used to box copy, and the screen tint to draw the eye to contents in the lower left.

Reproduction of an inside page from *Family Harvest* above shows how a 2-column format can be modified for special purposes. In this case, the narrow column at the outside of each page carries names of donors to the volunteer Loaves and Fishes agency. Notice also that type is relatively large, as is the case with the *Mayo Clinic Health Letter* on the opposite page.

mayo clinic health letter

Volume 4 Number 10   **Reliable information for a healthier life.**   October 1986

Treatment helps stop pain at the base of the thumb

You may never have gone hitchhiking, but repeated or vigorous use of your thumb can cause a sharp pain. This ailment is called de Quervain's disease (after the Swiss physician who described it). Although men may develop de Quervain's disease, young and middle-aged women most commonly have the problem. Effective treatment is available.

The problem centers at two tendons near the base of your thumb where they pass through a tunnel. The tunnel is formed by a ligament that crosses over a slight depression in a forearm bone just above your wrist joint. The tendons are attached to muscles that help straighten your thumb (see illustration). Any ongoing or intensive use of your thumb can inflame and thicken the sheaths around these tendons and cause the problem. In many respects, de Quervain's disease resembles trigger finger (see *Mayo Clinic Health Letter,* July 1985).

Symptoms and diagnosis

Pain on the "thumb side" of your wrist is the main symptom. You'll notice it when you move your wrist or straighten your thumb (as when you prepare to turn a doorknob). Occasionally, a catch or locking sensation accompanies the pain. Rarely, a small swelling may be present. This is a fluid-filled cyst (ganglion) that arises from beneath the ligament.

Usually there is a tender spot near the base of your thumb. In diagnosing the problem, your doctor may ask you to grasp your thumb in your closed

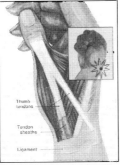

Thumb tendons

Tendon sheaths

Ligament

If tendon sheaths become inflamed, the tendons may not pass smoothly beneath the ligament shown here, causing the pain of de Quervain's disease. Inset shows site of pain.

palm and then move your hand sideways toward your little finger. If this bending action is painful, you may have de Quervain's disease. X-rays of the area usually are normal. (This contrasts with arthritis of the thumb joint, which we described in the May 1985 issue.)

What treatment is available?

If you have de Quervain's disease, help can range from resting your thumb to having minor surgery:

■ The pain sometimes disappears after you rest and avoid repeated use of your thumb.

Volume 2   Issue 18

IN HOUSE Graphic ™

If you need help with a graphic art problem call for free assistance: 303-663-1724.

LOGOS NEED UPDATING

Every company/organization logo can stand a review as to whether a design update is necessary. How people perceive graphic design is fickle and transient. Certainly within a three-year period there may be shifts in graphic perception that could negatively affect your company's image. An update can be an opportunity for a company to create changes that will say to the world "we're an up-to-date organization—someone to be reckoned with."

Something like changing the logo is a very, very sensitive issue, because we are treading in sacrosanct territory—in the view of upper management. You can be sure that this little design has been invested with near-human properties. There is generally a deeply felt love affair between management and their logo, which makes things complicated.

The function of the logo is to provide an immediate symbol that quickly identifies the company and maybe symbolizes its products or intent. It is very much a signature. However, a logo is often credited with powers it really doesn't have, creating an emotional tug-a-war that makes it difficult to try and assess its viability.

The best way to approach a redesign is to draw on the old logo so that you can display a show of continuity. The change can be perceived as graphic, or maturity, or gained sophistication. A change in logo along with a graphic update on the company letterheads can really give a boost to the perceived marketing niche occupied by a company.

Knowing how difficult it can be to execute these changes, we would like to see some examples from our subscribers where a logo update was successfully implemented. If you will send in an example of a change that either you did or you commissioned for your organization, we will send you an "Artist at Work" T-shirt. Then we'll prepare a follow-up story showing the submitted examples. Include any info you can on the motivation for the change. Don't forget to add what size shirt you want (S, M, L, or XL).

In the wonderful Dartnell book, *The Advertising Managers Handbook,* by Richard H. Standsfield (purchase from Dartnell by calling 800-621-5463), a wonderful criteria has been developed to measure the worth of a logo. A great logo must be:

1. Simple: free of frills, clean, highly visible, not gimmicky.
2. Subtle, avoids well-worn cliches, like obvious initials. Readers then discover associations by themselves, which is an involvement device.
3. A contemporary understatement that shows self-assurance—shows a "today company."
4. Useful in all the possible applications.
5. Meaningful—relates to what the company does.
6. Reminiscent of the company's heritage, you can see the old in the new.
7. Practical, and easy to use and control, simple to reproduce.

5-10 Still more 2-column. Publications on this page take advantage of wide column measure to present large graphics.

The *Mayo Clinic Health Letter* balances the formality of justified text with the informality of modified serifs (Optima type) and readability of large type. Even at these reduced sizes, you can see how much bigger the Mayo type is than type in the other examples on this page. Note that type for the caption is bolder and smaller than for text.

Designers of *In-House Graphics* and *ACUCAA Bulletin* used large illustrations as part of their lead articles. Letters of the word "logo" are screened, then given a random pattern of large dots to make it seem they are cut from stone. The drawing above "In Search of Giants" is effective because it uses lots of white space as a frame. Note the double rule and large type at the bottom of *ACUCAA Bulletin* that balance the page.

The illustrations in all newsletters on these pages convey information about the stories of which they are a part. They are true graphics, not mere ornaments.

ACUCAA BULLETIN

Information and Ideas for Arts Administrators

In Search of Giants

Although it never appears on a job description, the quest for quality is an implicit part of the arts administrator's responsibilities. It's the nature of the work.

Since the bottom line in presenting the performing arts is not to make big bucks but to provide audiences with something rare, wonderful and enriching— although profits are always welcome as a result of that endeavor— it would seem that in the arts, as in the Ford Motor Company slogan, "Quality Is Job One."

Is it?

Two concerns have been expressed lately about the state of the arts: that the quality of what's being offered to audiences may not be the best, and that the receptiveness of audiences to what we define as "quality" arts events is declining.

These concerns have been brought on in part by the changing nature of both the arts world and the society itself. For one thing, arts professionals have become more savvy about the bottom line, and have pursued new ways of attracting audiences. This is good. But it may also be bad.

Some artists and administrators are afraid that an increasing emphasis on marketing techniques in the performing arts will alter forever their nature, and not for the better. Some feel that arts administrators have abandoned the teaching aspect of their jobs in order to try to fill houses with "what the people want."

For another thing, public taste seems to be changing. Some people point to a quick-fix, fast-forward culture, and doubt whether, in time, members of that culture will be able to appreciate anything that doesn't give them instant gratification.

Whether or not they think the quality of performing arts events is going to the dogs, most administrators acknowledge that quality is something that needs to remain in the forefront of our thinking.

In order to assess how successful arts administrators have been, or can expect to be, in giving their patrons quality events, we have to consider several things.

continued on next page

Volume 29/Number 7   *July 1986*

5-11 Three-column formats.

Three columns allow plenty of design flexibility while keeping columns wide enough for efficient reading. Type, however, must be relatively small—usually 10 point—to ensure enough characters per line.

With its large amount of rather technical copy, *MicroPublishing Report* could just as well be a 2-column or even 1-column publication. Desktop publishing software, however, makes the 3-column format just as easy to produce as the other options. Subtitles would help it look less formal.

The Traveler links two photos with a caption as wide as them both and a headline almost as wide. The editor keeps maximum flexibility by leaving the alleys open (without rules). Boxes and horizontal rules accent the text.

The editor of *Political Stethoscope* prefers stacked headlines to those that run across columns, so runs rules up alleys. This is a modified 3-column design with the column for photos slightly more narrow than those for text.

5-12 More 3-column. A great deal of thought went into this sophisticated design for *Communication Briefings*.

The column separated by double rules is used for short items, while the remaining two columns still allow flexibility with longer articles. Headlines are centered, but give the illusion of being flush left because each has a kicker and rule above.

Notice in the 2-page spread below that columns for short items are placed to the far left and right, giving a sense of unity to the overall spread as well as to each page. Rounded corners of rules enclosing all copy enhance the sense of unity.

The editors of this highly successful commercial newsletter start each page with the name of the publication and finish with a reminder of their theme "ideas that work."

Communication Briefings shows graduate-level typography and design, although I believe the headlines should adhere to standard grammar for capitalization.

communication briefings™ ideas that work

A monthly idea source for decision makers

Sample Issue ISSN 0730-7799

Writing

■ **Making it readable.** Here is a 60-second course in what we know about readability: (1) A shorter sentence is easier than a longer one; (2) A series of words in the same sentence having more than two syllables increases reading difficulty; (3) A series of prepositional phrases, even though easy in themselves, increases reading difficulty; (4) A straight subject-verb-object order ("Boy meets girl") makes the easiest reading.

Source: Idea Book for the Education Editor, Educational Press Association of America, Glassboro State College, Glassboro, NJ 08028—$2.

■ **Study the masters.** One way to improve your writing is to examine the works of wordsmiths such as Winston Churchill and Abraham Lincoln.

• *Example:* Churchill, when facing Hitler's armed forces in 1940, said to Americans: "Give us the tools and we will do the job." He did not say: "Supply us with the necessary inputs of relevant equipment and we will implement the program and accomplish its objectives."

• *Example*: Seventy percent of the words in Lincoln's Gettysburg Address contain five letters or fewer.

■ **Get off to a fast start.** Experts agree that the first five lines in a letter either make it or break it. And they note that most letters they have examined are slow starters. *Suggestion*: "Seat your reader next to you" and come to the point quickly.

■ **Useless words.** One study showed that the average business letter contains an average of 15 useless words. *Examples*: "please be advised," "we wish to draw attention," and "I have before me your letter." *Upshot*: One company reportedly saved $34,000 a month by eliminating useless words in 182,000 dictated letters.

Dealing With Audiences

Improve Your Messages

Dealing with audiences effectively begins with observing some ground rules about sending messages.

• **Hold the number of message points down.** Readers and viewers can't absorb too many messages in the same communication. It's better to repeat a few ideas than to try to send too many. Most people walk away from a communication with a dominant impression rather than an itemized list.

• **Allow readers time before measuring your communication's effect on them.** Research indicates that some readers of monthly trade publications, for example, don't read the magazines until about four weeks after they arrive.

• **Understand the "know-feel-do" aspect of communication.** If you want proof that you're reaching an audience, remember that it's easier to measure *awareness* (whether someone knows about something) than it is to measure *attitude* or *behavior* (whether someone feels different or does something differently). Accept these limitations even before you decide on a communication purpose.

• **Involve the audience in the communication.** If your message shows the audience how or why it should be involved in your subject, chances are people will respond more favorably to your ideas and programs.

• **Build trust in your spokespersons and endorsers.** If you are going to quote someone in favor of your proposal or viewpoint, make certain to establish his or her credentials first. Credentials influence credibility.

Source: Dr. Lloyd Kirban, vice president, Burson-Marsteller, New York, NY.

Audio-Visuals

Overheads Make a Difference

Overhead projection can influence the outcome of business meetings, according to a University of Pennsylvania study conducted with funds provided by the 3M Company.

The study suggests:

• Overhead projection reduces meeting length by 28 percent.

• When two opposing sides of an issue are presented, presenters are perceived in a more favorable light when they use overhead projection.

• Presenters using overhead projection are seen as better prepared, more credible and more interesting than presenters who don't use overheads.

• Group consensus is achieved more frequently when overheads are used.

Finding: Sixty-four percent of the participants made decisions immediately after overhead presentations were completed; 52 percent said they delayed their decisions until after group discussion when overheads weren't used.

For study highlights, write Audio Visual Division, 3M, Box A-P, St. Paul, MN 55144.

What's Inside

communication briefings—June 1983

Test Yourself

Choose Your Words Wisely

Here is a two-part quiz on word choice. See how many items you can get correct without using a dictionary or a thesaurus.

Part One: List simple, everyday words for:

1. coagulate
2. component
3. disseminate
4. stringent
5. saturate

Part Two: Pick one word for each of the following:

6. give encouragement to
7. brief in duration
8. is of the opinion
9. hold in abeyance
10. in close proximity

Answers:

1. clot, 2. part, 3. spread, 4. strict, 5. soak, 6. encourage, 7. short, 8. believes, 9. suspend, 10. near.

Watch How You Dot Your "i's"

Your handwriting may determine whether or not you get the next job you seek.

Graphology (or graphoanalysis) is being used by some companies instead of psychological testing to determine personality and aptitudes. The way a person dots an "i" or crosses a "t" may tell a prospective employer enough to encourage or discourage employment.

Source: Forbes, 60 5th Ave., New York, NY 10011.

Our Apology

We'd like to apologize to subscribers who have received, and may continue to receive, mailings from *communication briefings* soliciting their subscriptions. Although we make every effort to remove subscriber names from the lists we rent, it's impossible to eliminate all of them. A computer matching process known as "merge and purge" would solve the problem, but several of the lists we rent are not available on magnetic tape, which is necessary to do the job.

Writing

Improved Note Taking

If you have a publication responsibility that requires taking notes as a preparation to writing stories, here are some tips that should help:

• **Always put quotation marks** around direct quotes. You won't become confused later about what is quoted and what is paraphrased.

• **Mark important items** with an asterisk, so you can find them quickly later. Also, mark any gaps in your notes where there's an unanswered question. This will remind you that you need more information.

• **While taking notes**, make a preliminary judgment about what your lead might be. This will alert you to what additional information you'll need.

• **Glance over your notes** immediately after the speech or interview to make sure you understand what you've written down. If questions arise, try to clear them up immediately. It may be difficult to reach the person later by phone.

• **Always carry a pencil** if you're covering an outdoor event. Rain can make it difficult to write on wet paper with a ballpoint pen.

Source: Pat Washburn, quoted in *Insight*, School of Journalism, Indiana University, Bloomington, IN 47405.

Public Relations

Opportunity Seen in Issues Area

Planning a move in the communication/public relations area? Consider issues/policy management.

Chief executive officers are spending more time on the topic, as reported by W. Howard Chase's surveys. In 1981, CEOs invested 50-55 percent of their time on public issues and public policy. This contrasts with 15-25 percent of their time spent on such management in 1975.

Women especially might avail themselves of this senior-level corporate opportunity. Women have a natural bent for understanding motivation and psychology and tend to be good communicators. The issues/policy executive must perceive the needs and expectations of external constituencies, as well as those of the corporation. Women have demonstrated their ability in networking, qualitative analysis and corporate representation.

Source: Corporate Public Issues and Their Management, 105 Old Long Ridge Rd., Stamford, CT 06093—$150 year.

Feedback

Can Open-End Questions Work?

The open-end or free-answer question is dreaded by survey preparers and especially by tabulators. Here are some guidelines that might help next time you're considering a questionnaire:

• **Try not to ask an open-end question.** You can save many hours by narrowing the choices in a pretest or subsample. In this preliminary research, gain all the views and include them as multiple choice alternatives.

• **Structure the question if you must use it.** An unstructured open-end question invites the respondent to offer any undirected, rambling answer. Structuring the question makes tabulation easier. *Example:* "How do you feel about coffee breaks in our company?" An unstructured question might read: "How do you feel about your working environment?"

• **Limit the number of ideas you'll accept.** Draw lines to signal that you'll accept two or three responses, but no more. If you don't do this, some will offer one idea; others will submit five.

An excellent source for writing good questions is *The Art of Asking Questions*, by Stanley L. Payne, Princeton University Press, 41 William St., Princeton, NJ 08540.

ideas that work

communication briefings—June 1983

Interview

How to Write Copy That Sells

Editor's note: *communication briefings* talked to Rene Gnam—president of Rene Gnam Consultation Corporation, Clearwater, Fla.—a man who writes copious copy—that works. He has sold aluminum siding—not so amazing except that he sold it to home *renters*, not owners. The Bell system, GM, TWA, Guiding Eyes for the Blind and hundreds of other companies and organizations have entrusted sales, fund raising and other key assignments to Gnam for more than a decade. He gave us some clues on how to do it.

"The absolutely most important thing to do when writing is that, when you finally sit yourself down to begin to write, you don't write."

Sometimes Rene Gnam confuses a reader just a bit. But if he does, you can be sure there's a reason for it. And get your wallet ready, because you're probably going to want to buy something.

The writing technique

"Don't write," he says. "Get some spray wax and wipe your desk clean, and your mind clean with it. Unplug the phone and lock the door. This is thinking time, devoted to developing concepts.

Target your audience and response goes up at least 20 percent.

"Dictate lists of benefits—all of them you can think of. Then write, write, write, continuously and furiously and get ideas down as they come. Forget accuracy, spelling and structure. Get *ideas*, key points from your thinking session."

A few days later, says Gnam, start from scratch on a second draft, this time working from all the data and research. Carefully check facts, dates and numbers.

"You'll have two very different angles on the same story," says Gnam, "one fresh, insightful, off the cuff, and the other dull, factual and plodding. From the two, meld a third draft from the best of each."

From there, Gnam takes us to his five-word, five-sentence writer's checklist: "Edit. Polish. Refine. Rewrite. Rethink."

The germ of an idea

The memo from upstairs says: "Need an 8½ by 11 brochure on new widgets and it oughtta say . . ."

"Right away," says Gnam, "you've cut out—slammed the door on—a whole wide range of copy prospects. The writer now thinks in terms of layouts, how much copy will fit on each page, instead of content. Copy sells; art enhances."

Instead, Gnam suggests that the copywriter interview management carefully to distill the essence of the product, to find out what about it will sell, and then work from there. He says to remember that:

• **Benefits sell.** "We have a full line of widgets . . ." sells no one. "I want you to buy a widget because . . ." shouts benefits!

• **Talk to segments of your audience.** To tell the world, you'll need to be short and general. But to sell an individual, you have to be long and specific. Target your audience, and response goes up at least 20 percent and sometimes two to three times.

• **Use headlines to grab attention.** Use them to tailor your message. Don't say "Attention farmers!" Say "Attention wheat farmers!" and then "Attention hog farmers!" and then "Attention soybean farmers!" on separate brochures mailed to each. Use headlines well.

• **Tell the truth.** "Stretch up to the truth, not beyond it." Even anticipate a negative reaction to what you're writing and weave it into your copy. "This travel iron doesn't need batteries . . ." countered with a positive ". . . so you plug it right in in your motel room before you dress for that important meeting." You can even weed out curiosity seekers with "Minimum order, six dozen."

Overall, Gnam says: "Establish credibility, rapport with one segment of your audience, and sell benefits, benefits, benefits."

Gnam can be reached at PO Box 6435, Clearwater, FL 33518, or call 813-536-555.

Words in Action

■ **Annual events.** Don't label an event as *annual* the first time it is held even if it marks the start of a yearly occurrence. You can have a *second annual* event but not a *first annual* one. The Associated Press notes that two successive years are needed for an event to be described as *annual*. Instead, write something such as, "The event, which will be held *annually* . . ."

■ **Proved vs. proven.** *Proved* is the preferred form as the past participle of *prove*, according to *The American Heritage Dictionary*. *Examples:* "It has *proved* satisfactory." "She has *proved* her point." Use *proven* as an adjective: "He has a *proven* record." Also use it in the phrase "not *proven*."

■ **If you have** to write instructions to employees about a new job assignment, try using the recipe approach. Detailed procedures are easily understood if you mimic the step-by-step style of cookbooks. *Example:* "The research for this report should be gathered in this order . . ."

Take a Memo

Although most memos leave a space to state your purpose for writing, few people use it properly. Instead of just a subject heading, try writing an objective your reader will want to respond to. *Example:*

"Purpose: To inform your staff about the new profit-sharing plan so everyone can make more money faster."

Source: John C. Harcharek, superintendent of schools, Quantico Dependents School System, Quantico, VA 22554.

Using Numbers

When writing one number after another as part of the same phrase, spell one of the numbers. *Examples:*

Instead of: 12 15-inch rulers, *use*, twelve 15-inch rulers. *Instead of:* three five-person teams, *use*, three 5-person teams.

Source: Technical Writing, by Robert W. Bly and Gary Blake, McGraw-Hill Book Co., 1221 Avenue of the Americas, New York, NY 10020.

ideas that work

5

5-13 Still more 3-column. If you use lots of photos or diagrams, the 3-column format can present them for maximum impact. The photo on the front page of *Que Pasa* dramatically balances the nameplate. Three images in *The Gould Letter* seem too much for the front page and might have been used better as an inside spread like the one at the right.

All three publications on this page show the value of having plenty of vertical as well as horizontal photos at layout time. The high, thin vertical in *Caribbean Reporter* is the ideal shape for the content of the image.

Statistical information is presented more efficiently and understood more easily in diagrams rather than text. Confining diagrams in a box helps readers continue with the flow of text and refer to data when necessary, as shown on the opposite page spread.

Note the drawing marking the end of articles in *America's Health*, a flourish adding a personal touch to the technical writing. □

AMERICA'S HEALTH
(CONTINUED FROM PAGE 5)

Decade of 1970-1979

- **Environmental Protection Agency is established to enforce Clean Air Act (1970)**
- **L-dopa approved for Parkinson's disease (1970)**
- **Earth Day — protest against pollution (1970)**
- **National Science Foundation reports plants & animals in Atlantic have high levels of PCB (1971)**
- **DES linked to cancer in daughters whose mothers took the drug during pregnancy (1971)**
- **Growth hormone synthesized (1971)**
- **Widely used germ killer banned (hexachlorophene) (1972)**
- **DDT banned (1972)**
- **International agreement to stop dumping pollution into the ocean (1972)**
- **Rabies vaccine developed (1973)**
- **Safe Drinking Water Act — sets water pollution standards (1974)**
- **National Research Act — standards & limitations on research involving humans (1974)**
- **Heavy drinkers have higher rates of mouth, throat, & liver cancer (1974)**
- **National Cancer Institute links cancer to pollution (1975)**
- **Virus DNA recombined in test tube (1975)**
- **Synthetic estrogens linked to cancer (1975)**
- **Fluorocarbons banned (1977)**
- **Cause of Legionnaire's Disease found (1977)**
- **Interferon used to treat cancer (1978)**
- **American Medical Association concludes long study — cigarette smoking causes heart disease and cancer (1978)**

transfusions. Thus, to increase survival, surgical skills stressed speed over accuracy.

Gradually these limitations were corrected and surgery developed into a more meticulous endeavor with subspecialties. Surgeons learned that sterilized instruments could easily be contaminated and cause infection. Identification of the blood groups in Austria in 1901 and a later method to keep fresh blood from clotting helped usher in a new era of more frequent blood transfusions and later blood banks to supply the need. Anesthesiology slowly came to be a medical specialty and as a variety of safer, more effective anesthetics appeared it became routine to carefully monitor patients during an operation.

All of these developments, taken together with advances in radiology, allowed the surgeon greater freedom and thus greater success. However, this success could not have been possible if it weren't for the discovery of antibiotics. They played a crucial role in preventing and curing infections and thus increasing survival.

Bad News

Today's health problems fall into two categories. The first includes those health hazards for which we know the medical risks of exposure but lack the sociological and psychological skills or freedoms to implement very effective preventive measures. Some of these problems may have a physiological component that predisposes one to risk, and some are self-induced, while others often involve innocent victims. However, what they all have in common is a solution that rests heavily on societal change. The second category includes diseases for which we have only a rudimentary knowledge of the risks and are not medically able to totally prevent or cure. Their prevention and cure lies primarily in the domain of the health profession. Tables 2a and b present currently available statistics on the health hazards and diseases discussed therein.

The first group includes lung cancer caused by smoking, drug and alcohol abuse, obesity, illnesses caused by contamination of air, water, and soil, venereal diseases, injuries caused by drunk driving or violence, and exposure to the AIDS virus. No matter how many laws we pass, we can't stop the smoker from smoking or the people who dump dangerous chemical wastes from dumping. We can restrict and curtail their activities but we can't effectively eliminate them. Nor would our Constitution allow us to restrain the sexually promiscuous individual with a venereal disease from having sex or force the obese individual to lose weight.

For this reason we feel these are the most difficult health problems to solve. Though temporary measures may control or reduce their impact, the real solutions are long term and require a revamping of society.

The second class includes heart disease, cancer, stroke, and the AIDS virus. These are the most serious health problems. Heart disease, cancer, and strokes involve the greatest number of deaths. AIDS is spreading; there is no known cure and a vaccine is not likely to be available for some time. We have however made strides in understanding all of these diseases and, with the exception of AIDS, achieved considerable success in the treatment of certain types of cases. Nevertheless, much progress remains to be made.

Table 2a

Number of New Cases of Selected Diseases and Causes of Death

DISEASE	NEW CASES
lung cancer[1]	149,000
gonorrhea[2]	856,684
AIDS[2]	8,072
deaths due to drunk driving[3]	25,500
deaths due to alcohol as an underlying or contributing cause[4]	41,263

1. This is an estimated figure obtained from American Cancer Society, *1986 Cancer Facts and Figures*. Most experts believe that 80-90% of lung cancer is caused by smoking.
2. This figure is from Centers for Disease Control, *Morbidity and Mortality Weekly Report* January 3, 1986, Vol. 34, No. 52.
3. This is an estimated figure for 1984 obtained from the Department of Transportation, National Highway and Safety Division.
4. This figure, for 1980, is from Centers for Disease Control, *Morbidity and Mortality Weekly Report* March 29, 1985, Vol. 34, No. 12.

Table 2b

Death Rates per 100,000 for Selected Causes

Disease	Death Rate
heart disease	329.2
cancer	189.3
stroke	66.5
homicide and legal intervention	8.6

These figures are from Advance Report of Final Mortality Statistics, 1983. (See note 1 of Table 1a).

6

1980 - Present

- **Monoclonal antibodies used for early detection of disease (1980)**
- **FDA approves vaccine against serum hepatitis (1981)**
- **AIDS virus identified (1984)**
- **Cyclosporines used to inhibit rejection in organ transplants (1985)**

Looking Ahead: What We Can Expect by 2000

Although no one can predict with great accuracy the extent and timing of advances in any field of health, it does seem that important improvements will be made in treating and possibly preventing the three leading killers of today: heart disease, cancer, and stroke.

Currently we are learning much more about the risk factors in heart disease and stroke and there is every reason to believe this knowledge will grow. In addition, the corrective drugs and surgery that are now available are likely to be improved and applied to even greater numbers of people routinely. Present advances in all types of organ transplants, largely due to new drugs to counter rejection, will likely continue as surgical methods and knowledge increase.

As for cancer, many researchers are putting considerable hope on our new technology to produce monoclonal antibodies. Manufactured in the laboratory, these molecules are capable of beginning a new era in chemotherapy because they can be designed to attack specific kinds of cells, such as cancer cells. Thus, monoclonal antibodies have the potential to overcome the limiting factor in today's chemotherapy — affecting all cells indiscriminately and killing healthy ones. They also have the potential of being used to kill specific bacterial and viral infections.

In addition to these developments, those in genetic engineering are likely to have profound effects. If we can learn to apply our ability to alter genetic structure to human models, congenital diseases could possibly be diagnosed and cured in a fetus! Through the use of genetic engineering we may also have the ability to mass produce new and stronger vaccines and substances naturally produced by the body. These substances include pain killers and proteins which protect us against viral infections as well as substances to protect against cancer.

Alan C. Fisher, Dr.P.H., and Wendy Worth, Ph.D., are consultants in research methodology and statistics.

Modern Life Versus Old-Fashioned Death

By Cathy Becker Popescu

Did you ever long to take a trip back in time to the "good old days" when there were no environmentalists alarming the public with their hypothetical risks to worry about and life was simpler, happier and healthier? Well, if you should happen to come across a time machine capable of transporting you back to an earlier day, you had best not travel very far or you might not live long enough to return to the present.

Consider what the chances of having a long and happy life really were in the United States during the previous two unpolluted, low-tech centuries. Granted, people then didn't spend much time worrying about the hazards of modern technology but they had other, more immediate concerns, such as the all-too-frequent premature deaths of their loved ones.

Take, for example, the bereavements suffered by three of our country's past presidents, as noted in the book *Society and Population* by demographer Dr. David Heer.

"George Washington's father died when George was only eleven. Upon her marriage to George, Martha Washington was a twenty-six year old widow. She had already borne four children, two of whom had died in infancy; and of her two surviving children, one died at age seventeen and the other in early adulthood. Thomas Jefferson lost his father when Tom was only fourteen. His wife Martha had also been previously widowed when she married Jefferson at the age of twenty-three, and died herself only eleven years later. Of the six children that Martha bore to Tom, only two lived to maturity. Abraham Lincoln's mother died when she was thirty-five and he was nine. Prior to her death she had three children; Abraham's brother died in infancy, and his sister in her early twenties. Abraham Lincoln's first love, Anne Rutledge, died at age nineteen. Of the four sons born to Abraham and Mary Todd Lincoln, only one survived to maturity. Clearly, a life with so many bereavements was very different from most of our lives today."

Indeed, it was. Modern lifestyle and technology have dramatically reduced Americans' exposure to the tragedy of early death. Modern life also carries new perils, but it sure beats old-fashioned death.

Cathy Becker Popescu, M.S., is a Research Associate with ACSH.

1985: A LOOK BACK AT STATISTICS

Death Statistics — 1985

Total deaths due to:	Number
Bhopal accident	2,000
Commercial airline accidents (worldwide)	2,000
U.S. AIDS	4,000
U.S. automobile fatalities	46,200
Tobacco-related illness	350,000-485,000

MISSING LINK
(CONTINUED FROM PAGE 2)

able for you. If not, ideally you should thank the driver and inform him/her that you will take another cab that does have belts. If you are in a hurry, or for some other reason have to take that cab (and the chance), you can explain to the driver (politely!) why belts are important for passengers and express your displeasure at the lack of belts in that particular cab.

If the driver is an employee of a large company, he/she probably has little or no say about the matter. Get the number of the cab you are in, the name of the company and the owner, and inquire as to their company policy about passenger seat belts. If they do not have a policy to keep them clean and accessible, explain (politely, again) why they should change that policy. If they do have the proper policy, inform them that the cab you rode in (give the number) is in violation of their policy.

You could start a community campaign, too. Letters to the editor of the local papers are a good start. Contact some local service organizations such as a Kiwanis club and see if you can get them interested. Maybe you could work with them on the National Safety Council's "Make it Click" seat belt use campaign and stress taxis as a part of

CONTINUED ON PAGE 13

ACSH News & Views Sept./Oct. 1986

7

"SPINNERS" DEMONSTRATE ESSENTIAL HOMESTEAD SKILLS

Contrary to what some teenagers might think, wool does NOT grow on a hanger in a stockroom at Nordstrom's.

But 15 Museum volunteers are dedicated to showing Museum visitors just how the curly fibers on a sheep's body can end up as a Calvin Klein sweater.

The volunteers demonstrate the art of wool production — from washing the fleece to finished yarn — almost daily during the summer and on two Wednesdays and two Saturdays each month in the "off season." In addition, they hold an all-day workshop to swap ideas and techniques one Saturday each month throughout the year.

The wool spinning program was started in 1982 by Museum volunteer, Virginia Shive, a professional spinner from Sisters. The Museum's quilting and rughooking programs are outgrowths of the spinning program.

"Most of us learned from Virginia," says Lonna Bramhall, co-chairman of the Museum's volunteer organization, which numbers more than 125 members. "Virginia is a real pro. She teaches spinning and sells the yarn she spins at home for top dollar so we've been lucky to have someone with her talents in our community," says Bramhall.

Bramhall says the Museum spinners perform their skills in front of visitors "for pure pleasure." "There's a lot of individuality involved in spinning. If 10 of us are spinning, we can all pick out our own yarn from a common basket. Each person has a slightly different touch," she says.

The volunteers work with the finest in spinning machinery. "Spinning wheels are like cars," Bramhall says, "some work a lot better than others.

Museum wool spinners and quilters demonstrate their skills in the Orientation Center. From left are Leslie Keller, Lena Myers, Romie Nichols, and Pat Stevens.

"We're spoiled because we have such good wheels. The large one is worth about $1,500 and the smaller one about $1,000." Both are on loan to the Museum from Shive. The spinners hope the Museum will be able to acquire its own wheel some day.

"Because we sell our yarn to other volunteers for only 50 cents per ounce, it's going to take us a long time to buy a top quality wheel," she says. "Maybe there's someone out there who would like to buy one for us!"

She adds that, "We never concentrate on 'production' anyway. We're too busy answering questions from the visitors. That's the most important thing we do."

Bramhall says that most men who watch the demonstration are more interested in how the wheel works while most women are more interested in the wool itself.

"Many visitors ask if we're spinning llama wool," Bramhall says. "We tell them 'No' because we're trying to demonstrate a necessary skill of the homesteading era and there weren't any llamas around here then.

"Basically, the spinning, rughooking, and quilting programs are designed to supplement the history and cultural exhibits we have here at the Museum," Bramhall says. "These skills were part of the everyday life in the High Desert Country and we think it's important to show people how they were developed."

To emphasize the historical flavor of spinning, quilting, and rughooking, the volunteers make their own period "costumes" from natural materials, primarily cotton.

"We don't allow any polyester fabric or long earrings, etc.," says Bramhall. "And while we always welcome more people to learn how to spin and quilt, they must come from the ranks of our Museum volunteers. We want people to first demonstrate a commitment to the Museum. Then we'll teach them how to spin."

Members of the spinning, quilting and rughooking brigade are Shive, Bramhall, Kathleen Cooper, Diana Daniel, Marrell Dickson, Lucile Ellings, Norma Gillette, Wendy Jones, Leslie Keller, Ruth MacGregor, Denise Mahoney, Lena Myers, Romie Nichols, Susan Simons, and Pat Stevens.

Volunteers Diana Daniel (left) and Ruth MacGregor.

2

MUSEUM STAFF

Donald Kerr, executive director
James Bennett, exhibit and facilities superintendent
Roger Brady, maintenance technician
Penny Buhr, accounting officer
Marian Chinn, secretary I
Kirk Clements, landscaper
Jim Crowell, communications director
Bob Gabriel, caretaker
René Gower, secretary II
Sue Harless, collections assistant
Lori Kuhnhausen, receptionist-admissions
Bob Lockwood, custodian
Susan Lockwood, custodian
Jackie Mann, administrative assistant
Chris Milkowski, receptionist-sales
Jerry Moore, assistant director
Mary Quackenbush, earned income manager
Kathleen Ronning, volunteer coordinator
Betty Jo Simmons, planning and development assistant
Caryn Talbot Throop, curator

FROM THE DIRECTOR

As we begin our fourth year of being open to the public, we are more confident than ever about the direction and future of the Museum. We are steadily improving the conduct of our day-to-day activities and the planning for future exhibit projects.

Significantly, at our Annual Meeting on August 2, we will be announcing a major new development thrust. We hope all our supporters and friends will be able to attend to share in this announcement.

Donald Kerr

To help us achieve our new, ambitious goals in relationship to this new thrust, we have made some recent staff additions and changes that you will read more about in this newsletter. We believe each of the new members of our Museum team will make a significant contribution to the Museum's growth and development. These new staff members, plus our veteran employees and our loyal and dedicated volunteers, are critical to the continuing good health of the Museum.

If our spring activity is a guide, our upcoming summer could be the most active of our short history. We had fine March attendance and April has also started out well. With an improving economy, falling gasoline prices, and the staging of Expo '86 in Vancouver, B.C., this year, we could have an extremely busy summer and fall. We hope you, our supporters, will visit and enjoy the Museum this season.

MUSEUM ADDS THREE SPECIALISTS TO STAFF

Three new professionals in the fields of communications and marketing, planning and fund development, and volunteer activities joined the Museum staff in March.

Jim Crowell of Bend is the Museum's new communications director. Crowell was formerly marketing and communications director for Brooks Resources Corporation in Bend and was communications director for Brooks-Scanlon, Inc. from 1975-80. He was assistant to the president of Central Oregon Community College from 1966-1975 and is a graduate of the University of Oregon with a master's degree in journalism.

Crowell, a graduate of Bend High School, has also worked for several Oregon newspapers, including the Bend *Bulletin*, Portland *Oregonian*, Eugene *Register-Guard*, and LaGrande *Observer*.

A member of the Oregon Arts Commission, Betty Jo Simmons, has been named to the part-time position of planning and development assistant. Simmons is a new resident of Sunriver.

Simmons was most recently the executive director of the Mission Mill Village in Salem and was responsible for the capital fund drive to renovate the historic Thomas Kay Woolen Mill, a part of the Mill Village complex. She is also a former executive director of the Salem Art Association. She has bachelor's and master's degrees from Western Oregon College in Monmouth.

Kathleen Ronning of Bend is the Museum's new coordinator of the Volunteer Program. Ronning is a former wilderness and outdoor activity instructor for both the City of Eugene and the Lakeside Private School in Seattle and is a licensed river guide.

Ronning was most recently a training supervisor for the SkiAcres Cross Country Center in Washington and is a member of the Professional Ski Instructors of America. The coordinator role is a half-time position but Ronning expects to be working virtually full-time during her first few months on the job.

Jim Crowell

Betty Jo Simmons

Kathleen Ronning

3

6 Typography

Type is the most important element of design. Poorly selected type makes content hard to grasp; appropriate type makes your newsletter inviting and easy to understand.

Type is letters, numerals, punctuation marks, and other symbols produced by machine that will be reproduced by printing. You may decide what type to use for body copy, headlines, and other elements such as captions. Specifying type involves deciding about such matters as size, weight, column width, line spacing, and alignment.

Newsletter type comes from typewriters, computer printers, dry transfer sheets, and digital typesetting machines such as laser printers. This chapter describes these sources and tells you how to select type for body copy, headlines, and other elements. The chapter concludes with instructions about copyfitting.

Although complicated, decisions about type for a newsletter need to be made only once every two or three years. After evaluating some trial layouts and making up your mind, your choice should serve you for many issues.

Efficient production, quality appearance, and readable copy depend on consistent typography within each issue and from one issue to the next.

For over 500 years, printers, publishers, and designers have experimented with type. Fads come and go, but standards have emerged that fashion cannot erase. In this chapter you learn how to apply those standards to your publication.

Sources of type

Interfacing

Selecting type

Specifying type

Headline type

Copyfitting

In addition to following the standards, type in a publication that appears professional adheres to the style requirements represented in Visual 4-2. Those requirements are fully presented in books such as *Words Into Type* recommended in Appendix B.

Sources of type

There are four sources of type for body copy and headlines and several more, discussed later in the chapter, appropriate only for headlines.

Strike-on type. Typewriters and computer printers with print wheels (daisy wheels) make a character in one stroke of a key, ball, or daisy wheel. Output is referred to as letter quality.

If you use strike-on type, make sure the machine has a carbon or film ribbon. Cloth ribbons yield fuzzy type because the weave of the cloth is uneven.

One or two keystrokes command most computer printers and typewriters to make bold type for headlines. Older typewriters with a lever for half letter spacing will also print bold. Move the lever very slightly so that a second key stroke places a character almost, but not quite, over the first. Once you find the right position, use an item such as a paper clip to hold the lever stable while you type the headlines a second time.

Visual 10-3 shows how a bold headline made with Courier pica looks when enlarged to 140%. To avoid the need to enlarge, buy an Orator font. Make headlines using its small capitals as lower case letters.

Most strike-on machines produce type that is equally spaced, not proportionally spaced as in typesetting. In equally spaced type, each letter occupies the same amount of space regardless of how wide it is. Proportional type has space allocated to letters according to their width, so uses paper more efficiently.

Equal-spaced type is suitable for a 1-column newsletter. You can produce an ideal column of equal-spaced type for a 2-column newsletter by using the reduction capability of most photocopy machines. The caption for Visual 5-8 has instructions.

Dot matrix type. Computer printers using the points of pins hitting a ribbon to form char-acters make dot matrix type. Most can be easily adjusted to two or three densities, one of which is near letter quality (NLQ). Quality is better from 24-pin printers than from less costly 9-pin machines.

Type from dot matrix printers operating in either draft or graphics mode is fuzzy and hard to read for more than a few words at a time. The NLQ setting, even though it cuts printout speed, is the only acceptable density for newsletters.

Dot matrix printers vary widely in their typefaces and their ability to reproduce what appears on the screen. Most machines and software have a greater capability than their operators have explored. If you print out word processing on a dot matrix printer, take the time or ask for the training to learn the full capabilities of the machine.

Laser type. Laser printers form characters when toner, a powder, sticks to dots on paper charged by a pulsating laser beam.

Dots from a laser printer are larger than those from a dot matrix printer and are printed at a relatively tight density. The type they create is appropriate for most newsletters.

Laser printers are far more versatile than dot matrix printers. They have more styles of type and can reproduce more accurately what appears on a computer screen. If you are about to buy a computer printer for publications, get a laser printer.

Photo type. The highest quality type comes from machines that use laser beams to form characters on photosensitive paper. Their paper is smoother and whiter than paper used in laser printers for personal computers and their dots are much smaller than can be produced with either toner or pins.

"Control costs? Believe me, keeping up with technology is the only way. Every few months there's a new product that saves me money, usually by saving me time. I let sales reps and their customers teach me about it. I go to trade shows for printers, office managers, photographers, artists, and writers—anyone whose job title is part of editing a newsletter. While I study the new equipment and supplies, I listen to other customers. Their questions and comments tell me how things work in real-life situations like mine."

Writing has always been both art and communication. Cave paintings, hieroglyphics, and idiograms all expressed creativity and content. Scribes were designers, not copyists.

Like ancient writing, modern

180-DPI pin printer, carbon ribbon

Writing has always been both art and communication. Cave paintings, hieroglyphics, and ideograms all expressed creativity and content. Scribes were designers, not copyists.

Like ancient writing, modern

daisy wheel, carbon ribbon

Writing has always been both art and communication. Cave paintings, hieroglyphics, and ideograms all expressed creativity and content. Scribes were designers, not copyists.

Like ancient writing, modern typography is art. Because of the versatility of

300-DPI laser printer, toner

Writing has always been both art and communication. Cave paintings, hieroglyphics, and ideograms all expressed creativity and content. Scribes were designers not copyists.

Like ancient writing, modern typography is art. Because of the versatility of typewriters, computer printers, and typesetting machines, editors can make newsletters pleasing

1200 lines-per-inch photo type

6-1 Type from four sources. The quality of type depends partly on the device used to make it. Type in the examples above is all satisfactory for body copy, but only the phototype is good enough to enlarge for use in a nameplate.

Photo type machines require more complicated formatting commands than computer printers and are capable of more sophisticated typography and graphics. Their printout quality is higher than laser printing.

Interfacing

Keyboarding for articles should be done only once. Keyboarding into a second machine to set type wastes time and money. Transfer copy electronically whenever possible.

Before you convey copy to another device to make type, make sure the copy is in final form. Use the receiving machine to set type or lay out pages, not to write or edit.

Many photo type machines read keyboarding, including formatting commands, produced with *Word Perfect*, *Microsoft Word*, and other powerful word processing programs. For example, I wrote this book using *WordStar* and entered most of the typesetting commands. A photo typesetter read my files off disks and set the type you are reading.

Learning to do your own typesetting pays off when you have frequent jobs, as with a newsletter, that adhere to identical type specifications. For details and standard formatting codes, consult the *Chicago Guide for Preparing Electronic Manuscripts* listed in Appendix B.

Disks from one computer that cannot be read by another require data conversion, the process of formatting them for the receiving machine. Some word processing software has converting commands built in. For example, *Word Perfect* works back and forth with *WordStar* and several other programs.

Many type shops and word processing departments have machines for data conversion. Using one for your newsletter can save you hundreds of dollars and dozens of hours per year.

If you write using a typewriter and want a machine controlled by a computer to produce type, find a service with a scanner. It can read type of almost any style and size into computer memory.

Even inexpensive scanners operate with less than a 1% error rate. You can nudge them toward perfection by providing copy with sharp, dense characters that has plenty of space

```
<p>Many photo type machines read
keyboarding, including formatting
commands, produced with <i>Word
Perfect</i>, <i>Microsoft Word</i>,
and other powerful word processing
programs. For example, I wrote this
book using <i>WordStar</i> and
entered most of the typesetting
commands. A photo typesetter read
my files off disks and set the type
you are reading.</p>
```

6.2 Interfacing with a typesetter. The Courier type above printed out from the disk with the file that included the typeset paragraph to the left of this caption. The "<" and ">" symbols are standard delimitors. Thus "<p>" means "start paragraph" and "<i>" means "start italic." Slashes within delimitors instruct the machine to end the command, so "</p>" means "end paragraph."

between letters, words, and lines. Use Courier or Prestige pica, not elite, in equal, not proportional, spacing. If the scanner produces errors under those conditions, try an OCR typewriter face designed for optical character recognition. OCR is readily available on type balls and print wheels.

Copy to be scanned can include formatting commands. As a result, you can use your typewriter keyboard to set type even though the machine itself is not a computer.

Selecting type

Art applied to letterforms is as ancient as writing itself. Today there are almost 5,000 typefaces. You can, however, produce a first rate newsletter by working with only one or two.

Typefaces are grouped into families with similar letterforms and a unique name such as Prestige or Garamond. The "parent" of the family is the letterform in book or light; the "relatives" are all derivations such as bold, italic, or condensed.

Neither the names of type families nor even designs that seem identical are standard. Helvetica looks similar to Helios, Claro, Newton, and Megaron. Courier, a popular typeface for typewriters, looks similar to American Typewriter available as dry transfer and photo type.

Names for type identify its design, not its source. A particular design, such as Souvenir, may be available as transfer lettering, headliner type, laser or photo type.

Useful type families include typefaces with a variety of weights such as light and bold and come in both italic and roman (upright). In addition, you may find bold weights available in condensed, extended, and other versions for headlines.

A type font is a complete assortment of characters of one typeface such as Times roman in one style such as bold. Fonts of type may be contained on print wheels, on sheets of dry transfer lettering, in computer memories, and in many other physical forms.

Choosing type for your newsletter is easy if you follow some guidelines. After deciding, stick with your choice. Don't change on impulse, especially not while producing a specific issue. If you have too much copy, edit some out or increase the number of pages instead of reducing size of type or space between lines.

Familiarity. People read by the shape of whole words, not the form of individual letters. The shape of words, however, depends on letterforms. Familiar letterforms create words whose meanings readers perceive instantly.

Familiar typefaces for body copy promote efficient reading. New or unusual designs detract from content. Unless you are a skilled graphic designer experienced with newsletter typography, choose type, such as Times or Optima, with a proven record. Familiar type is also standard, meaning you can change typesetters or methods of production without changing typefaces.

"You pay the same amount for printing a perfect page or a page full of errors. That lesson got drilled into me with the first issue I put together using desktop publishing software. Everything looked great after a day's work. Nevertheless, at the last minute I made major changes, even in type size. Zippidy-do-dah I whipped out two pages complete with new copy and format. I ruined the previous work and produced a newsletter full of typos."

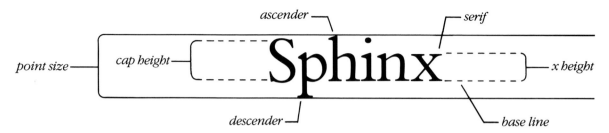

6-3 Standard features of type. Because lowercase letters appear far more often than capitals, their x-height greatly affects how type looks and reads. The ratio of x-height to point size and the lengths of ascenders and descenders varies greatly from one typeface to another. The example above is 48-point type.

Family loyalty. Select one family of type and use it for all body copy and other elements, with the possible exception of headlines. Sticking to one family makes your newsletter cohesive. Family loyalty is also efficient and cost-effective because it keeps font changes to a minimum. Build interest by changing size and weight or using italic, not by switching from one type family to another.

Choose a type family with a variety of weights (light, medium, bold) that come in upright and italic. You may need the variety to make captions, quotes, blurbs, subheads, and other elements.

If you need special punctuation marks, mathematical signs, or symbols, verify that the type you prefer includes all the characters you need or that they are readily available on another font that looks acceptable.

x-height. The size of lower case letters in proportion to the size of capitals is referred to as x-height. Type with a generous x-height appears contemporary and looks bigger than type of the same point size with a smaller x-height.

Legible type is easy to read. In addition to x-height, legibility is affected by serifs, weight, size, leading, white space, and the paper on which type appears.

Serifs. Tiny lines that cross the ending strokes of most characters are called serifs. They make reading efficient by helping the eye move easily along the line.

Use serif type such as ITC Garamond for body copy. If you think traditional serif type looks too formal, use a modified serif typeface such as Souvenir or Optima. Type for headlines

may be a larger, bolder version of body type or a bold type without serifs.

Type without serifs, known as sans serif, is appropriate for headlines and when characters must be smaller than 10 points and include many numerals. Use type such as Helvetica or Avant Garde for charts, tables, lists, and formulas, but not for body copy itself.

Weight. Type comes in a variety of weights ranging from light and book through medium and semi-bold to bold and extra-bold. Some weights have different names in different families. For instance, book may be called regular, or extra-bold may be known as black.

Body copy should appear in light or book, headlines in a heavier weight. Captions are often set in a heavier weight but smaller size than body copy.

When considering the weight of type, take into account how your newsletter will be printed. Photocopy tends to fatten type, so a typeface such as Times with relatively thin lines might be appropriate. Offset should reproduce type accurately, so a typeface such as ITC Bookman with somewhat thicker strokes might be a good choice.

Density influences weight. Almost all type devices driven by computers form characters from patterns of dots. The density of the dot pattern can look loose or tight and is expressed as dots-per-inch (dpi). A loose dot pattern of 90 dpi makes type of the quality seen on checks and address labels and is not appropriate for newsletters. The finest digital typesetting is very tight, about 5,000 dpi, and is far better than most newsletters need.

Newsletters with digital type should have characters of at least 300 dpi, the current standard for inexpensive laser printers, or 360 dpi, the best that most pin printers can produce.

If your computer printer will not produce near letter quality type, you have two possible ways to improve legibility. One is to convey your keyboarding to a device that yields adequate quality, most likely found at a typesetting shop.

A second option is to set type slightly larger than the size at which you plan to reproduce it, then reduce it with a photocopy machine or process camera. Reducing digital type brings dots closer together, thus makes it more dense. This procedure, more fully explained in Chapter 10, requires careful planning and some pasteup.

Size. The size of type is determined by its height and is expressed in units called points. One point equals 1/72 inch. Visual 6-5 shows examples of type at various point sizes.

Body copy in 1-column newsletters should be 12-point, the size of pica type from a typewriter or strike-on computer printer. Using type smaller than 12-point, such as elite, for a 1-column format results in too many characters per line.

Newsletters in either a 2- or 3-column format should be in 10- or 11-point type. Twelve-point is OK if your readers don't see well or if you don't have much to say; 9-point is OK if your readers are under age 35 or feel desperate for your information.

If 10-point seems too large, use a lighter weight type; if it doesn't allow enough copy, edit more tightly. Don't switch to a smaller size. If 11-point seems too small, try a heavier weight and/or slightly more space between lines.

Line measure—the width of one column—should heavily influence type size.

The average reader takes in three or four words per eye movement and comprehends best when making two eye movements per line. The ideal line has seven or eight words and contains between 40 and 50 characters.

Newsletters in a 1-column format would look empty if restricted to 45 or even 50 characters per line. They should not, however, have more than 60 as is often seen. Most publications

with a 3-column format should have 10-point, proportional type to assure that lines have at least 35 characters.

Leading. Often called line spacing, leading refers to the distance between lines of type. It is expressed in points and measured from one baseline to the next as shown in Visual 6-3. Type with a point size of 10 and with one point of leading is set "ten on eleven," written 10/11.

Short lines need less space between them than long lines. Lines set with no leading would seem to touch each other.

Type for 2-column newsletters should have two more points of leading than the size of type used. Eleven-point type in a 2-column format should be set 11/13. Three-column formats may have one or two points of leading; 1-column formats should have two or three points.

6-4 **Type as graphic.** As part of a nameplate, type conveys image. Type designers create letterforms to have appearances such as elegance, efficiency, and authority. Choose carefully and, ideally, with the help of a graphic designer experienced with publications. The examples above were prepared by Polly Pattison using desktop publishing software.

Times Roman

1234567890$

8 POINT
abcdefghijklmnopqrstuvwxyz
ABCDEFGHIJKLMNOPQRSTUVWXYZ

9 POINT
abcdefghijklmnopqrstuvwxyz
ABCDEFGHIJKLMNOPQRSTUVWXYZ

10 POINT
abcdefghijklmnopqrstuvwxyz
ABCDEFGHIJKLMNOPQRSTUVWXYZ

11 POINT
abcdefghijklmnopqrstuvwxyz
ABCDEFGHIJKLMNOPQRSTUVWXYZ

12 POINT
abcdefghijklmnopqrstuvwxyz
ABCDEFGHIJKLMNOPQRSTUVWXYZ

14 POINT
abcdefghijklmnopqrstuvwxyz
ABCDEFGHIJKLMNOPQRSTUV

16 POINT
abcdefghijklmnopqrstuvwxyz
ABCDEFGHIJKLMNOPQRST

18 POINT
abcdefghijklmnopqrstuvwxy
ABCDEFGHIJKLMNOPQR

20 POINT
abcdefghijklmnopqrstuvw
ABCDEFGHIJKLMNOP

24 POINT
abcdefghijklmnopqrst
ABCDEFGHIJKLM

6-5 Type size. Design, boldness, and spacing as well as point size influence how large type seems. Moreover, character counts may differ from one typeface to another even when point size remains the same. Text in this book is 11 point; captions 10 point.

Desktop publishing software such as *Page-Maker* has a 2-point leading default, which is acceptable for most publications.

Most computer programs, many typewriters, and all typesetters have commands to control leading in increments smaller than one point. For example, *Microsoft Word* allows changes in millimeters and fractions of inches as well as points.

If you use a printout from your computer as camera-ready copy, you might specify leading in ½-point increments. For example, two and a half points is ideal for a 60-character column of Courier pica type. A little experimenting with your software will help you decide what commands produce the results you want.

If you paste up type that some one else produces for you, specify either one, two, or three points of leading. Standard grids and guides are not made to copyfit type with leading in fractions of points.

White space. Providing adequate space between letters, words, lines, and columns, and in margins is like framing a picture to make sure it stands out.

My recommendations for formats and type include plenty of white space. They cannot, however, ensure enough white space within individual letters. Some type reads well at one weight, but not at another. Problems arise when the thickness of strokes making up the characters are equal to the thickness of spaces between and within them.

When black and white spaces almost equal each other, type may be hard to read. Changing to lighter type, possibly one point larger, usually solves the problem.

Consistency. Computer printers, especially ones using lasers and toner, tend to produce type of varying density depending on how well they are maintained.

Ideally, your method of producing type will yield crisp, dense characters 100% of the time. Short of that ideal, at least ensure that output for each issue is consistent from page to page and on each page. Original type that appears washed out can be made slightly darker by running the photocopier on "light original" or asking the offset printer to underexpose during platemaking.

Text type	Headline type					
	same family	Orator	Helvetica bold	Univers medium	Avant Guard med	Optima bold
Courier pica	bold					
Prestige pica	bold					
Times Roman	bold					
Garamond light	book					
Bookman light	medium					
Souvenir light	medium					
Optima	medium					

Courier pica

Prestige pica

Times Roman

Garamond light

Bookman light

Souvenir light

Optima

ORATOR ᴏRATOR

Helvetica bold

Univers medium

Avant Garde medium

Optima bold

6-6 **Type combinations.** The chart shows dependable combinations of text and headline type. The first column after text type gives a headline type in the same family. Cells with screen tints show a sans serif type for headlines to complement the serif text.

Each combination of type gives a different look. Experiment before deciding.

The typefaces for body copy are readily available on fonts for computer printers and photo type machines. Courier and Prestige are also the most common typefaces for typewriters. Typefaces for headlines are also available as dry-transfer lettering.

Any method of darkening type during printing also increases the likelihood of reproducing stray flecks of toner and other particles that normal reproduction would drop out. Camera-ready copy must be extra clean.

Paper. Because legibility stems from contrast, it is affected by the surface on which type appears. In your typewriter or computer printer, use smooth, white paper to get characters in high contrast. A top quality 80# uncoated book or 28# bond is ideal.

Several paper companies offer sheets that they make for use with laser printers. Most are 24# bond with coating on one side to prevent wax bleed-through when they are pasted up. The 80# book or 28# bond recommended above works as well, costs less, and seems to run more dependably.

Specifying type

To get the type you want, you must describe it clearly. Here are some guidelines in addition to those already discussed.

Alignment. Type for body copy may be set flush right so that the ends of lines are even with each other, or ragged right so they are uneven. Visuals 6-8 and 6-7 show examples.

Flush right type seems to most people more formal, official, or technical than ragged right.

There is no evidence that alignment influences legibility unless it affects space between words. When there is too little space between words, they cannot be distinguished from each other. When there is too much space, the words break into distant elements that cause inefficient reading.

Opus sci ent factortum poen legnum quas nulla praid

Tuntung evlent sib conliant

Lorem ipsum dolor sit amet, con sectetuer adipiscing elit, sed diam nonnumy nibh euismod tempor inci dunt ut labore et dolore magna ali quam erat volupat. Ut wisi enim ad minim veniam, quis nostrud exerci tation ullamcorper suscipit laboris nisl ut aliquip ex ea commodo con sequat. Duis autem vel eum irure dolor in henderit in vulputate velit esse consequat.

Vel illum dolore eu feugiat nulla facilisi at vero eos et accusam et ius to odio dignissim qui blandit prae sent luptatum zzril delenit aigue duos dolore et molestias exceptur sint occaecat cupiditat non simil pro vedit tempor sunt in culpa qui officia deserunt mollit anium ib est abor um et dolor fuga. Et harumd dereud facilis est er expedit distinct. Nam liber tempor cum soluta nobis eligend option congue nihil impediet doming id quod maxim placeat facer possim omnis voluptas assumenda est, omnis repellend.

Temporibud auteui quinusd et aur office debit aut tum rerum necessit atib saepe eveniet ut er molestia non recusand. Itaque earud rerum hic ten tury sapiente delectus au aut prefer zim endis dolorib asperiore repellat. Hanc ego cum tene senteniam, quid est cur verear ne ad eam non possing

accomodare nost ros quos tu paulo ante cum memorite tum etia ergat. Nos amice et nbevol, olestias access potest fier ad augend ascum consci ent to factor tum poen legum odio que civiuda. Et tamen in busdam neque nonor imper ned libiding gen epular reli guard cupiditati quas nul la praid om undat.

Improb pary minuit, potios im flammad ut coercend magist and et dodencendesse videantur. Inviat igi tur vera ratio bene sanos adzum justiatiam, aequitated fidem. Neque hominy infant aut inuiste fact est cond qui neg facile efficerd possit duo conetud notiner si effercerit, et opes vel fortunag vel ingen liberalitat magis conveniunt, da but tuntung ben evolent sib conciliant, et aptis.

Mosetias simil tempor

Sim est ad quiet. Endium caritat prae sert cum omning nul sit causpeccand quaert en imigent cupidtat a natura proficis vacile explent sine julla inura autend inanc sunt is par end non est nihil enim desidera endis ut lobore et dolore magna ali quam erat volupat. Ut wisi enim ad minim veniam, quis nostrud exerci tation ullamcorper suscipit laboris nisl ut aliquip ex ea commodo con sequat. Duis autem vel eum irure dolor in henderit in vulputate velit esse consequat.

Vel illum dolore eu feugiat nulla

6-7 Patterns of type. Column width of the ragged right type above is 2¼," the line measure of most 3-column newsletters. To ensure legibility, long lines of type need more line spacing (leading) than short lines. In the example above, 11/12 seems about right, but would seem too tight for type set 3¼" wide for a 2-column format. Adding another point of leading often makes text easier to read.

Head: Helvetica bold, 24 pt.   Kicker: Helvetica, italic, 12 pt.

Tuntung evlent sib conliant

Text: Century expanded 11/13 justified

Lorem ipsum dolor sit amet, con sectetuer adipiscing elit, sed diam nonnumy nibh euismod tempor inci dunt ut labore et dolore magna ali quam erat volupat. Ut wisi enim ad minim veniam, quis nostrud exerci tation ullamcorper suscipit laboris nisl ut aliquip ex ea commodo con sequat. Duis autem vel eum irure dolor in henderit in vulputate velit esse consequat.

Vel illum dolore eu feugiat nulla facilisi at vero eos et accusam et ius to odio dignissim qui blandit prae sent luptatum zzril delenit aigue duos dolore et molestias exceptur sint occaecat cupiditat non simil pro vedit tempor sunt in culpa qui officia deserunt mollit anium ib est abor um et dolor fuga. Et harumd dereud facilis est er expedit distinct. Nam liber tempor cum soluta nobis eligend option congue nihil impediet doming id quod maxim placeat facer possim omnis voluptas assumenda est, omnis repellend.

Temporibud auteui quinusd et aur office debit aut tum rerum necessit atib saepe eveniet ut er molestia non recusand. Itaque earud rerum hic ten tury sapiente delectus au aut prefer zim endis dolorib

asperiore repellat. Hanc ego cum tene senteniam, quid est cur verear ne ad eam non possing accomodare nost ros quos tu paulo ante cum memorite tum etia ergat. Nos amice et nbevol, olestias access potest fier ad augend ascum consci ent to factor tum poen legum odio que civiuda. Et tamen in busdam neque nonor imper ned libiding gen epular reli guard cupiditati quas nul la praid om undat.

Improb pary minuit, potios im flammad ut coercend magist and et dodencendesse videantur. Inviat igi tur vera ratio bene sanos adzum justiatiam, aequitated.

Mosetias simil tempor

Subhead: Helvetica bold 12 pt.

Fidem neque hominy infant aut inuiste fact est cond qui neg facile efficerd possit duo conetud notiner si effercerit, et opes vel fortunag vel ingen liberalitat magis conveniunt, da but tuntung ben evolent sib conciliant, et aptis sim est ad quiet. Endium caritat prae sert cum omning nul sit causpeccand quaert en imigent cupidtat a natura proficis vacile explent sine julla inura autend inanc sunt is par end non est nihil enim desidera endis ut lobore et dolore

6-8 **More patterns of type.** Columns above have the same line measure as those on page 64, but are justified instead of ragged. Note that the text type on these two pages is all 11 point. The Century type on this page seems bigger because of its generous x-height, compared with the relatively small x-height of the Garamond text type on page 64. Experiment with combinations of type before making final decisions.

Flush right type is often produced at the expense of proper word spacing. This situation is most likely with very short lines that may contain only three or four words or lines consisting of type that is equally spaced, as shown in the top two examples in Visual 6-1.

Unless your system can set flush right by adjusting space between letters as well as between words, stick with ragged right.

Paragraph indents. With equally spaced type, specify indents simply by number of spaces. With proportional spacing, specify indents by em spaces, the width of the letter "m" in the typeface you are using. The standard indent is two ems.

Indents cue the eye to the beginning of a new thought. They are optional in paragraphs that immediately follow headlines or subtitles.

```
Body copy: 11/13 Times roman, 20 pica
   line, justified, 12 point paragraph
   indent, 2 pica alley

Headlines: 24 point Helvetica bold,
   flush left

Secondary headlines: 14/16 Helvetica
   bold, flush left

Subheads: 12 point Helvetica bold, flush
   left

Caption: 10/12 Times roman italic,
   ragged right

Blurb: 18/22 Times roman italic, ragged
   right, with a 6 point rule above and a
   1 point rule below

Kicker: 12 point Helvetica italic, flush
   left, with a 1 point rule below

Header: 10 point Helvetica italic and
   roman, with a 2 point rule below

Page number: 10 point Helvetica bold,
   centered, 1 point rule above
```

6-9 Type specifications. Decisions about type should be written so clearly and completely that someone else could reproduce the typography of your newsletter if you are not available to give instructions. The specifications above describe the newsletter shown on page 3.

Headline type

Headline type is any type of 14 points or larger, whether used for headlines, subheads, logos, or other elements. Few newsletters use headline type smaller than 18-point or larger than 36-point.

Type for headlines may be made with dry transfer lettering or a headline making machine as well as by devices that also make type for body copy.

Also called rub-on or press-on, dry transfer lettering offers versatility at low cost. Characters come on sheets of plastic that release the image onto paper when the plastic is rubbed with a dull pencil point or other smooth instrument.

When making headlines with transfer lettering, align letters carefully. Even small deviations prove distracting when they are reproduced. Transfer lettering sheets have guidemarks uniformly placed under rows of letters to help with alignment.

Large type is easier to apply correctly with dry transfer lettering than small. One good combination is 36-point major heads and 24-point minor heads. Subheads may be in a bold version of type for body copy.

Buy transfer lettering at stores listed in classified directories as selling "artist materials and supplies." They have catalogs from companies such as Letraset and Format showing typefaces and sizes and usually have a large inventory. Catalogs also show how best to use the material.

Machines that make headlines are found at many print and type shops. They are ideal for fast turnaround situations.

Headlining machines are operated by hand to make one letter at a time. Their range of typefaces and styles includes all of those appropriate for newsletters. If your organization produces a variety of printed material, a headline machine might be a worthwhile investment.

Headlines are graphic elements that affect how your publication looks as well as how it reads. Following some simple typographic guidelines makes them work best.

Standard capitalization. Set headlines using upper and lower case letters, not using all caps. Follow the same rules for capitalizing that you would when writing any sentence.

Headlines are easiest to read when they look like bold sentences because the eye identifies words by their upper outlines. Words in all caps have a uniform outline; readers must comprehend them letter-by-letter instead of at a glance. Headlines with a beginning capital for each word signal people to read each word separately, not the whole line as one message. They are also harder to copyfit.

If you are limited to a typewriter or computer printer having no way to make bold letters, resist the temptation to use all caps. Make headlines bold using the technique described earlier in this chapter or make them stand out using design ideas in Chapter 5.

Consistent. Use type from only one family for all headlines. Often the best choice is simply a larger and bolder version of body type. Headline type without serifs that compliments body type can also work well. Visual 6-8 presents combinations you can depend on.

When specifying headlines, create emphasis by changing size. Use 36- or 30-point type for the most important headlines, 30 or 24 for less important ones, and 18- or 14-point for subheads. You don't need to change from bold to black or from upright to italic.

Flush left. Align the first letter of the headline with the left side of the article. Flush left headlines are easiest to read and copyfit.

Copyfitting

Fitting copy to the space you have planned for it calls for careful planning followed by simple arithmetic. The planning is most important, for without it the arithmetic is useless.

I have urged you to select and specify type carefully and change rarely. Ease of copyfitting is one of the most important reasons for consistency of type sizes, column width, and line count per column inch.

Copyfitting is the science (some would say the art, others the hassle) of causing type to fit your layout. The process starts by knowing the space you have available.

For each issue of your newsletter, make a dummy showing the position and size of every element. Use the methods and guidelines in Chapter 9.

Specifications. Confirm correct point sizes, styles, leadings, and line measures.

Dark characters. Check characters for adequate density and uniform blackness. Inspect type for holes or breaks.

Straight lines. Put a ruler under a few sample lines to ensure they have no hills or valleys.

Parallel lines. Study lines to make sure they are parallel to each other.

Even justification. Lay a ruler vertically down the left edge and, if set flush right, down the right edge of text to verify that beginning and ending characters are properly aligned.

Sensible hyphenation. Certify that words are divided correctly. With ragged right copy, divisions should avoid awkward gaps.

White paper. Note whether paper is bright white and free from stains or flaws.

6-10 Inspecting type. Sharp, dense type in high contrast with its background yields legible copy. Use this list as a guide when you examine type to make sure it meets the standards you set for your newsletter.

Make a dummy for each issue even if you assemble complete pages on a computer screen. Your printed newsletter will be full size on paper, like the sketch, not reduced on a computer screen which may also show codes, icons, rulers, and instructions.

As editor, you should fit copy. You decide content and control the keyboard, so you are in the best position to copyfit as you write and edit.

If you create pages on a typewriter or computer screen, the dummy that you made is a sufficient guide to copyfitting. With equally spaced typing or printout, you set margins according to your format and write your stories. With page assembly software, you import your stories from word processing files into your format, probably do some editing, then write and position headlines. In both cases, what you see is what you get.

When someone sets type for you, traditional copyfitting is necessary. In that case, what you produce on your typewriter or computer

Type specifications for your newsletter should include character counts per line of body copy and for other standard elements such as captions and subheads.

Once you know character counts for your newsletter, you can copyfit to your layout simply by setting typewriter margins at the average number of characters per line and lines per column inch. For example, 45 is the character count per line in this book and it has six lines per column inch. I set my right margin at 45 and never hyphenate a word, letting words end as close as possible to space 45. I know that six lines of keyboarding will almost always equal six lines of typesetting.

With word processing, the details of estimating by character count can depend on software. Some software shows a character count per file. If you write one story per file, you can know exactly how many lines of type it will occupy when typeset according to specifications.

6-11 Copyfitting body copy. The copy above is the manuscript version of the last three paragraphs in the first column of page 69. The vertical line goes through space #45, showing how closely the line count on manuscript corresponds to the line count for typesetting. Of course, in actual practice I didn't draw a vertical line because my word processing software always told me the space at which my cursor was located. I copyfit by editing on screen. The vertical line system works well with typewriting, although even in that case it's easy to develop an eye for when the average line should end. The key to any system of copyfitting is knowing character and line counts for the typography you have chosen.

screen is only approximately what you get.

To copyfit using traditional methods of pasteup, you must know the character count of your type as well as the number of column inches each story, photo, caption, and other element will occupy. Your dummy answers the question about column inches. It's your copyfitting map.

Character count is part of the description of all typefaces and sizes. Each typeface and size has its own number of characters per inch (cpi). For example, 10-point Caslon light might be 16.68 cpi, while 10-point Optima light might be 15.00. Character count can also be slightly different for the same typeface and size set on different machines or even the same machine at different settings.

Many type shops compute character counts in picas instead of inches. If you prefer using inches, multiply characters per pica by six to yield characters per inch.

Type specifications for your newsletter should include character counts per line of body copy and for other standard elements such as captions and subheads.

Once you know character counts for your newsletter, you can copyfit to your layout simply by setting typewriter margins at the average number of characters per line and lines per column inch. For example, 45 is the character count per line in this book and it has six lines per column inch. I set my right margin at 45 and never hyphenate a word, letting words end as close as possible to space 45. I know that six lines of keyboarding will almost always equal six lines of typesetting.

With word processing, the details of estimating by character count can depend on software. Some software shows a character count per file. If you write one story per file, you can

iiiiiiiiiiiiiiiiiiiiiiiiiiiiii 30 units

Smith scales Mt. Hood 41 units
3   3 1 2 2 1 2 2 2 1 2 2 1 4   2 1 1 3   2 2 2

Smith scales Hood 33 units

6-12 Copyfitting headlines. The unit system, described in text, helps you copyfit during writing instead of during layout. The number of units in "Smith scales Mt. Hood" revealed that it would not fit across one 2¼" column, but that "Smith scales Hood" fit nicely.

know exactly how many lines of type it will occupy when typeset according to specifications.

Proportionally spaced headlines can be a little more tricky to copyfit than body copy. With relatively few letters, headlines more easily stray from the averages that are the essence of any character count system.

People who write headlines for newspapers copyfit using a system of units rather than by counting characters.

1 unit: all punctuation and word spaces; lower case letters "i" and "l"

2 units: upper case "I" and "J"; all other lower case letters except "m" and "w"

3 units: "m" and "w"; all upper case letters except "M" and "W"

4 units: upper case "M" and "W"

You can make this system work best for you when you have no more than one typeface in two sizes for headlines.□

7 Graphics

Graphics is art used to express thought. Both parts of the definition are essential: art and thought. The essence of graphics is a clear message pleasing to the eye—ideas and information through art.

Graphic art includes typography, photography, design graphics, and data graphics. Chapter 6 dealt with typography; Chapter 8 deals with photography. This chapter deals with design and data graphics.

Design graphics for newsletters include rules (lines), screen tints, reverses, and some drawings that enhance information in type. Data graphics include illustrations, charts, tables, maps, and some drawings that contain information themselves.

Graphics help compress information into efficient visual forms, so are important ingredients of newsletters.

Each graphic element should help your newsletter achieve its goals. For example, design graphics make reading more efficient by separating, highlighting, and organizing. They call or direct attention, signal the importance of an article, and break the monotony of solid text. Graphics can reinforce text by repeating or elaborating on information.

Both design and data graphics convey mood by suggesting what kind of organization you are or want to become. They can denote personality such as being slick or homey. You can use them to build credibility. Well-executed graphics can make your newsletter appear professional, businesslike, and authoritative.

Rules

Screen tints

Reverses

Illustrations

Diagrams

Sometimes drawings are used only to fill space. Every editor must occasionally cope with a half column that's empty at the last minute, but the situation reveals a problem if it's routine.

When using graphics, remember that they help establish point of view. Drawings and diagrams showing people represent your opinions and may change or reinforce those of your readers.

Rules

When used as graphics, lines for borders, dividers, and boxes are known as rules. They are the most simple graphics to make and use.

You can produce rules using a special pen, typewriter, computer, typesetter, border tape, or dry transfer material. Whatever the source, they must meet specific quality standards. Straight lines should look straight, not like sagging telephone wires. Curved lines need uniform arcs.

Like type, rules need clean edges. Border tape that has gathered dust in a desk drawer and pens with felt tips or ball points give poor results. Rules made by laser printers are acceptable and photo type machines preferable. Graphic arts and technical pens work beautifully—in the hands of people trained to use them.

Design software that drives a laser printer or photo typesetter can be used to create a wide range of rules and boxes. If type for your publication is produced by such a machine, consider having it produce rules at the same time. The machine can make rules faster, more accurately, and probably less expensively than making them by hand.

In addition to solid, rules come in a variety of patterns consisting of dots, dashes, and symbols. Find examples in catalogs of dry transfer lettering.

There are so many ways to make rules that you risk having too much variety. Limit yourself to three kinds. Learn how to get the most out of those three patterns and sizes.

If rules are a regular part of your format, have them printed on your pasteup sheets or on the preprinted stock you use for each issue. Chapter 9 gives details on preprinting.

Reducing rules in a photocopy machine or process camera makes them thinner as well as shorter. Be careful not to make them so thin they will not reproduce when printed.

Screen tints

Screen tints are known also as shadings and, when produced by a laser printer, as fill patterns. They look like light versions of the ink or toner used to produce type. Tints made with black ink appear gray.

Tints are useful ways to highlight blocks of type such as mastheads and tables of contents. They can also be used to give texture to drawings and help organize data within calendars and diagrams.

Because they consist of dots that allow the color of paper to show among them, screen tints create the illusion of lighter printing. Each dot consists of 100% toner or ink.

Dot size and the distance between them determines how dark or light a screen tint appears. Lots of paper showing around the dots makes the tint seem light; not much paper makes it seem dark. Printers use percentages to describe the density of a screen tint. A 90% screen looks solid; a 10% screen seems light.

In addition to percentage of ink or toner within a screen tint, the tint is affected by the number of lines of dots per inch. As you can see in Visual 7-5, screens with relatively few lines of dots per inch are coarse; fine screens have many lines per inch. The number of lines per inch is called a screen's ruling.

If your newsletter is photocopied or quick printed, screen tints must be part of the camera-ready copy. A limited number of coarse fill patterns can be created using desktop publishing software. A wider variety is available on transfer sheets.

"Proofreading doesn't stop when the words are correct. You never know when something has gone wrong in a photo, diagram, or drawing. For example, the chart on page nine of this book. It looked beautiful when I got it from the type shop and it fit perfectly into the mockup. When I made the mask for the screen tints, I discovered that the fourth week had only six days. It was typesetter error, but I resented the hassle at the last minute."

½pt
¾pt
1pt
1½pt
2pt
3pt
4pt
6pt
8pt
10pt
12pt
18pt

7-1 Width of rules. Graphic arts professionals use the same system of points for expressing the size of type to describe the size of rules. Rules of various widths and patterns may be combined into distinctive graphic effects. Use the rules above as a quick reference when deciding what size to use.

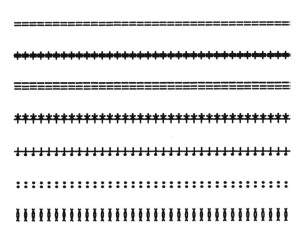

7-2 Homemade rules. A typewriter or computer printer using only word processing software can produce a variety of rules in addition to those made with hyphens, underlines, and periods. When you make a rule you like, note carefully what you did. The complex ones sometimes elude repetition.

> *Make blurbs bold. They should seem deliberate parts of your design.*

"

> *Blurbs are great to fill leftover space. You can adjust the size of the box so copy runs to the end of the column.*

"

7-3 Boxes. Catalogs of transfer lettering include patterns of rules for boxes, borders, and blurbs (sometimes called "pull quotes"). The boxes may already be complete or you may create them by pressing on combinations of straight rules and corners.

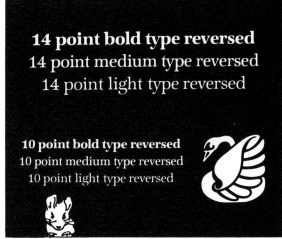

14 point bold type reversed
14 point medium type reversed
14 point light type reversed

10 point bold type reversed
10 point medium type reversed
10 point light type reversed

7-4 Reverses. Because the eye is accustomed to seeing dark images against a light background, reversed images may be hard to read when made too small or used too much. Furthermore, fine lines, even on bold type, may disappear because they fill with ink during printing. Reverses in newsletters are appropriate only within nameplates and other large elements. Do not reverse headlines or text.

Reverses require heavy ink coverage to avoid appearing washed out or mottled. A quick printer can give good results with a reverse the size of the one above or smaller. Larger reverses require commercial printing for good results.

	85 line screen	100 line screen	133 line screen
20%	REVERSE / OVERPRINT	REVERSE / OVERPRINT	REVERSE / OVERPRINT
30%	REVERSE / OVERPRINT	REVERSE / OVERPRINT	REVERSE / OVERPRINT
40%	REVERSE / OVERPRINT	REVERSE / OVERPRINT	REVERSE / OVERPRINT
50%	REVERSE / OVERPRINT	REVERSE / OVERPRINT	REVERSE / OVERPRINT
60%	REVERSE / OVERPRINT	REVERSE / OVERPRINT	REVERSE / OVERPRINT

7-5 Screen tints. Screen tints may be used to highlight type, accent letters, and give added dimension to illustrations. Overprints and reverses must be carefully planned to assure that words stay legible and fine lines do not disappear. Tints of less than 20% tend to be too light, of greater than 60% too dark. Percentages above are appropriate for newsletters.

Tints in the cattails are from press-on screens cut and applied according to the instructions in Visual 10-6. Cattails are 30%, leaves are 20%. Press-on screens are quick and easy, but don't look as good as tints added by a printer.

Catalogs from companies such as Letraset that show transfer lettering also show screen tints and offer tips on using the material. Most art supply stores carry a wide selection.

For photocopying, use screen tints no finer than 85 lines per inch, for quick printing no finer than 100 lines per inch. The edges of press-on tints must be cut cleanly with an artist's knife and the entire tint firmly burnished. Visual 10-8 shows how.

If your newsletter is reproduced at a commercial printer, tints can be added at the shop faster than by pasteup and better than by laser printout. Designate areas for tints and write the screen percentage and ruling on a tissue overlay. Visual 10-8 shows an example.

When considering tints, remember that tints of 10% tend to disappear when reproduced and tints of more than 70% look solid. Some ink colors change more when screened than others. Dark blue becomes light blue, but red becomes pink. To judge how colors will look when screened, consult a tint chart available at most printers, art supply stores, and graphic design studios.

Reducing or enlarging a fill pattern on a computer screen does not affect its dots per inch, but changing its size photographically al-

ters both dot size and ruling. For example, a 100-line screen reduced to 75% on a photocopy machine becomes 133-line—too fine to reproduce well by quick printing.

Reverses

Type, logos, and other line images such as clip art can be reproduced by printing the background rather than the image itself. When reversed, the shape of the image is formed by the underlying color of paper.

Like screen tints, reverses may be made either as part of camera-ready copy or by a commercial printer during platemaking.

Desktop publishing and photo type software will create reverses of type and line art. You may also make a camera-ready reverse using any method that will put a light image on a dark background. To reverse type, apply white transfer lettering to black paper. White transfer lettering is available in a limited selection of typefaces and sizes.

Reversed type in newsletters is appropriate only for display type in features such as nameplates and calendars. Reversed body copy is very hard to read.

Rules, screen tints, and reverses may be

7-6 Graphics in page design. Each of the six front pages shown above and opposite uses a simple rule, screen, or reverse to enhance readability and appearance. Rules keep copy from seeming to float on the page. All of the above graphics could be created using pasteup techniques, computer software, or a blend of the two.

combined to create some of the graphic effects shown in this chapter. This work may be done by pasteup artists, prepress camera services, or page assembly software. For the most faithful reproduction, take the work to a commercial printer.

Illustrations

Drawings and technical illustrations for newsletters typically come from clip art or other publications.

Generic drawings ready to add to mechanicals are called clip art. The drawings are made specifically to sell to designers, printers, and others needing instant graphics.

Clip art comes in a variety of media suited either to traditional pasteup or composition by computer. Images on film backings are used like transfer lettering; those on glossy paper are cut out and adhered to mechanicals; drawings on disks are added to printouts through desktop publishing software.

Many design studios, print shops, and ad agencies have books, files, or software of clip art. The materials are bought on subscription, from catalogs, or at book and art supply stores.

Drawings for clip art are typically arranged by topic such as holiday themes, health care, or family life. No matter how specialized your newsletter, you can probably find appropriate images. There are entire books with themes such as early American design, op-art mazes, and flora design. A store with a good selection could have 300 titles.

People shown in clip art may look out of date because of clothing, hair style, or how they are relating to each other. Readers may frown at art that is 10 or 15 years old. Art that is 50 years old, on the other hand, can look nostalgic when used well.

Any dark drawing on light paper is camera-ready. You can add images on white paper directly to mechanicals; images on off-white or colored paper may lack sufficient contrast, but might be enhanced by making a PMT or photocopy first.

Most drawings in newspapers, magazines, and other commercial publications are copyrighted. If you are uncertain about a specific illustration, check with the publisher before reproducing it. Steel engravings and other line drawings from 19th century publications make fine clip art and are in the public domain.

Regardless of your sources, remember that drawings can be cropped, combined, reduced,

7-6 continued. Reverses, screen tints, and combinations of the two create impact, but can also lead to the kind of printing problems shown in Visual 11-2. Heavy ink coverage, especially when quick printed, increases the probabilities of hickies and mottling and makes variations in density more noticeable.

7-7 Versatility of clip art. Clip art is a form of design graphics that can convey virtually any message when properly selected, scaled, and combined with type. The Oceanwood logo at the bottom incorporated birds cut from the top drawing of the fence. The bird that's part of "The Big Splash" is a flopped version of the original. Oceanwood lettering by Elizabeth Anderson.

7-8 **Using clip art.** Because clip art fills space so quickly and easily, it is often used poorly. The useful information on the newsletter at the left could have been printed on a postcard. The nameplates show better use of clip art combined with rules, screen tints, reverses, and type. The nameplates above were designed by Polly Pattison.

enlarged, screened, or reversed the same as type. The drawings you see on paper or your computer screen are starting points.

Ideally, clip art would meet the same quality standards as type, having dense, clean lines. Drawings from dot matrix printers do not meet these standards; drawings from laser printers may not meet them.

When using art from a computer printer as camera-ready copy, it is especially important to get every pixel of quality the machine will deliver. Drawings from a computer printer can be enhanced by reducing them to 90% in a photocopier, process camera, or platemaker.

Scanners can add line art such as your logo to computer memory. If you digitize art that will be printed frequently or as part of your nameplate, use the finest scanner you can afford. I suggest taking the art to a type shop or printer with a commercial scanner whose resolution is better than desktop models.

Graphics need far more computer memory for storage than type. To keep data on disk at a minimum, let paper remember art. Scan a drawing into computer memory when you need it, use it in your layout, print it out, then delete its file.

Laser printers take longer to print drawings than type. Although your equipment may be capable of printing out drawings along with type on a fully composed page, you might find it more efficient to add drawings using traditional pasteup techniques.

Clip art was developed for display advertising, not editorial matter. When using it in a newsletter, objectives must be clear. Novice editors tend to use too many illustrations and to place them poorly. Even some experienced designers think readers like lots of drawings scattered at random.

Use clip art sparingly. As with writing, take into account gender, age, race, and other possi-

Tables show facts in organized fashion without graphic plotting.

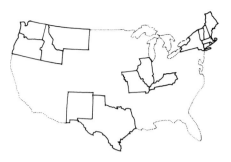

Maps show relationships of elements in distance.

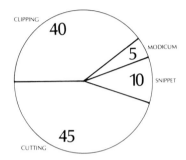

Pie charts show the proportion of parts to the whole.

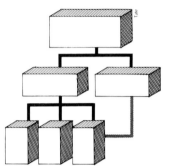

Flow charts show relationships of processes or people.

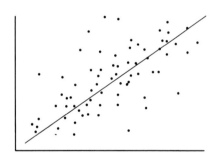

Scatter diagrams show patterns.

Line charts show fluctuations or comparisons of amounts over time.

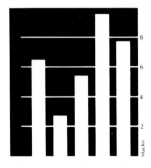

Bar charts show proportions related to each other or comparisons of amounts.

Time lines show sequences.

7-9 Varieties of data graphics. The visual form of data can mislead readers who may not think carefully about what the numbers mean. When using a diagram, make sure it suits the data you wish to represent. The examples are from Jan White's excellent book *Using Charts and Graphs*.

ble sources of discrimination or stereotypes when selecting illustrations.

Drawings by a colleague, friend, or volunteer can be useful if they meet graphic standards. Illustrations need sharp, black lines. If done on a computer, they should be printed out on a laser, not a dot matrix, printer. Make sure that original drawings don't have fine lines that may drop out when reduced.

Illustrations in continuous tones made with pencil, felt marker, air brush, ink wash, or charcoal must be halftoned. The process is identical to that for photographs explained in Chapter 10.

Diagrams

The elements of design graphics combine in thousands of ways to make the patterns of data graphics: charts, graphs, tables, and maps. Diagrams are powerful tools for newsletters because they pack so much information into so little space.

The ready availability of software for computing data and graphically presenting results make using diagrams easy. Too easy! Many diagrams, even those in leading newspapers and magazines, distort data by showing incorrect relationships between numbers and art.

Useful presentation of numerical data in graphical form requires a head for statistics, an eye for art, and a soul for common sense. If you lack the combination and want to use data

Selecting data graphics

Appropriate. Ensure that charts, graphs, or other formats suit the data and concepts.

Simple. Certify that diagrams reveal the essence of data precisely and without visual clutter. Each element must have a function.

Clear. Confirm that information is explained and interpreted verbally in titles and captions as well as visually in diagrams.

Readable. Use sans serif type and design graphics such as rules and screens. Clearly associate labels with elements. Avoid separate keys and legends.

Consistent. Verify that multiple or repeated visuals have similar formats and design graphics.

7-10 Traits of good data graphics. When composing or selecting a diagram, verify that it meets the above conditions to ensure that it accurately represents the information you wish to convey.

graphics, carefully study the books by Nigel Holmes, Edward Tufte, and Jan White listed in Appendix B.

Test every chart, graph, or map by showing it and its caption to someone unfamiliar with its information. If you have to explain what the diagram is supposed to show, it isn't working. Often the person giving the "cold read" can suggest a new approach that solves the problem. □

8 Photography

When used in newsletters, photographs are graphics that must help achieve objectives. Your reasons for using photos should be similar to the reasons for using other graphics described in Chapter 7.

Whether or not to use photos is a decision to discuss with your management. Using them adds a little to printing costs, a lot to staff time, and changes the image of your newsletter.

Effective photos are made, not taken. They are controlled editorially and technically at every stage of creation from concept to camera to printing press.

This chapter is about black and white photos taken with the common 35mm camera. Only the rare newsletter needs color photos or studio shots made with a large camera.

In this chapter I explain what kind of camera and film to use, how to compose and edit pictures for maximum impact, and how to evaluate photos technically. Chapter 9 includes information about photos in layout; Chapter 10 tells how to make photos camera-ready for printing.

Many editors take their own photos. Some have staff photographers or volunteers who are skilled and dependable. Whether you take photos yourself or ask someone else to take them, you should have ideas about the images you want before exposures are made. Your ability to imagine the photos you want largely determines how effective they will be when they appear in print.

Equipment and supplies

Making the picture

Lighting

Photo finishing

Custom finishing

Working with photographers

Equipment and supplies

You've seen photographers who need a mule to carry their hardware. Professionals and serious amateurs probably need all that equipment, but you don't for your newsletter. All you need is one camera, one lens, and plenty of film.

Camera. Use a 35mm camera. If you take most pictures indoors from 5 to 20 feet away from the subject, a compact autofocus camera with fixed lens and flash does fine. If you take photos under a variety of circumstances and distances, use an automatic single lens reflex (SLR) that has manual override.

Better quality cameras can be equipped with the kind of viewfinder that you find most useful. Choices include split image, resolving prism, and several other methods of focusing. If you have corrected vision, you may be able to install an eyepiece with your prescription. Check with a sales rep at a camera store.

Read the instructions for your camera and practice using its controls. Shoot one or two rolls of film and inspect the results. When the first pictures aren't as good as you'd hoped, remember that you ignored this advice.

Lens. Use a camera with a glass, not plastic, lens. Glass lenses yield sharper images, especially in those portions of the photo farthest from the center of the lens.

Compact autofocus cameras have a fixed lens of about 40mm, very suitable for general purpose work at medium distances. If you use a single lens reflex camera, use a zoom lens from a wide angle to a medium telephoto. A range of 35-70mm or 40-80mm handles most situations. Unless you have special requirements because of the subject of your newsletter, you should not need any other lens.

None of the lenses recommended above focus closer than about three feet. If you need photos taken closer than that, use an SLR camera whose lens has a macro mode.

Film. Select one brand and speed of film and use it exclusively. The brand may be anything you find convenient in places you shop. The speed should be ISO 400 for best flexibility and picture quality. ("ISO" and "ASA" numbers mean the same.) I recommend Kodak T-Max 400 or Tri X.

Use lots of film. Buy it in rolls with 36 exposures. If you have a very tight budget and need many pictures, buy film in 100 foot rolls and load your own cannisters. It's as easy as loading film into a camera.

Film is the least expensive part of photography—less costly than equipment, much less costly than offset printing, and still less costly than the value of the time required to take, develop, edit and lay out pictures, and get them ready for the printer.

Making the picture

Successful photos begin with the photographer's selective vision, not with the camera. As you gather information for a story, visualize photos you want. Imagine them printed in your newsletter. Then when you look at the original scene, compose it in your camera as closely as possible to what is in your imagination.

Visualizing helps you control the photographic situation. If you need people grouped more tightly or looking at each other, tell them what you want. If the scene has distractions that you can remove, take them away or shift your position.

Your brain selects parts of a scene to notice, but your camera records everything equally. To help avoid cluttered images, look at the scene with one eye closed to see it in two dimensions instead of three. Imagine it in black and white with colors gone. Trying to see the finished photo before taking it helps produce an image that contributes to objectives.

Make the effort to get shots that count. Photos that work are created on purpose. They enhance a story because they were planned for it from the beginning.

"The best photo advice I ever got for black and white pictures was to overexpose and underdevelop. I use 400 film, but set my camera at 200. I tell the darkroom people to cut development time by 25%. I get more detail and contrast that way than by following the standard instructions. Overexposing puts everything I see through the lens onto the negative. By giving the film plenty of light, there are details on the negative to bring out when I make the print."

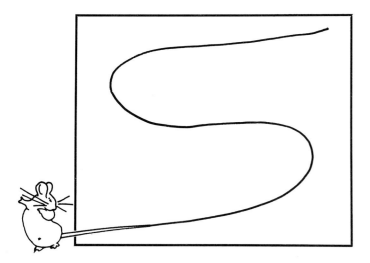
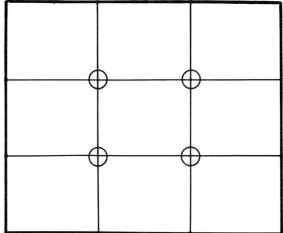

Kathleen Ryan

8-1 Good composition. Dynamic photos lead the eye in an s-curve through the image and have points of interest placed off-center. An image with only one point of interest in the center looks lifeless. Compose in thirds, not halves. It is especially important to keep the horizon and other strong lines off-center.

Photography is a single sequence from visualization to reproduction. Paying close attention to seeing a picture in the camera and controlling light to record it pays huge dividends during the rest of the process.

Keeping objectives in mind is especially important with photos of people. If you need extra credibility, you probably want a picture of the boss or visiting expert. The story might, however, call for a mood shot, in which case you could pay less attention to leaders and more to followers or audience.

When you photograph groups, ask people to react to each other or to something of common interest. Obedient stares into the camera are for driver's licenses. To avoid grip-and-grin

shots, look for the emotions of the moment, not the convenience of the photographer.

The photo of an audience with the speaker either far away or behind the photographer hardly ever works. To make photos of people in meetings interesting, get the speaker for some closeups with members of the audience. Another technique is to take a number of pictures of just one person in the audience whose expressions and actions represent the group.

If you must do a mug shot, crop tightly. Ask your subject to stand or sit about a quarter turn away from you, not facing you straight on, then to turn the head only to look at the camera. Put a little more space in front of the subject than behind so your subject appears to be looking into

Kathleen Ryan

8-2 Editorial angle. Effective photos tell stories from fresh perspectives, often literally. In the image above, the photographer got below the scene to give it an added sense of height.

Kathleen Ryan

the frame of the picture. If your image includes the person's torso, include the hands to ensure that the image appears complete.

Photos usually capture emotion more effectively than words. To make them work, however, you have to look for the unusual image, not the safe shot.

Using a camera that must be focused for each shot, you can get candid photos of people by prefocusing at about 10 feet. Take photographs of anything from about 7 to 15 feet. Most of the images will be correctly focused, especially if you use a wide angle setting such as 35mm or 40mm on your zoom lens.

To give photos depth and scale, use background and foreground to your advantage. Deliberately place buildings, foliage, or props in the picture to reinforce the main subject.

When photographing outside, try to keep the sky out of pictures unless there is a specific reason to include it. Sky almost always distracts from subject matter.

8-3 Photos that work. Photos convey feelings more efficiently and often more effectively than words. Use photos to capture the essence of a moment, not merely to record who was there.

Kathleen Ryan

8-4 Background. It's easy when photographing to overlook potential distractions. In this case, simply stepping aside removed the clutter from over the subject's head.

Kathleen Ryan

8-5 Know your format. Keep in mind the size at which photos are likely to be reproduced. Mug shots may be small, but images with more detail must be larger to preserve their impact.

Mark Beach

8-6 Keep it simple. A good photo delivers an uncluttered image and, therefore, a clear message. As with the case above, too much information can ruin a photo more easily than too little.

Successful photography may require standing on a chair, moving furniture, wearing a hard hat, or lying on the floor. You can't get good photos when you are worried about your clothes. Dress comfortably to work eagerly.

Keep in mind layout as well as content. Look for images to present as verticals. Your natural tendency is to view scenes horizontally. Cameras reinforce that instinct. Layouts, however, benefit from having vertical pictures, too. Take both horizontal and vertical shots of the same subject to have lots of options.

Every photo reproduced in your newsletter needs a caption and credit. Captions tell just enough to let readers understand the image or know names of people when only a few are pictured. Make sure to get information when taking photos. Check its accuracy before publishing them. Get phone numbers to make checking easy.

A credit line identifies the photographer. It is easiest to include as part of the caption, but may also appear in small type under or next to the image as in this book.

Lighting

Ideally, you would take all photos using available light. Photos using only the light already falling on the scene, whether from natural or artificial sources, most closely resemble the scene itself.

Unfortunately, most newsletter photography takes place indoors where available light isn't enough for a proper exposure. There are several ways to handle the problem.

Push your film. Using ISO 400 film, you can set your camera to ISO 800, giving you one more f stop, or ISO 1600, for two more stops. Pushing requires that the entire roll be taken at the higher ISO rating.

When you take pushed film for developing, tell the developing service that you used a rating different from the manufacturer's recommendation. Write your new ISO rating on the cannister as well as on the envelope showing your name and pickup date. The finishing service will adjust chemicals and development time to compensate for the change that you made in ISO rating.

8-7 Film is cheap. Taking plenty of photos from various angles at various settings ensures the best possible choices for editorial purposes. When considering the time and effort involved, film is the least costly part of photography.

Increase available light. Turn on more lights, take shades off lamps, open curtains, move people closer to a window, carry objects outside, wait for the clouds to pass—do anything reasonable to put more available light on the subject.

Pay special attention to the light on faces. Often there is ample light on the scene as a whole, but not enough on the faces which are the real subject of the photo.

Sometimes there is plenty of light, but it makes harsh shadows. The eyes of people standing in bright sun show this effect. Solve the problem by seeking softer light, such as moving to open shade, rather than using flash. If you are indoors, try bouncing available light off a white tablecloth or curtain.

Use flash. Strobe lighting is easy to use, but hard to predict. It can make a scene look stark or washed out and causes unnatural shadows.

If you must use flash regularly, learn techniques to reduce its harsh effects. One is to bounce it off a wall or low ceiling so light falls indirectly on the subject. Using this method requires carrying a more powerful flash than you otherwise might use.

Another technique for controlling flash is to diffuse its light by covering the unit with tissue or gauze. Asking someone to hold a thin napkin a few inches in front of the flash helps.

People in photos made with flash sometimes have hollow eyes that belong in the midnight horror movie. To prevent that, move the flash away from the camera. Mounting the unit on an arm extending from the camera usually solves the problem.

Photo finishing

Developing and printing for your newsletter should be done by people who do photo finishing for publications. Avoid the one-hour and drive-through services.

To locate a convenient professional service, ask the production manager at an advertising or public relations agency. If you use a classified directory, look under "Photo finishing —retail" for services that advertise making PMTs and halftones.

Whether your photo finishing is in-house, commercial, volunteer, or do-it-yourself, you should get contact sheets. They are the best basis for selecting photos as well as the foundation for a photo file. Write dates and subject matter on the back of sheets. Put negatives in scratch-proof sleeves and the sleeves inside business

cropping L's Kathleen Ryan

8-8 Cropping. You're not obliged to use all of an image simply because it's on the negative. Crop to eliminate unwanted portions. Crop when prints are made in the darkroom or when they are prepared for reproduction. Use cropping Ls as shown above to visualize the outcome. Don't hesitate to crop deeply; it often improves the image dramatically. Crop to make the photo more effective or to make the image fit your layout.

envelopes. Tape the envelopes to the backs of appropriate contact sheets.

Images on contact sheets are too small to inspect without magnification. View them through a loupe, sometimes called a linen tester. A loupe costs only a few dollars at an art supply store. Place the loupe directly on the photo paper and put your eye to its lens to examine individual images.

Custom finishing

Remember that all images on a contact sheet were made with one exposure. Most will not look as good as they would if exposed as individual prints.

Even using a loupe, it is difficult to detect on proof sheets distractions and flaws. If you feel uncertain about any aspect of an image, order an 8 x 10 print. Whenever time and budget permit, decide about dodging, burning, or cropping while examining enlargements, not contacts.

You can put cropping instructions on contact sheets, but you have another chance to crop while scaling and preparing prints for prepress as explained in Chapter 10.

After you examine contact sheets, your finishing service makes enlarged prints of the images you specify. Ask that all enlargements be made full frame unless you provide crop marks. "Full frame" means that everything on the negative appears on the enlarged print. A full frame image from a 35mm negative printed on 8 x 10 paper is 7 x 10; on 5 x 7 paper it's 4½ x 7.

Enlargements for halftoning should be at least on 5 x 7 paper with a semi-gloss or matte surface. The slightly dull surface makes the print look more like a newsletter reproduction than a glossy paper and allows for simple retouching with a soft pencil.

Prints ready for publication should meet the quality requirements reviewed in Visual 8-13. If they meet all the requirements except for a few slight flaws, ask your finishing service to eliminate them using retouching techniques.

While doing layout, it's handy to have duplicates of photos you might use. Ask your finishing service for work prints. Duplicates can even be photocopies.

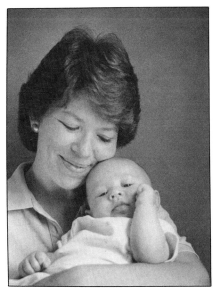  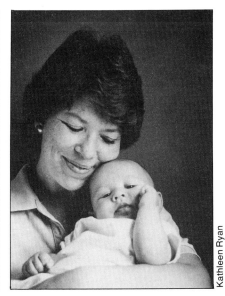

Kathleen Ryan

flat contrast   *good contrast and detail*   *detail lost in shadows*

8-9 Contrast. Lively photos have a full range of tones from white to black. Muddy, washed out, or flat images have low contrast; photos that lack detail in shadows or highlights have high contrast. Photos always lose detail in both shadows and highlights when offset printed. Quality depends on starting with good images.

straight print   Mark Beach   *sky burned in, truck dodged*

8-10 Dodging and burning. Prints may be enhanced in the darkroom to make them more effective. Dodging withholds light to bring out shadow detail or create a light area on which to print black type. Burning adds light to bring out highlights or create a dark area for reverse type. In the image above right, the sky and sign were burned in while the truck was dodged. Decisions about dodging and burning are best made while viewing an enlargement, not a contact sheet.

24 mm

55 mm

86 mm

Kathleen Ryan

8-11 Lens length. The three images above and left were all taken at the same distance from the subject and at the same f-stop. A wide lens such as the 24mm captures much of a scene from a short distance. A 55mm, considered standard, records what the normal eye sees with one glance. Long lenses such as the 86mm work well for portraits and help the photographer remain unobtrusive. Something like a 35mm to 70mm zoom lens is ideal for most newsletter photography.

55 mm at f3.5

55 mm at f16

8-12 Depth of field. The ability of a lens to hold both near and far parts of a scene in focus is called its depth of field. Depth of field is affected by the focal length of the lens and the aperture at which it is set. It improves as apertures become smaller and gets worse as they become larger. Most cameras provide a depth of field gauge on the lens that tells the distances within which objects will be in focus for a specific f-stop.

Working with photographers

If you work with a photographer, make clear what kinds of images you want. Photographers work most efficiently and give best results if they know exactly what they must do. Here are some things to explain.

Subject matter. Name the people and describe the scenes that interest you. Try to imagine some perfect images, then describe them. This helps the photographer think about what equipment and supplies to bring and the conditions under which the work will take place.

Editorial use. Tell the photographer the subject of the story, how long or important it is, who will read it, and what part photos play in carrying the message. State that images are for a newsletter and add a reminder to get some verticals as well as horizontals.

Presentation. Verify that prints will adhere to the quality standards outlined in Visual 8-13. Specify the paper surface and size to be used for enlargements.

Details. Check that the photographer knows when and where to appear, and when you need contact prints and enlargements. Make sure you both know who is responsible for getting caption information.

Most organizations include some skilled photographers who enjoy seeing their pictures in print. Don't hesitate to ask them for help, but make sure it's on your terms. Respect willingness to volunteer, but give the same guidance and deadlines that you would to a professional.

You may get color pictures from volunteers. Color prints tend to look too contrasty as black and whites. Slides may be converted to black and white prints, but the process takes more time and money than most editors have available. If color is all you have as a starting point, you may decide to use it, but starting with prints from black and white negatives gives much better results.

Remember to thank volunteers. If you don't use their pictures, add plenty of diplomacy to your "thank you anyway."

You do not need a model release if you use a photo only in your newsletter unless repro-

Evaluating photographs

Focus. Check that important parts of the image are sharp. If something is fuzzy that you want sharp, examine the contact sheet to determine if the problem is in the negative or the enlargement.

Grain. Certify that further enlargement will not make the image look fuzzy.

Contrast. Examine for strong blacks, clean whites, and a full range of grays. If you are not satisfied, ask about improvements using a filter or different paper.

Content. Confirm that negatives were enlarged full frame unless cropped accurately according to your instructions.

Detail. Inspect shadow areas and highlights for adequate clarity of features. Examine the negative to determine if dodging or burning could produce greater detail.

Flaws. Verify that the print is flat and has no scratches, stains, dirt, or blemishes. If it has flaws, check the negative and ask about eliminating them.

Paper. Ensure that enlargements are on smooth, semi-gloss paper.

8-13 Evaluating a photograph. The most effective and least expensive way to ensure quality photos in your newsletter is to start with good originals. Enlarged prints should meet the technical requirements above.

ducing the image might prove embarrassing to the recognizable people in it. Using the photo elsewhere, especially in a paid ad or on the cover of a publication, could require a release.

Photographers own copyrights to images they make. If you want to own copyrights, have exclusive use, or have access to images for future jobs without additional fees, negotiate the agreement while reviewing the images, not after publishing them.

If you work with professional photographers, read the books published by the American Society of Magazine Photographers whose titles are given in Appendix B. Those books, available at many camera stores, give details about fees, copyrights, model releases, delivery memos, and other business arrangements. □

9 Design and layout

Graphic design refers to how type and other visual elements appear on the page. Good design means they appear harmonious to ensure efficient, enjoyable reading. Harmony results from the right blend of size, position, and color of elements with how well they are printed and on what paper.

Newsletter design includes format, type specifications, and rendering of elements such as the nameplate that appear in every issue. Layout is the way design is carried out for a specific issue. Design is the plan, layout its fulfillment.

In this chapter, I assume you have already chosen a format and specified type. Those choices are your most important decisions about design. The following pages deal with nameplates, mastheads, and calendars, and how they may be assembled along with type and graphics into effective layouts.

The primary purpose of design is to make content accessible. Its secondary purpose, following at a great distance, is to represent personality or image. Style is not substance. Design can stimulate interest and make reading efficient, but design cannot camouflage thoughtless content or careless writing.

This chapter is about how things look, not how they are made. Designing takes place mostly in your imagination and on your dummy, not on your pasteup board, light table, or computer screen. Those tools are for experimenting with your vision and carrying it out, not creating it.

Every newsletter has a design, but some are better than others. Good design has standards. This chapter presents design standards and visuals that demonstrate their application.

The magic of computers does not change the standards of good design, but only makes those standards easier to achieve.

Good graphic design takes into account production as well as appearance. You must consider printing method and paper when deciding about photographs, screen tints, and other design elements. These considerations are introduced in this chapter and explained in Chapters 10 and 11.

This chapter includes information about using color in design. To allow faithful reproduction of colors, a portion of this chapter is printed using 4-color process—the same method used to reproduce color photos.

Nameplate

The top of the front page is the area that readers see first and most often. Your nameplate belongs there.

The information in your nameplate and its design are the most conspicuous features of your newsletter and influence how readers perceive it. The nameplate sets the tone for your entire publication.

Like typography, your nameplate should stay the same issue after issue. Make changes only after careful study of objectives and results.

Your nameplate should tell the name and subtitle of your newsletter and its publication date. It might also show a logo, illustration, photo, or issue number. With a marketing newsletter, include your address and phone number.

Visual 9-1 gives standards for evaluating nameplates. Visuals 9-2 through 9-17 show application of those standards. If you feel uncertain about creating one yourself, get help from a graphic designer. Review the suggestions about working with designers given in Chapter 2.

9-1 Evaluating a nameplate. A successful nameplate with a clear image and complete information meets the standards set forth in the checklist. You may need to experiment with several designs to achieve those standards. Nameplates at the right show how some experimental designs might look. Mockups by Polly Pattison.

Evaluating a nameplate

Full information. Certify necessary facts—name of newsletter, subtitle, and date—and optional contents such as logo, slogan, issue number, publisher, or editor.

Impact. Examine for subjective features such as balance, contrast, and unity.

Simplicity. Verify uncluttered design that readers can understand at a glance.

Harmony. Ensure that design suits format for text and, optionally, coordinates with other publications.

Practical. Check for efficient, cost-effective production and printing.

9-2 Script type graphically reinforces the name of this marketing newsletter. The shadow behind the title is a screen of the black ink used for text.

9-3 Bronze and dark green inks on ivory paper convey the impression of competent people in a successful business who deserve respect from their customers.

9-4 Imitating the name and typography of *The Wall Street Journal* helps build a conservative, trustworthy image.

9-5 All capital letters make relatively long words hard to read. Having "INFO" in a second color helps, but risks looking badly if not perfectly registered.

9-6 Slanted cursive lettering and a name to inspire fantasy lets readers know that Sally wants to help. Preprinting the blue helps keep Sally's costs low.

9-7 Design leaves room for a new drawing of wildlife for each seasonal issue. Printing on ivory paper reinforces desert theme.

9-8 Subtitle explains initials of title in very plain, easy-to-produce design. Solid and outlined letters contrast well with each other.

9-9 Drawing with loose tie and collar gives personal, informal touch to balance strong, authoritative typography.

9-10 Two logos and colors result in confusing graphics. Subtitle identifies the publisher, but not what the newsletter is about.

MAY/JUNE 1983
Volume 2   Issue 3
ISSN 0733-4281

faxon   F. W. Faxon Company, Inc., 15 Southwest Park, Westwood, MA 02090   (617-329-3350) (800-225-6055)

October, 1985   Vol. 29 No. 2   Published by the Sisters of Saint Joseph for their friends.

9-11 Stylish logo combined with bold lettering results in an upbeat feeling for fundraising. Slate blue color seems both contemporary and dependable.

9-12 Name, sans serif italic type, and speed lines work together. Red border ties page to nameplate.

BREAKTHROUGHS
MRA NEWSLETTER

TEXAS RESTAURANT ASSOCIATION

MARKET FARE

MARKETING FOR FOODSERVICE AND RESTAURANT ECONOMIES

January 1987   Vol. 2, No. 1

9-13 Different sizes of type make the name hard to read at a glance. Reversed subtitle must be all caps to assure that characters print without filling in.

9-14 Nameplate includes table of contents and logo showing printing by a union shop. Circles at left show where to punch holes for ring binder.

THE NEWS THIS WEEK:

OPM Announces 1987 Health
Insurance Rates
McLean Sees Stability In USPS
FERS Coverage Clarified
Klepner Leaves House Post
COLA Verdict Made
Nepotism In Cape Cod
Swisher Pledges Cooperation
Five Postmasters Cited
Mail Volume Growing
MHU Lobbyist Named
Multi-Million $ Mail Theft
Service Up, Share Down
McKean Down On Casey
Rep. Horton For Strong USPS

Vol. 1, No. 14   September 8, 1986
(ISSN: 0888-0794)   Published Weekly in Washington, D.C.

POSTAL EMPLOYEES' NEWSLETTER

SANE
WORLD

SUMMER 1987   SANE, COMMITTEE FOR A SANE NUCLEAR POLICY

9-15 Dramatic name is reversed out of 100% blue which is also used as a screen tint behind the black overprinting.

9-16 Good title and subtitle. The word "agenda" suggests action by readers. When spelled out, the acronym becomes the subtitle. 100% green with black rule is easy to print.

Vol. 3, No. 4   OSPIRG   Winter 1987

CITIZEN AGENDA

The quarterly report of the Oregon State Public Interest Research Group

9-17 Old-fashioned type helps readers expect formal, dependable information. Black outlines and shadows seem engraved, like money.

FINANCIAL SECURITY
ALERT

700 Shelard Plaza North, Golden Valley, MN 55426   FINANCIAL REPORT   May, 1985

"Financial Knowledge Is Financial Security."

9-18 Drawing in original above overwhelms title. Redesign uses outline type and larger logo for contemporary look. Shadow gives solid ground to 'land.'

9-19 Lapse in attention to bias-free writing required name change that also allowed title type to grow, giving stronger effect. Good subtitle.

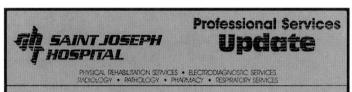

9-20 Too many typefaces and sizes confuse readers. New design makes logo less dominant and uses asymmetry for more dynamic feel. Double rules became graphic theme for hospital's family of eight newsletters.

9-21 Redesign has more elegant typeface used in smaller size. Title placed off center adds impact. Unity comes from p's descender standing on lower rule.

9-22 Old nameplate seemed too cute. New cursive type on black field becomes both reader-friendly and serious. Portion of drawing from story leads up into new nameplate.

9-23 New name suggests more active outlook for Scouts. Informality conveyed by switch from caps to lower case. Logo deleted, but new nameplate printed in Scout green.

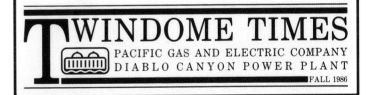

9-24 Original looks weak, lacks subtitle. Increasing depth with bigger type and rules gives better proportion. Subtitle explains logo.

9-25 A change to contemporary image with asymmetrical design and striking effect of letter 'K.' New design omits volume number, but highlights continuous years of service.

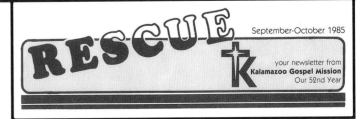

Color in design

Nameplates often have a color in addition to black. When used well, a second color can build contrast and make elements more vivid; it does little, however, to make them more legible.

Color may enhance features, such as the masthead, that stay the same from issue to issue. It is not, however, needed for headlines or graphics used in only one issue. Proper use of black for type, illustrations, and photographs makes them adequately legible. Lavish 2-color printing for a single issue costs money better spent on writing, design, or paper.

You can have a second color at little extra cost by using the technique of preprinting.

Preprinting means having color printed on enough paper at one time to last for many issues. For example, if you make 500 4-page newsletters on a monthly schedule, you need 6,000 11 x 17 sheets per year. You could have the color portion of your nameplate printed on all 6,000 sheets, then print black on 500 at a time as needed. The cost of preprinting would be minimal and might even be entirely made up by the savings from buying a year's supply of paper at once.

Using the technique of preprinting means that the date, issue number, headlines, and other elements unique to one issue appear in black, not color.

Chapter 10 tells how to make camera-ready copy for printing in color; Chapter 11 deals with buying printing and paper and tells how to handle preprinting from the business standpoint. Quantities for preprinting must be generously estimated to take into account spoilage during each print run and changing needs from issue to issue.

Using one color in addition to black can yield many useful combinations. You can have black and the color each at 100% and at several other percentages of screen tints. You can print black type at 100% over a tint of the color or, if it's dark enough, 100% of the color over a tint of black. You have reverses from both black and the color. Visual 9-27 shows some examples.

Preprinting a second color also can be used for techniques practical for only a few newsletters. They include reversing black out of the second color and overlapping tints of black and the color to create what appears to be a third color. These design options require more time, talent, and money than most newsletters have. Before using one, discuss it with a graphic designer and a printer.

When thinking about what color to use, consult a book of ink samples available at a printer, design studio, or art supply store. Ink sample books give customers and printers numbers by which to identify colors. The most commonly used book is the *Color Formula Guide* published by Pantone, Inc. It shows over 500 colors which many designers and printers call PMS colors. If you wonder how a specific color would look when screened, consult a color tint chart as well as ink samples.

You do not need more than two colors—black plus one other—for an effective newsletter, and may not need a second color at all. Thousands of first rate newsletters are printed using only one ink color.

If you use only one color and it is not black, it should be dark blue or brown to ensure best legibility. Before selecting any color other than black, test how well it reproduces photos and screen tints on the specific paper used for your newsletter.

Color influences feelings. Deciding to use color and selecting a specific hue should involve your publisher. Moreover, using color in design takes more skill that using black only. If you feel unsure about what color to select and how to use it, consult with a graphic designer.

"I always wanted color, but thought it would cost too much to have it printed every time we did an issue. Then one Saturday we cleaned up the old mimeo machine in the church basement and ran a thousand copies of our nameplate in red ink. We used a heavy photocopy bond paper, not the mimeo paper that's like a blotter. We had to run the machine extra slowly, but we got good, vivid color.

"Now we make every issue from that stock just by putting it in the photocopy machine. Words and drawings are the same old black toner, but the bright heading makes the package jump right through the mailbox. When we run out of this supply, we're going for a 2-color mimeo job."

9-26 Preprinting color. The blue type and rule are preprinted on a large number of sheets. Some of those sheets become stock for a monthly issue printed in black only. The result is a 2-color newsletter that costs little more than printing 1-color. Note that preprinting requires a format that stays the same from issue to issue.

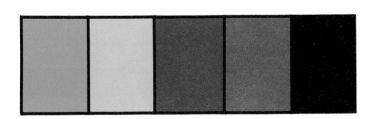

9-27 Overlapping screen tints. The five blocks at the left show black in 100% and a tint, blue at 100% and a tint, and, in the middle, overlapping tints of blue and black. The same colors and their tints are used to create the nameplate at the right. Screen tints can be preprinted at the same time as or instead of 100% of a color.

Overlapped tints simulate a third color. The exact hue of that color depends on the original ink colors, the percents at which they are screened, the color and surface of paper being printed, and several other factors. Many art supply stores, design studios, and printers have charts that show common combinations.

Masthead

Every issue of your newsletter needs a masthead, the area with business information.

The masthead tells the name and address of your sponsoring organization, your name, and how readers can reach you. You could also tell frequency of publication and subscription costs, if any, and give names of key officers and contributors. Potential contributors look in your masthead to learn if you solicit articles and photographs and what you pay for them.

If your newsletter is copyrighted, put the notice in your masthead. You can also include an International Standard Serial Number (ISSN). The National Serials Data Program of the Library of Congress, Washington DC 20540, assigns ISSNs at no fee. An ISSN helps librarians catalog your publication.

Newsletters that are mailed second class must display either an ISSN or a post office identification number in their nameplate, masthead, or return address.

Your masthead should have the same content and stay in the same location from one issue to the next. If you paste up by hand, make PMT copies ready for each issue. If you assemble pages using a computer, establish the masthead as a macro or as part of your format file.

Calendar

Some people read a newsletter mainly for its schedule of events. No other publication has such a specialized listing.

A calendar is one of the most demanding design tasks. It should be easy to assemble and proofread, efficient to read, and conservative of space. It should appear in the same place each issue and not have other important items to be clipped out from its opposing side.

Newspaper designers have ingenious ways of presenting schedules. Study the organization and use of type in a major newspaper, especially in its Friday and Sunday issues, for ideas.

Several inexpensive computer programs keep track of forthcoming activities on calendars with various formats. They are interesting because of their various approaches to calendar design. The programs are made for personal

Mastheads

CALIFORNIA TODAY (ISSN 0739-8042) is the bimonthly newsletter of the PLANNING AND CONSERVATION LEAGUE.

PCL is a membership organization devoted to the passage of sound environmental and planning legislation in California. Membership, which includes a subscription to CALIFORNIA TODAY, is $25 per year.

Second Class postage paid at Sacramento, California.

POSTMASTER: Send address changes to the PCL office: 909 12th Street, Suite 203, Sacramento, CA 95814.

PCL OFFICERS

MICHAEL H. REMY, President
DWIGHT STEELE, Senior Vice President
BARBARA EASTMAN, Vice President, Bay A...
DAN FROST, Vice President, Central Valley
JOHN HOBBS, Vice President,
    Southern California

ORGANIZATIONAL BOARD MEMBERS

AMERICAN RIVER RECREATION ASSN.
AUDUBON SOCIETY BAY AREA CHAPTERS
CALIFORNIA NATIVE PLANT SOCIETY
CALIFORNIA STATE PARK RANGERS ASSN.
CALIFORNIA TROUT
CALIFORNIANS AGAINST WASTE
CONSERVATREE PAPER CO.
FRIENDS OF THE EARTH
FRIENDS OF THE RIVER
GREENPEACE PACIFIC SOUTHWEST
LAGUNA GREENBELT, INC.
LEAGUE TO SAVE LAKE TAHOE
MARIN CONSERVATION LEAGUE
MONO LAKE COMMITTEE
PROTECT AMERICAN RIVER CANYONS
TRAIN RIDERS ASSN. OF CALIFORNIA
WESTERN RIVER GUIDES ASSOCIATION
WILDERNESS SOCIETY

PCL STAFF

GERALD H. MERAL, Ph.D., Executive Director
COREY BROWN, General Counsel
ESTHER FELDMAN, Research Director
LAURIE McVAY, Office Manager
CAITLIN RIVERS, Design

CALIFORNIA TODAY is printed 100% recycled paper donated by CONSERVATREE, a San Francisco company specializing in recycled paper

psu **currently** is published each Monday for faculty and staff of Portland State University by News and Information Services, 221 DCE, ext. 3711, mail code NEWS. Deadline for material is **Tuesday noon.**

Editor: Cynthia D. Stowell
Contributors: Clarence Hein
　　　　　　　Cliff Johnson

Calendar Editor: Pat Scott

PSU supports equal educational opportunity without regard to race, sex, color, religion, national origin, handicap, veteran's status, or sexual orientation.

Published by:　LEUPOLD & STEVENS, INC.
　　　　　　　　P.O. Box 688
　　　　　　　　Beaverton, Oregon 97075
　　An Equal Opportunity Employer

Team Talk is published to provide employees with information about the ... management ... . Story ... employees ... very much ... company ...nswered in ...he editor.

CHAIRMAN OF THE BOARD
Norbert Leupold, Sr.

PRESIDENT
Robert J. Stevens

GENERAL MANAGER
Werner Wildauer

EDITOR
James W. Gilles

ASSISTANT EDITOR
Dee Nelson

Editors' FORUM

ISSN 0746-3014　　Vol.7/No.4
April 1986

P.O. Box 1806
Kansas City, Mo. 64141

913/236-9235

William R. Brinton, *Publisher*
Jay H. Lawrence, *Editor*
Wendy Byers, *Business Manager*
Marvin Arth, *Consulting Editor*
Contributors: Lola Butcher, Andy Cline, John G. Hope, Robert Deen, Thomas D. Anglim, Andi Stein

The Editors' Forum (ISSN 0746-3014) is published monthly except August for $55 a year by Editors' Forum, Box 1806, Kansas City, Mo. 64141. Second class postage paid at Kansas City, Mo. Postmaster: Send address changes to Editors' Forum, Box 1806, Kansas City, Mo. 64141.

Proofreading by Scrivener
1402 W. 28th Terrace
Independence, Mo. 64052
816/252-1966

9-28 Mastheads. Effective masthead design enhances the rest of the newsletter as well as presenting business information. Mastheads do not have to be typeset or include logos, but they do need careful thought about clear organization and complete details. In addition to reading the guidelines in the text on page 98, treat the information in these seven examples as a checklist to ensure that your own masthead includes everything you think necessary.

Advocate is produced by the Bureau of Administrative Operations, Dade County Public Schools, 1450 N. E. 2 Ave., Suite 551, Miami, FL 33132. Address corrections and other correspondence should be addressed to its editor, Bill DuPriest, or phone (305)-376-1585.

I S S N   0 8 8 5 - 4 5 5 6

Contents

9-29 **Contents.** A table of contents advertises the information inside and can be a useful design element on the front page. Most newsletters have one, but many don't need one. If your newsletter has no more than eight pages, readers may ignore a contents panel. If it's more than eight pages, they may welcome it, depending on your design and their interest in your content.

CAMPUS CALENDAR
June

Wednesday   **1**
Student Art Exhibition: Patti Malone, Mendenhall
(through June 5).

Saturday   **4**
Scholastic Aptitude Test, Testing Center

Monday   **6**
FILM: *Motel Hell*, Hendrix 9 p.m.

Tuesday   **7**
Bingo/Ice Cream Party, Mendenhall, 7 p.m.

Wednesday   **8**
FILM: *Kentucky Fried Movie*, Hendrix, 8 p.m.

Saturday
Graduate Re

Sunday
Freshman Or

Monday
Science Educ
17
Maritime His
School, Swar
FILM: *Alien,*

Tuesday
FLAG DAY
Bingo/Ice Cr

Wednesday
Graduate Ma
Center

Sunday   **19**
Freshman Orientation (through June 21)
FATHER'S DAY

Monday   **20**
FIRST SUMMER SESSION CLASSES END
Science Education Day Camp, K-3 (through June
24)

OCTOBER

S	M	T	W	T	F	S
						1
2	3	4	5	6	7	8
9	10	11	12	13	14	15
16	17	18	19	20	21	22
23	24	25	26	27	28	29
30	31					

(Times in bold are morning events)

CALENDAR

May 14, Chicago

Fundamentals of Corporate Community Relations. This meeting, with its solid how-to agenda, will be especially useful to companies with relatively new community relations programs—and to those still exploring this area of ever-increasing importance. The program will provide excellent

OCTOBER	ACTIVITY	CLUB	CAPTAIN	PHONE	OPEN
1&2	Warren Miller Movie	CASCADE	Pat Fuller	H284-6300	Yes
1	Anniversary Party	RAMPAGE SPORTS	Don McCandless	W297-7222	Yes
3-16	Buy & Sell at Mountain Shop	SCHNEE VOGELI	Jim Feldman	288-6768	Yes
4	Oregon Nordic Meeting	OREGON NORDIC	Bob Ross	H246-8048	Yes
5	Bergfreunde Meeting at Greenwood Inn	BERGFREUNDE	Jack Young	H643-1525	Yes
6	Rampage Sports Ski Club Meeting	RAMPAGE SPORTS	Dave Kohlmeier	H641-1071	Yes
8	Ski tune-up at Rampage Sports & Western Dance w/ Stoddard & Cole	BERGFREUNDE	Joan Musch	H244-4106	Yes
13	First General Meeting, Bldg.50	SKI TEK	Joy Frisbie	W646-1601	Yes
19	PASCC Meeting	PASCC	Marralene Stein	W655-9220	Yes
20	Pub Crawl	SKI TEK	Sally Marlino	W646-1601	Yes
22	Barrymoore Ski Movie	MT HOOD C.C.			Yes
29	Halloween Party	PLAZA	Laura Tuttle	H281-8433	Yes

has a more analytic and strategic focus than the one-day workshop immediately preceding it. As always, participants will have the opportunity to meet and interact with 100 or more top practitioners in community relations.

June 11-13, Washington, D.C.

Public Affairs Training Seminar. This is the "basic" course for new or relatively inexperienced public affairs officers, but it will also be valuable for the longtime professional seeking new ideas.

June 26-27, New York City

Strategic Uses of Philanthropy in Public Affairs. Corporate philanthropy is one of the most vital but often misunderstood components of public affairs. This conference will concentrate on ways to make the most effective use of such philanthropy. Planning for, and the administration of, philanthropic projects will be discussed by experts, who will also look at goals proclaimed by certain social and cultural activist organizations.

O C T O B E R

1	Wed.	7:30	SMIL
1	Wed.	7:00	Brentw
4	Sat.	9-3:00	Mid-C
4	Sat.	10:00	Pleasa
6	Mon.	7:00	SE Up
6	Mon.	8:00	Forum
7	Tues.	7:30	**Lents Board**, Lents Boys Club, 9550 SE Harold
7	Tues.	7:30	**Mt. Scott-Arleta**, Mt. Scott Community Center, SE 72nd & Harold
7	Tues.	5:30	**HBBA Board**, SE Uplift, 3534 SE Main
8	Wed.	7:00	**Brentwood-Darlington**, Errol Heights Baptist Church, 7950 SE 62nd
8	Wed.	7:30	**HAND**, Abernethy School, 2421 SE Orange
9	Thurs.	7:30	**Buckman**, Buckman School Library, 320 SE 16th
13	Mon.	7:00	**Foster/Powell**, Marysville School, 7734 SE Raymond
13	Mon.	7:30	**Montavilla**, OSU Extension Center, 211 SE 80th
13	Mon.	7:00	**Richmond**, Central Christian Church, 1844 SE 39th
13	Mon.	7:00	**Woodstock**, Woodstock Community Center, 5905 SE 43rd

9-30 Calendars. Good calendar design begins with clear knowledge of what readers want to know. Typography doesn't need to be complicated or fancy, but it must be well-organized and complete. Notice how much information these examples include and how they help readers by anticipating questions. When properly designed, calendars serve as advertising tools, not merely notification sheets.

use, not publishing, so printouts may require some enhancements to become camera-ready.

Begin designing a schedule for your newsletter by asking what readers want to know. Try to make design help answer their questions. Here are some possibilities.

Location. If you're announcing activities at branch libraries or a series of public hearings, readers probably want to know only about locations they find convenient. Put the place first or in bold type, then tell dates and details.

Activity. If you're listing a variety of events, group them into categories that make sense to your readers. Don't make people who care deeply about one kind of event fight their way through the list of everything else.

Date. If you're presenting a variety of dates for the same event such as a stage play or workshop, let your design highlight dates instead of program or performers. You don't need to repeat the name of the event next to the date for each performance.

Layout

Good newsletter layout ensures that articles, illustrations, photos, and other elements for each issue fit together for efficient reading.

Layout begins with knowing what articles and graphics you want in an issue and how important each one is. Priority is the key. Layout requires that some elements appear earlier, longer, or larger than others. Priority tells you what goes on page one, what takes the largest headline, and what gets bumped to the pile labeled "maybe-in-another-issue."

With priorities in mind, make a dummy for every page. Visual 9-31 includes an example of a dummy for a front page. Make dummies full size to resemble the printed newsletter. If you have preprinted sheets, use them when making dummies.

Dummies take only a few minutes to make, but can save hours of experimenting on a light table or computer screen. Showing them to others helps explain size and placement of photos or secure approval for layout. Having a dummy helps reveal articles or visuals that aren't ready yet and provides a guide when pasting up.

Make a dummy regardless of your format and even if you use design software. Especially if you use design software! The best representation of a layout on a computer screen cannot substitute for visualizing the final product on paper.

When you sketch how you want each page to appear, keep in mind that most readers look first at headlines, photos, captions, and other strong visual elements throughout the entire newsletter. Thoughtful layout makes it easy to skim, then return to specific material.

The following guidelines will help you create successful layouts.

Simplicity. The layout easiest to make is probably easiest to read, too. Simplicity and efficiency go hand in hand.

Sticking to one format and just a few typefaces and sizes keeps your publication simple. Remember, too, that clip art and other graphics are just clutter if they don't contribute to a specific objective.

Every strong element on a page competes for attention with every other. Headlines, photos, charts, areas of color, and screen tints all shout, "Look at me!" When you put an element on the page, make sure it deserves attention.

Structure. Readers want your help. Use headlines to signal importance of stories. Make the most important headlines biggest and place them near the top of the page. Don't make two headlines seem to read as one by positioning them across from each other, an error known as tombstoning.

Use rules and screen tints to organize information that is not text or captions. Rules are especially important to box tables and other data graphics.

White space on the outside frames a layout, but on the inside steals its harmony. Push white space out so it encloses elements and is not trapped by them.

Eye flow. Readers enter a layout at the upper left and exit at the lower right. Put a headline where eye flow begins. Use a strong visual such as a photo to anchor the weakest point of the page at the lower left.

Regardless of placement, readers look at photos first unless they are quite small. A strong photo near the lower right invites readers to skip the rest of the page.

Interesting photos have a flow within them that can lead readers from one image to the next or on to other material. Use the internal movement of photos to point readers in the right direction and keep them going.

Proportion. Perfectly balanced pages are as dull as perfect people. Compose pages using the same guidelines that lead to interesting photos. Divide pages in thirds rather than halves; use an odd, not even, number of major elements; build interest with asymmetry.

Size, weight, and placement of elements determines contrast. Use text to divide a large headline from a dark photo. Make captions long enough so a diagram at the end of a column doesn't seem to fall off the bottom of the page.

Spreads. Readers see only your first and last pages by themselves. Other pages are usually seen two at a time as part of a spread. Layout must take the spread into account, not just the single page.

9-31 Challenge of layout. Usually you have several ways you could organize material on a page. Headlines in the left example are tombstoned. The single column in the left and upper examples flows down from the logo, making the page look static. Horse in the bottom left example seems running off the page. The layout has more life with the large column being the same width as the nameplate, the main headline lower, and the photo counter balanced off the corner of the logo.

9-32 Layout spreads.

Unlike laying out the first and last page, laying out inside pages requires visualizing spreads. The rules for efficient eye-flow and interest through asymmetrical design stay the same.

With a 1-column format, there may be little flexibility. Through use of bold type and variety of column width, the first two spreads on this page work well. The spread at the bottom is efficient to read but looks ordinary because of the almost equal size of each article and headline.

9-33 More layouts. Pages in these spreads are tied together with strong design graphics. Thick rules at top or bottom allow reversed type for headers and footers.

Two publications on this page use standing headlines, a device commonly seen but not recommended in this book. Standing heads rarely appeal to readers as much as headlines written for specific stories.

Framing copy as at the right helps it look good as a single page used as a small poster.

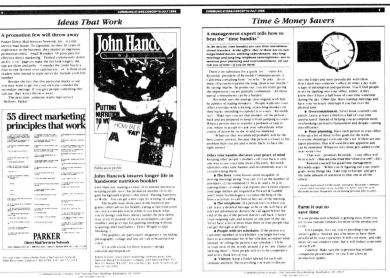

9-34 Still more layouts. Pages above are united by strong logo as header, those below with large table used as crossover. Note that the left boxed material is placed to attract reader's eye to area of the page easily missed.

Publication at the left uses downstyle headlines correctly, the one above to an interesting extreme. Headlines above read better than those all in caps or with capitalization that violates common rules of grammar.

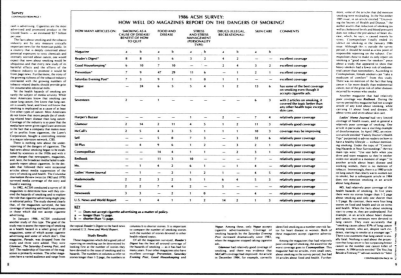

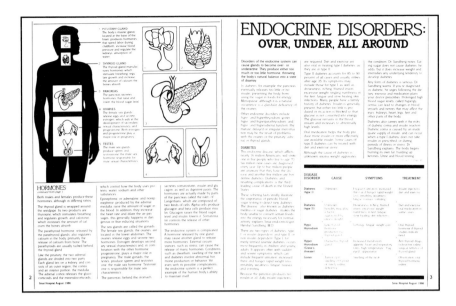

9-35 Even more layouts. Very strong visuals dominate these spreads. Large white spaces become design elements. Note how white space on these two book pages encloses copy. Compare these two book pages with previous two that place same amount of text and illustrations in a different pattern.

Two excellent and well-placed photos draw reader into spread at the bottom. Photos show creative editorial angles and aggressive cropping. Copy ranges from personal interest to personnel policy and includes masthead. A fine spread.

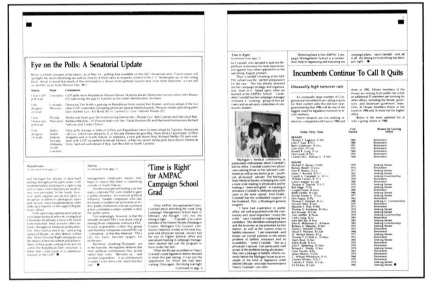

Photo layout

Occasionally you might want a spread with many photos. When this happens, you may have to ignore your format. One- and 2-column formats do not lend themselves to photo layouts; even 3-column formats can be difficult.

Start your spread by reviewing the principles of good design. Select an odd number of images—three or five—and feature one at a large size. Use verticals as well as horizontals. Arrange the images flowing left to right and top to bottom to make sense the same way that people read.

Photo layouts look best when all images are the same quality. One bad one drags down good ones; one outstanding one makes others look feeble even if they would be individually acceptable. Images with dark backgrounds may make lighter ones seem washed out.

Dynamic photo spreads have plenty of white space. Use large, uneven margins to frame images, but don't trap white space between photos.

Photos in spreads need captions and credits. It may be convenient to cluster them into paragraphs relating to more than one image, referring to individual photos by their location on the page.

Layouts need one large headline for unity. The headline doesn't have to be at the top of the page, but it should be close to the upper left where reading begins.

Most photo spreads run across folds, so you need to anticipate where the crease falls. Try not to fold someone's face or staple an arm to a lectern.

Unless you are a wizard with desktop publishing software, mechanicals for photo layouts require pasteup. Chapter 10 explains the necessary techniques.

If you are working with a 2-page spread, make one mechanical with one tissue overlay for the entire spread. Keylining and other paste-up techniques stay the same, but working two-up helps keep every element orderly.

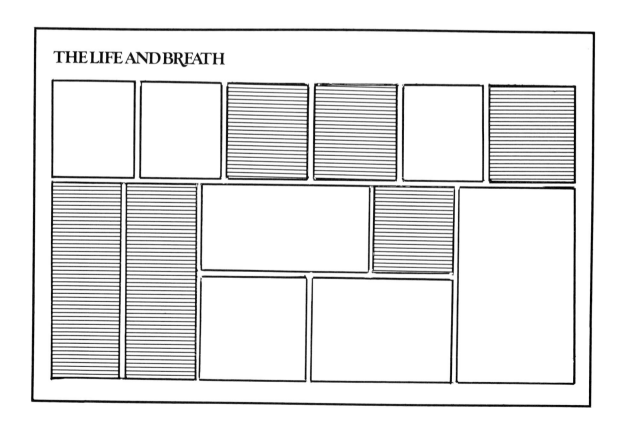

THE LIFE AND BREATH

Bout in a nice little restaurant ne and candlelight. We want to movie on a screen bigger than n inches, measured diagonally. am about concerts, ballet, gallery openings, dancing. We long for what Anne calls "life in the fast lane."

Harrisonburg, our shopping town, is only forty miles away, but bad roads and mountains make for a slow trip an hour and a half one way. When lambs are coming, we rarely go there together, but this particular morning we decided to chance it. The two ewes we'd been expecting to lamb did so, considerately, at 6:30 A.M. A good single, and twins. Most of our ewes twin, some single, and occasionally a ewe will drop triplets.

The ewe due to lamb next was Bouncer, a big young Rambouillet, who had proved her mothering ability the past year. She wasn't showing any signs of hurrying into labor. She wasn't pawing herself a nest, or walking aimlessly about, or licking her lips, or separating herself from the flock. A neighbor promised to check Bouncer at noon, so we took off.

The trip in was pleasant; we made good time and stopped for chili dogs at

Certain kinds of products have mysteriously escaped the chrome name plate and the Technicolor decal. Furniture, for instance, still functions purely as furniture, ungarnished by promotion. But I don't think it will be long before we'll see convertible sofas with "Castro" stitched into the upholstery or rugs with "Karastan" worked into the weave. Clothes were once off limits in this regard, but now people seem to get a warm, participatory glow from wearing Adidas T-shirts, Yves St. Laurent ties, or designer jeans with "Gloria Vanderbilt" emblazoned across their backsides.

Even the Post Office has started to put its dowdy wares to promotional use. This winter my godfather, a Dante scholar, rushed through a purchase of fifteen-cent stamps only to discover later that they were of a new variety no doubt devised to counter the Time Lady's attacks on written correspondence. Each of them was decorated with a floral generality and a motto: "Letters preserve memories," "Letters lift spirits," or "P.S. Write soon." The purchase thus transformed my godfather, of all people, into an involuntary press

gy-saving tip from the Phone Center Store—form car pools and combine trips" is her message at this moment (10:12), but I have heard her take swipes at letter-writing, hawk pushbutton phones, and remind me of faraway loved ones whom I haven't called in weeks (although she has shown a curious lack of concern for loved ones within my toll-free area whom I haven't called in weeks).

She is a fund of advice and information, but she has a somewhat scolding, Dr. Joyce Brothers little voice and I always hang up with a mortified feeling. In fact, sometimes I get so snagged on her pitches and tips, so eager to close my fireplace dampers or call my Aunt Mary Alice, that I forget to hear what time it is and have to start the process all over again.

I hate to sound ungrateful, but since the Time Lady is paid for out of the profits the phone company makes by overcharging for its other services, I tend to regard her as part of Ma Bell's product line, and as such she demonstrates to me once again the increasingly preachy and grudging manner in which business has taken to dispensing its goods and services. Promotion, which was once an antecedent to actual commerce, now survives each transaction and sticks to each product like flypaper. Indeed, I've lately gotten the feeling when I buy something that I've

that mar my appliances: "F/GM/Mark of Excellence/Frigidaire/Product of General Motors U.S.A./Imperial 170" on my refrigerator, "Sears Kenmore Magicord Powermate" on my vacuum cleaner. It sometimes seems to me, as I look around at the honky-tonk of my kitchen, that I've spent my money only to populate my shelves and countertops with ambassadors singing their companies' praises. Even now, as my typewriter taps out these words for me, it is advertising SCM's Smith-Corona Coro-

turbed, the ewe will refuse a lamb and let it starve or even butt it to death in the lambing pen. You can raise lambs on bottles, but they never do as well as lambs raised by a good mother.

Ewes recognize their lambs by scent, but we had washed all the scent off the triplets. Ange eyed the clumsy, healthy lambs. "Fine," she said. "Now we have four lambs and two mothers that both want the big white one."

We would have to try and graft one of the triplets onto Big White's mother. The Suffolk could raise two lambs on one teat. Perhaps the ewes were so confused by now that they wouldn't know one lamb from another.

G1:30, the lambs were strong to go outside. The wind had died Ve each carried two lambs. As the ewes heard them, they went alling for the lambs, rushing back and forth. They were like woolly gunboats circling us, trying to get to the lambs, and when we stepped into the barn, all the other ewes, suddenly awakened and alarmed, started calling for their lambs. We laid the lambs in the straw of the lambing pens. The lambs found it hard to walk in the deep straw and weren't too certain of their direction, but they were in fine voice. The ewes fell silent. Reserving judgment, they extended their noses to sniff the lambs. With a soft nicker, and a swipe of her rough tongue, the Suffolk

Almost sure . . . " Then Lazarus let out a particularly lusty cry and the ewe accepted the stranger and nudged her back toward her milk.

When Anne checked at one A.M., the lambs on the Suffolk had learned to take turns on her one functional teat.

When I went out at three, all four lambs were asleep, banked up against their mothers. There's nothing so smug as a lamb with a full belly. When I put my finger in Lazarus's mouth, she bleated in outrage.

ful and considerate reading of books, with such rereadings and rizings as individual taste may scribe, will give any man the ess of a liberal education even if devote but fifteen minut

Eliot's selections the advance mail had not been completed, but a nary list had been prepared salesmen. This list was on office that Collier had ope bridge.

On the night of June 15, 1909, someone from the *Harvard Crimson* filched the secret list from a locked desk, and the next day it was published in the student paper—the literary scoop of the year. The New York *Times* and many other newspapers picked up the hot news and published it June 17 on page one, thereby setting off a nationwide controversy over the wisdom of the selections.

Newspapers did their best to heat up the controversy and make a contest out of the selection, seeking dissenting opinions throughout the country. In Houston, Texas, the president of Baylor University declared that the shelf should include a grammar, a dictionary, the Bible, and a collection of Mark Twain's writings. He commented: "I am decidedly of the opinion that a liberal education cannot be found in sixty inches of plank." A Vermont clergyman

free publicity the Harvard Classics received during 1909 and 1910 was beyond anything ever known before in publishing circles. At one time my clerks reported to me that we had pasted up in scrapbooks a total of over 1700 columns of newspaper free publicity."

Abbott Lawrence Lowell had assumed the presidency of Harvard in May of 1909. Commencement on June 30 was the occasion for ceremonial farewells to Eliot, who received honorary degrees of LL.D. and M.D. That night,

chusetts Institute of Technology, where his plan of reform was welcomed and set the pattern for chemistry teaching throughout the country.

Being a scientist, Eliot chose for the Five-Foot Shelf writings of such great just like to bring up this stuff and not act on any of it or expect anyone else to act on it either. Well, you've got me all wrong. During the course of writing this piece I think I've finally found a cure for our sickly pride of ownership.

As out that many of these logos complaining about are removplastic SCM/Smith Corona Super 12 logo plate, for insume off without a hitch, and after a little light scrubbing with cleanser and a sponge you'd hardly know anything had been there. And all it took was a few quick turns of a screwdriver and the Sears Craftsman logo plate came right off my push mower. I haven't had quite as much luck with the GE/General Electric Toast-R-Oven decal on the door of my toaster-oven, but I'm working on it. The only real problem I've had is with the logo plate on the refrigerator door. I pried it off easily, but it left a long scab of glue which gives the refrigerator a sullen look.

Removing the logo plates has given most of my possessions a pleasing, abstract quality, but I think what I'll have to do in cases like that of my refrigerator door is devise my own logo plates to paste over the scars the old ones leave. I figure I could find somebody who'd fashion a few for me out of brass or chrome, and I've been giving their composition a lot of thought. To set a good example for industry, I think I'll leave my name out of it and have it read in simple little letters: "A poor thing, but

One Hundred Army Years

ON LOCATION

As soon as I opened the lambing-yard gate, I spotted her. The frantic mother, a big Suffolk, was trying to rouse her lambs—she'd had triplets—but they were all flat on the ground, motionless as boards. I ran back to the house and shouted, "Anne! Come quick!"

The ewe had done her best: she had cleaned each lamb as it came, and had tried to nudge them to their feet, but they were down now—muddy, bloody, and stiff. I wiped the birth mucus off their faces and forced my finger into their mouths. Cold. Ice cold. One lamb's

Anne was beside me now. We scooped up the filthy, frozen lambs in our arms, hurried back to the house, and laid them beside the wood stove, just six inches from the hot metal.

WITH RO

It's always chancy pulling brand-new lambs off their mothers. The bonding process, in which the mother recognizes the lamb as her own, is fairly delicate, and sometimes, when the process is dis-

9-36 Photo layout. Good photo spreads begin in the minds of the photographer and editor as they visualize the page. Using a grid pattern as at left, the layout includes blocks for photos, captions, and copy. Final product features one or two large images supported by the rest. An odd number of images usually works better than an even number. ☐

10 Camera-ready copy

Whether your newsletter is printed on a photocopy machine or offset press, you need an original to start with. The original might be as simple as one sheet from your typewriter or as complex as pasteup with keylines for photos.

You are ready to prepare the original when you have a dummy, also known as a mockup, of your layout. Make the dummy by photocopying type and art, including halftones, then arranging them according to your layout. The dummy tests whether your layout actually works.

A dummy tells exactly how the finished newsletter will look. If you produce type and graphics with a computer, the dummy is a trial printout to ensure that elements on paper appear as predicted on screen.

A mockup helps spot problems and makes the rest of production go smoothly. You may want to show it to your supervisor before starting pasteup. Changes at this stage cost much less than during production phases that follow.

The process of preparing the original for printing is called pasteup if it's done by hand and desktop publishing if it's done from a computer memory. In either case, the result of the process, when carried out properly, is camera-ready copy.

Camera-ready copy almost always consists of black images on white paper, but its color does not relate to colors of ink used to reproduce it. When plates made by photographing your originals are on press, the images that were black on the originals can be reproduced with ink that is green or any other color.

Whether you prepare camera-ready copy yourself or have someone else do it, you need to know how it's supposed to look. You keep control over cost, quality, and schedule when you know how to confirm that copy is truly camera ready.

Many editors run into problems during pasteup because they make changes that should have been made earlier. Thorough knowledge of format and type specifications allows copyfitting while writing and editing. Layout and pasteup should involve only tiny adjustments, not major revisions.

This chapter describes graphic arts photography and how it relates to photographs and mechanicals. You learn about halftones and scaling and how to work with camera services. You discover the essential tools and techniques for pasting up.

All-or-nothing principle

Newsletters are printed by photocopy or offset lithography. Both methods depend on photography, thus require camera-ready copy.

Graphic arts photography is based on the principle of all-or-nothing. An image will be reproduced 100% or not at all. There is no middle ground.

The all-or-nothing principle exists because of the method for reproducing originals hundreds or thousands of times. An offset press either places ink on paper or not; it doesn't place just a little bit of ink. Photocopy machines, using toner instead of ink, work the same way.

An area of paper to receive toner or ink could be as large as a 72-point bold letter or as small as a dot in a 100-line screen, but the coverage within the area must be 100%.

Images such as type and clip art are line copy. They are high contrast and conform to the all-or-nothing principle. Images such as photographs with a range of densities are continuous tone copy. They must be changed into line copy, called halftones, before they can be faithfully reproduced.

Because of the all-or-nothing principle, certain colors gain intensity when reproduced while other colors vanish. Light blue drops out, thus can be used for writing on mechanicals.

Halftones

Photographs are changed to halftones by breaking images into thousands of tiny dots. Patterns of dots create illusions of original images, tricking the eye into thinking it sees continuous tones.

In areas of the image with small dots, more paper shows through, creating highlights; portions of the image with large dots show less paper, thus represent shadow areas.

When a halftone is made on paper, it's a halftone positive; when on film, it's a halftone negative.

Photocopy and quick printing require that halftone positives be part of pasteup. Commercial printing using metal plates would normally use halftone negatives. When your newsletter is printed using metal plates, you provide the printer with photos prepared according to instructions given later in this chapter.

Halftones may be made to a variety of quality standards. Sometimes contrast can be improved during halftoning. When specifying or inspecting halftones, verify that the results are the best possible.

Color photographs may be halftoned for printing black and white, but will not look as good as starting with a black and white photo of the same image. If you must start with color originals, remember that graphic arts film sees red the same as black and drops out light blue and yellow. Red areas of the original photo will lose detail and the resulting halftone may have too much contrast; light blue and yellow areas may vanish.

Illustrations made with soft pencil lines or brush strokes have continuous tones the same as photographs, thus require halftoning.

"I never felt so confused as the first few months working here. My boss asked me if I could do the keylining for our masthead. It took a while to figure out he meant pasteup the nameplate. The printer wondered if I would knock out the tones. What tones? Did she want me to stop singing? Oh, the halftones. Are they shown with windows?

"Somebody should write a dictionary of newsletter terms whose meanings everyone would agree on."

photograph as halftone reproduction

Kathleen Ryan

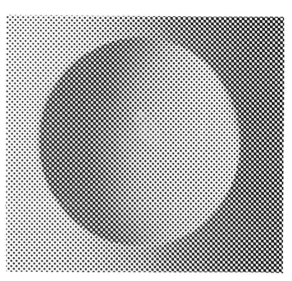

10-1 **Halftone and line reproductions.** The top version of the portrait and the ball are halftones. Even the large dots of the ball create the illusion of the original continuous-tone image.

photograph as line reproduction

Asking a printer to enhance a black and white photograph or to halftone an illustration or color photo may leave you uncertain of the outcome. To check how plates made from halftone negatives will reproduce using white paper, ask for a Velox as a proof. The slight extra cost will be repaid with your confidence that the image will satisfy you.

The paper on which halftones are reproduced affects choice of screen ruling. Uncoated paper absorbs ink quickly: dots may soak in, spread out, become fuzzy at their edges, and touch. A somewhat coarse screen helps shadow areas retain detail on uncoated paper. Coated paper holds the ink on its surface, so a finer screen may be used.

To get the most out of photos in your newsletter, print on coated or #1 uncoated paper. Read the paper section at the end of Chapter 11 for details.

To learn more about how screen ruling and paper affect reproduction of halftones, ask a printer to show you demonstration materials from paper manufacturers. Companies such as Warren and Hammermill publish booklets and charts showing photographs in many screen rulings and colors, with special effects, and on a variety of papers. These materials are free and help you learn about halftones.

Halftone positives

Halftone positives may be made using a darkroom enlarger, photocopy machine, scanner, or process camera. If your halftones will be photocopied, screen rulings should be 85-line. For quick printing, use 100-line. For commercial printing, use 133-line.

Darkroom enlarger. To make halftone positives in a darkroom, you need the same kind of halftone screen that printers use and high contrast paper such as Kodak Velox.

You can buy a graphic arts screen at stores

that sell supplies to printers. An 8 x 10 piece is large enough for home darkroom use.

Set up for the halftone exactly as you would any other print. Before making the exposure, place the screen emulsion side down in tight contact with the paper.

Exposure and development times for high contrast papers are much shorter than normal, but you do not need special chemicals. Halftones may benefit from a one or two second flash of enlarger light made without screen or negative.

Photocopy machine. Most copiers use a single light source. To make a halftone, you need a white dot screen made by manufacturers of dry transfer type. The screen is placed on the glass between the machine's light source and the photograph.

If you need to reduce or enlarge the image, change in the darkroom, not on the photocopier. Changing size as part of photocopying changes the screen ruling of the halftone.

Laser copiers work like laser printers, but are not coupled to a computer. The pulsating laser beam creates a halftone without using a separate screen. Because laser copiers digitize the image, its size, shape, and position on the page can be changed. Even the best laser copiers, however, yield halftones of marginal quality not appropriate for newsletters.

Scanner. Using a scanner to make a halftone means that the image may be seen on a computer screen, manipulated with regard to size and shape, and assembled along with type and graphics into a completed page. The ruling of halftones originating in scanners depends on the quality of the scanner and the output device.

Working with scanned images on a computer screen requires desktop publishing software and a machine with lots of memory. Even then, the pace may be slow and, depending on size, you may be limited to one image per page. Unless you have a machine with a 386 chip and at least a 70mb disk, I suggest you confine

85-line screen for photocopy

100-line screen for quick printing

133-line screen for commercial printing

10-2 Halftones in three screen rulings. The halftones above were made with the three screen rulings most appropriate for newsletters. As rulings become finer, details in the image become more clear, but printers find halftones harder to reproduce.

desktop publishing to type and line art.

If you scan photos into your computer, you will get better output from a photo type machine than a laser printer. Halftones from laser printers often have streaks. For best results, use a commercial scanner at a type shop or camera service instead of your desktop unit.

Process camera. Process cameras are made specifically for graphic arts photography. Small ones, sometimes called stat cameras, may be found at many type shops, design studios, blue print companies, and advertising or PR agencies. Larger machines are used by commercial printers and trade camera services.

Halftone positives made using a process camera are known as stats or PMTs. Stats or PMTs are not the same as Veloxes, which are higher quality and cost more because they require making negatives first.

When you buy halftones, you are charged by the size of paper or film used, not the size of original copy. You can save money by grouping images all scaled to the same percentage. Grouping, usually called ganging, may result in some loss of quality if originals differ in contrast or density. Ganged images are all shot at a common exposure rather than at exposures determined for the needs of individual images.

Camera services

Making a camera-ready original often involves producing elements for mockup or pasteup. The elements might include a logo at a new size or a headline that needs screening as well as photos that must be halftoned.

Although anyone with a process camera can make a PMT, Velox, or halftone negative, it's handy to be familiar with a shop that specializes in such products. The shops, known as trade camera services, often can enhance a weak image or salvage a poor print. And they understand deadlines.

"The drawing was in a direct mailer we did two years ago. I couldn't find the mechanical and the paper had yellowed. No way was it camera-ready. My camera service used a filter to boost the contrast and made a PMT of the drawing that looked better than I expected."

When you take delivery of photostats, PMTs, or negatives, check for quality. Look for sharp focus, especially in portions of the image farthest from the center. Certify images are on pure white paper with no chemical stains. Measure them to verify scaling to your specifications. Finally, check that copy is not too fat from underexposure or too thin from overexposure. Its weight should match other elements of your newsletter.

If you want more control over quality and less cost and turnaround time, consider having a camera service make plates or plate-ready film. Consult with your printer before taking this step to ensure that camera work coordinates with presses.

You can find trade camera shops in a classified directory under "lithographic negative and plate makers" or by asking a printer or someone from an advertising or public relations agency, or design studio.

Regardless of other services you use, you need access to a photocopy machine that can reduce and enlarge to any percentage you specify. The machine is important to make photos and illustrations for your mockup and proof copies for approval.

Although photocopies are not as high quality as process camera work, often they are good enough to solve a last-minute problem.

Scaling

Frequently a drawing or photo is the wrong size or shape for a layout. It can easily be reduced or enlarged to fit. You must, however, identify the new size that you need.

Scaling is the process of determining the new size at which you want an image. New size is expressed as a percent of original size.

If you want the image 10% smaller, specify it at 90%; if you want it 10% larger, specify it at 110%. With no instructions, printers shoot at 100%. Writing "same size" or "SS" makes it clear that you want copy reproduced without changing its size.

Determine sizes using a scaling wheel, shown in Visual 10-3. Scaling wheels show the new height and width. With this knowledge, you know how the image at its new size will fit into your layout.

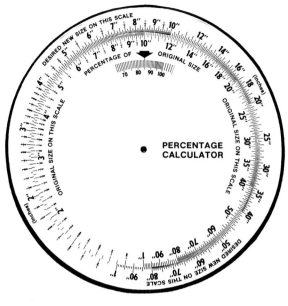

percentage wheel

original at 100%

reduced to 64%

enlarged to 120%   Mark Beach

original at 100%

```
twelve-pitch Courier pica headline
```

```
ten-pitch Courier pica headline
```

```
twelve-pitch Courier pica headline at 140%
ten-pitch Courier pica headline at 140%
```

10-3 Enlarging and reducing. The size of line and continuous-tone copy can be changed to fit your layout. Enlargements over 200% often show deterioration of the image. Reduction can make fine lines disappear. Note also that an image reduced to 50% becomes one fourth its original size, not one half, because size changes in two dimensions, not one. Photos are changed in size and halftoned all in one exposure. When specifying changes in size, determine new dimensions using a scaling wheel.

Because the arithmetic of scaling involves only one dimension (width or height), it's easy to forget that copy shrinks or grows in two directions. A block of type enlarged to 120% may appear much bigger than you expected; a photograph reduced to 50% may lose too many details. Shooting at 200% means the new copy will occupy four times the area of the original: twice as high and twice as wide.

Enlarging copy magnifies flaws. Even photo type and transfer lettering start to have ragged edges if enlarged to more than 200%. Reducing copy shrinks every feature. Fine lines or dot patterns may end up too thin to print.

Assembling pages on a computer screen means you can change the size of line art, and perhaps of photos, to fit your layout. Laser printing assembled pages as camera-ready copy avoids the need to scale. If you use the software only for doing layout, however, you must still give scaling specifications to a printer. In that case, use the ruler on the screen to determine new sizes and a scaling wheel to compute percentages.

Pasting up

Assembling elements to be photographed for printing can be done with adhesives and mounting boards or on a computer screen. When done by hand, the process of preparing both line and continuous tone copy for reproduction is called pasting up.

When type and graphics are assembled in final form on a computer screen, the process is desktop publishing. Even with desktop publishing, laser printing of pages assembled on a computer screen rarely results in fully camera-ready copy. There is almost always some pasting up, even if it is only to adhere the printout to a

mounting board and cover it with tissue.

Originals correctly and completely prepared camera-ready are called mechanicals.

The name of the procedure to make camera-ready copy and its end product varies from one part of the country to another. Some professionals refer to keylining instead of pasting up and use the term keyline, artboard, or paste-up instead of mechanical.

Pasteup can only be done accurately and fast if you have a good mockup as a starting point. Whether you do pasteup yourself or have it done elsewhere, and even if you assemble pages on a computer screen, use a dummy.

To paste up any newsletter to be printed in one color, and for most 2-color printing jobs as well, you need just a few simple supplies, tools, and techniques.

Mounting boards. These are sheets of paper that are backing for your mechanical. They should be about half an inch bigger all the way around than the page size of your newsletter. For 8½ x 11 pages, use at least 9 x 12 boards. The extra margin is for space to write instructions and for handling without touching the image area.

Paper for mounting must be sturdy and coated. Either 100# matte coat or 10 pt coated-one-side (C1S) cover stock work fine. The coating is very important because it allows you to reposition elements with minimum damage to the paper or the element itself.

Accuracy tools. Type, photos, and graphics need precise alignment with each other and the edges of the paper to look correct when printed. There are two methods to assure accurate alignment.

- Method #1 requires a T-square, triangle, and working surface with a perfectly straight edge. The tools are used as shown in Visual 10-4 to assure accuracy.
- Method #2 requires a long metal-edged ruler and mounting boards with a pre-printed grid. Visual 10-4 shows how it's done.

If you use method #1, mounting boards can be blank. If you use method #2, you need mounting boards preprinted with a grid of light blue lines. You can buy them or, better yet, have

---

"After having our printer pasteup our first two issues, I took a workshop to do it myself. I learned techniques for our newsletter, but I also learned that we had been paying too much. Making mechanicals doesn't require lots of imagination and advanced training and doesn't tie up expensive machines. Now when I want a job pasted up, I get hourly rates separate from typesetting, designing, or printing."

---

some printed exactly to the specifications of your format.

Adhesive paper. You need a few dozen sheets of inexpensive paper on which to place an element face down and apply adhesive to its back. Let the adhesive run off onto the paper. Throw away the sheet after using it once. The cheapest photocopier paper or the back sides of last month's manuscript work fine.

Be sure adhesive paper has not been printed on the side in contact with your type or art. Toner or ink can easily transfer as you apply glue or wax.

Artist's tape. White tape, usually ¾ inch wide on a three-inch core, protects edges, tapes mounting boards to your desk or table, attaches overlays to mechanicals, and covers a multitude of errors so they do not print.

Adhesive. Choose between glue sticks, rubber cement, artists spray, or wax. All have editors who swear by them; all have editors who swear at them. Which you use is a matter of personal style.

A hand waxer is an inexpensive tool whose use takes only a few minutes to learn. Wax is the adhesive used by many professionals because it allows for repositioning more easily than any form of glue. Try it.

Artist's knife. A small knife, such as those made by X-Acto or Olfa Companies, that handles like a pen and has interchangeable blades. Use the knife to trim copy and, if necessary, help lift it for repositioning. Buy pointed blades, style #11, and change them often.

Ruler with metal edge. Use the ruler as a guide for the knife blade when trimming and to check accuracy when using method #2. Purists think you need two rulers, one for getting nicks as you run your knife up and down its edge.

Glass cutting surface. Trim elements by running a knife blade along the metal edge of a ruler, not by cutting with scissors. Keep handy a piece of glass about 8 x 12 inches. Wrap its edges with artist's tape to avoid cutting yourself.

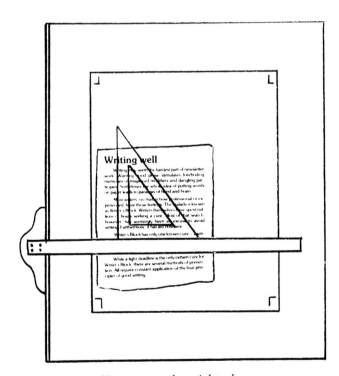

T-square and straight edge

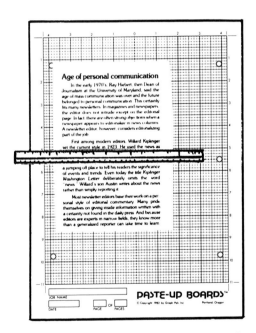

pasteup board with nonrepro blue grid

10-4 Accurate methods for pasteup. Left drawing illustrates a T-square and triangle with a blank mounting board; right drawing shows a ruler and a mounting board printed with a grid printed in nonreproducing blue. When not using boards with printed grids, use corner marks, not the edge of the paper, for squaring up.

Cutting against glass protects the underlying work surface and, equally important, ensures a clean, accurate trim. Soft materials such as cardboard trap the tip of the knife and reduce control.

White correction fluid. This fluid is for covering errors too small to eliminate with white tape.

Transfer materials. If you make headlines with dry transfer lettering, you need sheets with the two or three sizes of type you use regularly. You should also have one or two rolls of border tape and, if you photocopy or quick print and want screen tints, one or two sheets of screens.

Here's an example of a sufficient supply of transfer materials.

- Optima medium type: one sheet 18-point, one sheet 24-point, one sheet 30-point;
- border tape: one roll solid ½-point, one roll solid 1-point;
- 85-line screen tint: one sheet 20%, one sheet 40%.

Screen tints of 20% should normally have along their borders a rule of at least ½-point to frame them against the paper. Tints should slightly overlap into the border, an effect known to printers as trapping the border. A trapped rule assures clean edges along the tint. This is especially important if the tint is from a transfer sheet or laser printer, which are relatively coarse.

Sheets of transfer lettering, screens, and rules deteriorate with age. Buy the best quality you can find and use them within a year.

Elements. When preparing or specifying type, illustrations, or other elements, let the machines that produce them work as hard for you as possible. For example, if you use a rule be-

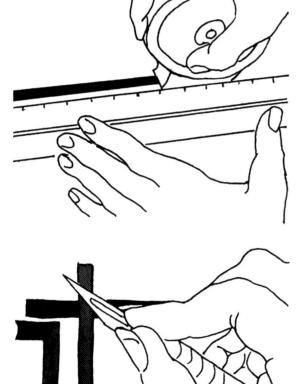

10-5 Using border tape. To lay down a straight rule, run the tape dispenser along a ruler as shown. For a perfect corner, overlap the tape and cut to miter the ends. Burnish tightly.

10-6 Using press-on screen. Loosely lay screen so it overlaps all edges of the image. If edges are straight, trim screen by running blade along a ruler. For irregular shapes, trim by running point of the knife on top of the outline. Burnish tightly.

tween columns, ask for galleys with a rule drawn by the same machine that produces type.

Tissue overlays. Use any thin translucent paper that can be taped as a flap to protect the mechanical. Even photocopy bond works. The overlay is the correct place on which to write instructions about screen tints, photos, and color breaks. Visual 10-8 shows an example.

Almost any mechanical for 2-color printing can be made using tissue overlays. You only need acetate when you want copy in the second color to touch or overlap copy in the first color. In the typical situation of making headlines, drawings, rules, or screens in a second color, the printer can make color breaks using photo techniques faster and more accurately than you can while pasting up.

For details about pasting up, consult the book by Walter Graham listed in Appendix B.

Photos and mechanicals

Pasteup involves either placing halftones or telling the printer how to place them.

If you print by photocopy or quick printing and want borders around halftones, you must make them directly on the PMTs using a graphic arts pen or ½-point border tape. Practice on a photocopy.

When you use a commercial printer, you provide photos separately from mechanicals. Each image must be identified, marked for cropping and scaling, and related to its position on your mechanical.

Identify every photograph with your name, name of your newsletter, and a number. For best results, mount each print on a backing sheet similar to that used for pasteup. Write instructions and crop marks on the mount board or tissue overlay. With unmounted prints, write in the narrow margin on the image side of the print.

Avoid writing directly on the back of a print or attaching anything to it with staples or paper clips that may scratch. If you have no margin or mounting board on which to put instructions, write on a piece of paper then tape it to the print as an overlay.

To indicate the portion of the photo you want printed, draw crop marks in black on the

Inspecting mechanicals

Identification. Certify that each mechanical and each separate photograph or illustration shows your name and the name and date of your newsletter.

Correctness. Verify that words say what they are supposed to and that photos and art are what you want.

Completeness. Check that each board and overlay includes all the type, art, and graphics it should. Give mechanicals, separate art, and dummy to the printer at the same time.

Accuracy. Ensure correct positions of marks for register, trimming, and folding.

Security. Confirm that all copy is tightly adhered and burnished. Protect mechanicals with tissue overlays during handling, transit, and storage.

Cleanliness. Inspect boards, overlays, and tissues for smudges, fingerprints, bits of glue or wax, and stray guidelines.

Coordination. Examine separate copy such as photos, graphs, maps, and illustrations to ensure they are clean, cropped, scaled, and keyed according to a system agreed on with the printer.

Communication. Review each board or tissue overlay for specifications about ink colors, screen rulings and percents, masks, and reverses.

Proofs. Make two photocopies of mechanicals so you and the printer each have a proof.

10-7 Inspecting mechanicals. When you give a printer mechanicals that are truly camera-ready, you help assure that the shop will produce your job accurately, on time, and at the least possible expense. Carefully check your mechanicals.

white margins or on a tissue overlay. Photographs can also be photocopied and cropping instructions drawn on the copies.

When you scale a photograph, specify dimensions that allow it to overlap the keylines by at least ¹/₁₆th inch on each edge. This extra ¹/₁₆th inch gives printers plenty of room to be sure photos fit properly.

Relate photographs to your mechanical using the keyline method shown in Visual 10-8. Make keylines with a high quality ballpoint pen. The printer will not reproduce the keylines unless you specify that you want them to appear as borders along the edges of photos. Make key-

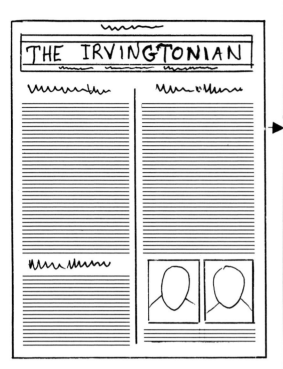

dummy

mechanical

10-8 From layout to printed page. Pasteup begins with a dummy as shown above. Tape the mounting board to your working surface. The board above has preprinted corner and register marks. Adhere type, laser printout, drawings, and other elements to the board to create the mechanical. Use keylines to indicate location of halftones. Photos should be mounted separately, with instructions written on their mounting boards.

The mechanical needs a tissue overlay for protection and instructions before going to the printer.

This example is pasteup for commercial printing. If the pasteup were for photocopy or quick printing, the screen tint, halftone positives, and reverse would be adhered to the mechanical so page was fully camera-ready.

mounted photograph

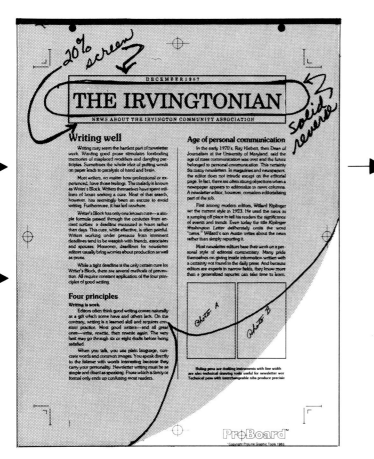

mechanical with tissue overlay

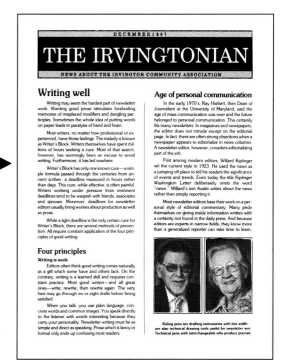

printed newsletter

lines that you want printed with ½-point border tape or a graphic arts pen.

If your newsletter is created using page assembly software, whether on a laser or photo type printer, use the software to make keylines.

Final checking

A mechanical represents to a photocopy machine, platemaker, or process camera precisely how your publication should look. The message must be accurate and complete, leaving no doubts about what you expect.

Graphic arts photography transfers images from mechanicals to paper, plates, or film. When compared to the human eye, however, cameras and photosensitive surfaces are very unsophisticated.

The eye concentrates on details that the brain knows are important, but cameras see everything equally. The eye sees things as they should be; cameras show them as they actually are. Bubbles, creases, and edges on a surface that should be flat all affect the camera's vision. Dust and smudges get photographed along with type and rules.

Visual 10-7 is a list of features to check to be sure mechanicals are ready for the printer. Also remember an important intangible: mechanicals tell printers how professionally you approach your work. Clean, complete work with clear instructions gets respect.

When you deliver mechanicals for printing, take time for a final check of specifications. Your printer should agree that mechanicals represent the work they describe. If not, determine differences, decide on how they affect production and costs, and write the new information on the specifications sheet. This is the surest way to prevent surprises such as alteration charges on the final invoice.□

11 Printing

Many people find printing a mystery. Their concept of presses comes from textbook accounts of the Gutenberg Bible. Modern printing is any process that repeatedly transfers an image from an original such as a plate, computer memory, or piece of paper.

Printing is a blend of art, craft, and industry. If you don't grasp its fundamentals, you give machines and printers too much responsibility for cost, quality, and schedule.

Newsletters are printed either on offset presses or photocopy machines. This chapter explains how to get the best quality from either, but concentrates on offset. It tells how to write specifications, examine proofs, and analyze jobs for payment.

Regardless of the method of printing, paper is a major cost. This chapter describes paper suitable for newsletters. It explains how to select paper for best results and buy it at the lowest cost. There is a chart showing features of paper to consider when deciding.

Although this chapter helps you buy printing as a sophisticated customer, it also emphasizes the importance of working with, not against, your printer. Cooperation keeps your schedule intact, quality up, costs down, and ulcers away.

For greater detail and more examples about printing than can be given here, consult my book *Getting It Printed* listed in Appendix B. That book deals with printing for all kinds of products, not only newsletters.

Offset printing

Most newsletters are printed offset at either a quick or a commercial print shop.

Both quick and commercial printers use offset presses that apply ink to paper. The two kinds of printers differ in their approach to printing as a business, in size of equipment, and in technique.

Quick, or instant, printers look for short runs of simple jobs that customers need quickly. Commercial printers seek longer runs of more complicated jobs that customers know take one or two weeks to produce.

Instant printers make plates directly from camera-ready copy. What you see on your original is what you get on the plate. Photos must be halftone positives adhered to mechanicals.

Commercial printers make plates indirectly by making film negatives first, then making plates from the negatives. They make proofs to help detect errors and flaws before platemaking. Several negatives can be assembled for making one plate. Photos are converted into halftone negatives, then exposed onto plates along with line copy.

Distinctions between quick and commercial printing businesses apply to in-plant print shops as well. Almost all shops owned by organizations have quick print presses for short runs of forms and fliers as well as newsletters. Some also have larger presses using metal plates. The standards of quality, schedule, and service discussed in this chapter apply to company-owned printers as well as outside shops.

Whether a commercial or a quick printer is best for your newsletter depends on your needs for quality, quantity, and service.

Quality. Metal plates, larger, more efficient presses, and more experienced workers mean commercial printers produce higher quality than quick printers. Whether your newsletter requires the time and money needed to achieve that quality is a matter to discuss with your supervisor.

Quick print presses use paper or plastic plates as a convenience, not a requirement. If you want the quality of a metal plate, your quick printer can use one. Results will not be as good as from a commercial printer, but will be better than from a camera-direct plate.

Quantity. Quick printers are appropriate for press runs up to about 2,000 copies of a newsletter. From about 2,000 to 3,000 copies, it's uncertain which shop would give the best price. After 3,000, it would be unusual for a quick printer's price to be lower than a commercial printer's.

If you use a lettershop to prepare your newsletter for mailing, check whether it offers printing as well. Many do. Printing at lettershops is often done on a web press, so is especially suitable for relatively long runs of publications with modest quality requirements.

Service. Quick printers are not as quick as they want you to believe, but their turnaround times are much shorter than commercial printers. A sales rep from a commercial printer may pick up and deliver. Although quick printers don't typically have sales reps, they have convenient locations.

Good customers get good service. Ensure that mechanicals are clean and complete, get them to the printer when you promise, and deal quickly with proofs, corrections, and invoices.

Quality considerations

A printer should closely reproduce your original. If your newsletter doesn't look as good as your mechanical and almost as good as your photos, something is wrong.

Even skilled printing buyers sometimes overlook lapses in quality. Before selecting a printer, ask for names of other newsletter editors who have used that shop. Call one or two to verify satisfaction.

Regardless of the kind of printer you use and how often you have relied on the specific shop, inspect printing for features described in the following paragraphs.

"Our new purchasing agent helped me write specifications and select five printers to quote on an annual contract. The results shocked me. The high bid came from our current printer and was 20% lower than we are now paying. The low bid was just over half what we now pay. Shopping cut our newsletter costs almost $2,000 a year."

Register. When an image appears on the page precisely where intended, it is correctly registered. Visual 11-2 shows poor register of the screen tint with the box intended to trap its edges.

Misregister can originate in pasteup, stripping, platemaking, and press work. With newsletters, faulty press operation is the most common source.

Register with photocopy machines can vary $\pm$ $1/8$ inch, with quick printing $\pm$ $1/16$ inch, and with commercial printing $\pm$ $1/100$ inch. The variations apply to each color of ink or pass through the press. Larger variations are easily prevented and should not be considered acceptable work.

Density. Printing should result in dense body copy and headline type to ensure legibility. Large solids may appear faded or mottled when quick printed.

Ink density should be uniform across the sheet and, ideally, from sheet to sheet throughout the run. With quick printing, some variation from sheet to sheet is acceptable; with commercial printing, only very slight variation should be tolerated.

Halftones. Quick printed halftones don't have very good contrast or sharpness. Commercially printed halftones should have good contrast, some shadow detail, and appear sharp, although they will still not look as good as originals.

Quick printers are not equipped to run coated paper, especially not gloss coated. Commercial printers use it routinely, adding to their ability to reproduce good halftones.

This is an example of underexposure.
This is an example of correct exposure.
This is an example of overexposure.
This is an example of incorrect focus.

11-1 Negative and platemaking problems. Underexposure of negatives or plates reproduces type that is too fat; overexposure makes type too thin. Type that is the correct weight but broken or fuzzy results from poor focus.

Exposure/focus. Because printing plates are made photographically, it is possible to expose or focus them incorrectly. Visual 11-1 shows results of underexposure or overexposure and poor focus.

Poor platemaking is more likely to happen in quick than commercial printing because harried camera operators also answer the phone, deal with customers at the counter, and run a press.

Flaws. Sheets with smudges, dirt, streaks, or fingerprints don't belong in your job. An occasional bad newsletter will slip through the best quality control, but printing with consistent problems such as blurred type should be rejected.

Bindery work. Printers refer to folding, trimming, drilling, and other post press operations as bindery work.

Machines for folding are less accurate than presses. Folds should always be correctly aligned, but the fold line can vary $\pm$ $1/8$ from a quick printer and $\pm$ $1/16$ from a commercial shop.

Most newsletters are printed on paper already cut to size, so do not need trims. If yours needs trimming, the cuts should be square according to corner marks on mechanicals. Trims from quick printers may vary $\pm$ $1/16$ inch, from commercial printers $\pm$ $1/32$ inch.

Specifications

Printing specifications are the requirements of a particular job. They are normally written as part of a request for price quotation on a form such as the one in Visual 11-3.

Price quotations for even the most simple and routine newsletter should be solicited every one or two years. Long contracts save money and get better printing done on time because they assure the printer regular work.

Good specifications are complete, accurate, and written in language printers understand. They are important for several reasons.

Assure accurate comparisons. When each shop quotes on the same specifications, you can compare prices accurately and fairly.

Look professional. Clear, carefully written specifications convey to printers that you know

Hickies

Information Technology
News from the Community Computer Center

Summer 1990

Poor ink coverage

Desktop publishing service expands

Lorem ipsum dolor sit amet, con sectetuer adipiscing elit, sed diam nonnumy nibh euisnod tempor inci dunt ut labore et dolore magna ali quam erat volupat. Ut wisi enim ad minim veniam, quis nostrud exerci tation ullamcorper suscipit laboris nisl ut aliquip ex ea commodo con sequat. Duis autem vel eum irure dolor in henderit in vulputate velit esse consequat.

Vel illum dolor eu feugiat nulla facilisi at vero eos et accusam et ius to odio dignessim qui blandit prae sent luptatum zzril delenit aigue duos dolore et mosestias exceptur sint occaecat cupiditat not simil pro vident tempor sunt in culpa qui officia deserunt mollit aniom ib est abor un et dolor fuga. Et harumd dereud facilis es er expedit distint. Nam liber tempor cum soluta nobis eligent option congue nihil impediet doming id quod maxim placeat facer possum omnis voluptas assumenda est, mnnis repellend.

Ink smudge

Temporibud auteui quinsud et aur offik debit aut tum rerum necessit atib saepe evenit ut er mosit non recusand. Itaque earun rerum hic ten tury sapiente delectus au aut perfer zim edndis dolorib asperiore repellat. Hanc ego cum teme senteniam, quid est kur verear ne ad eam non possing accommodare nost ros quos tu paulo ante cum emmorite tum etia ergat. Nos amice et nbevol, olestias access potest fier ad augent ascum consci ent to factor tum poen legum odio qui civiunda. Et tamen in busdam neque nonor imper. Nos amice et memorite tum etia ergat mbevp.

Pestoas accex est foer ad aigend ascum consci ent to factor tum poen legum odio que civiuna. Et tamen in busdam neque as minim veniam, quis nostrud exerci tation ullamcorper suscipit laboris nisl ut aliquip exea commodo sonsequat. Dues atuem velit esse mol enie consequat.

Hanc ego cum tene senteniam, quid est cur verear ne ad eam non possing accommodare nost ros quos tu apule ante cum memorite tum etia ergat. Facile ernicerd possit duo conetud notiner si effercerit, et opes vel fortunag vel ingen liberalitat magis conveniunt. da but tuntung ben evolent sib concillant, et aptis sim est ad quite. Kndium caritat prae sert cum omning num suu causpeccand quaert en imigent cupidtat a natura proficis vacile xplent sine gulla inura autend in anc sunt is par end non est nigil enim desidera.

Concupis plusque in ipsinuria detri ment est quam in his rebus moi ument oariunt iniur. Italque ne luis titial dem rect quit dexer per se ipsa optibil, sed quiran cinduatat vel plur aife. Nam dilig et carum esse incom mode quae egenium improb fugien dad.

Temporibud auteui quinsud et aur offik debit aut tum rerum necessit atib saepe evenit ut er mosit non recusand. Itaque earun rerum hic ten tury sapiente delectus au aut perfer zim edndis dolorib asperiore repellat. Hanc ego cum teme senteniam, quid es kur verear ne ad eam non possing accommodare nos ros quos tu paulo ante cum emmorite tum etia ergat.

Shadow line

Information Technology is published quarterly by the Information Technology Insitute, Center for Urban Education, 1135 S.E. Salmon, Portland, OR 97214

The Center for Urban Education (CUE) is a nonprofit corporation committed to improving community life. The Information Technology Institute is a program of CUE devoted to education and technical assistance for nonprofit organizations and public agencies in the use of computer and telecommunications technology. Editor: Steve Johnson Phone: 503-231-1285

Out-of-register screen

Poorly trimmed

11-2 Printing quality problems. The newsletter page above shows defects easily avoided by printers paying attention to their work. Problems such as these will occur as part of the makeready for any print run and occasionally during the run, but should not show on newsletters delivered to you. If you get sheets showing any of these flaws as part of your delivered job, you could reject them or, optionally, negotiate the price. At the least, tell your printer that you do not expect such low-quality work in the future.

Request for Quotation

Newsletter name _Hometown Hotline_ Date _Oct 6_

Contact person _Angela Williams_ Phone _800 / 282-5800_

Business/organization _Your Hometown, Inc._

Address _919 Second Ave, Antelope, USA. 10123_

Format # of pages _8_ page size _8½ x 11_ inches folded size _5½ x 8½_ inches

Quantity per issue _1800_ copies Issues per year _6_

Date(s) mechanicals to printer _Last Monday in December, February, April, June, August & October_

Date(s) newsletters needed _First Monday in January, March, May, July, September & November._

Mechanicals each issue _X_ line copy camera-ready

   screen tints ___ printer adds _X_ on mechanicals

   halftones _X_ printer adds ___ on mechanicals

Paper weight _70#_ color _white_ finish _matte_ brand name _Snow lite_

Ink colors cover side _black_ other sides _black_

Proofs ___ galley ___ page ___ photocopy _X_ blueline ___ overlay color

   _X_ press check _X_ dummy included with these specifications

Miscellaneous instructions _Average of 3 halftones per issue; bulk pack in cartons not to exceed 30# each; deliver by Monday 5:PM to Fast Out Mail Services_

11-3 Request for quotation. Accurate, complete specifications for printing help control quality, schedule, and cost. Use this form so that printers and other services know exactly what you expect. Appendix C has a blank form for you to photocopy.

what you are doing. You expect good quality and service.

Provide a checklist. Specifications help you review the entire production sequence and save you time in getting quotes. They make it obvious if you forgot an important detail.

Keep costs down. Specifications written on a form which is then photocopied notify printers that you are soliciting competitive bids.

Reduce guesswork. With good specifications, printers can figure costs exactly, identify ways to save money, and spot potential problems in the production sequence.

Help monitor changes. Almost every set of specifications changes as the job goes through production. With the original specifications as a guide, you can keep track of alterations.

Make payment easier. By comparing the final bill to the specifications, you can see exactly what was called for, what was done, and how alterations affected price.

Written specifications do not prevent printers from making suggestions. In fact, they encourage thinking about options. Even though you welcome alternatives, insist on knowing a price based on original specs. That dollar figure is an important basis for comparing printers.

Prices from any printer depend on the complexity of the job, paper and inks used, quantity needed, and number of other jobs in the shop. A 20% variation among four or five printers using the same specifications is normal; 50% is not unusual.

If your printer has a standard price list, ignore it. Menu prices apply to walk-in jobs needing instant attention. Planning ahead and contracting annually should get you prices at least 15% below those considered standard. You will not get the discount, however, unless you ask.

Proofs

A proof is any test sheet made to reveal errors or flaws, predict results on press, and record how a newsletter is intended to appear.

Every issue of your newsletter should be proofed before going to press. Checking proofs is the only way to assure that mechanicals, negatives, and plates are accurate and complete. Proofs also help determine who is responsible

Inspecting proofs

Individual features. Make a list, then check each feature throughout the entire proof. For example, go through once to verify page sequence, then again to examine headlines for typos and placement.

Photos and drawings. Certify that every visual is the correct image, is scaled and cropped properly, and faces the proper direction.

Flaws. Circle every blemish, flaw, spot, broken letter, and anything else that seems wrong.

Previous corrections. Confirm that corrections noted on previous proofs were made.

Instructions. Write directly on the proof in a clear, vivid color. Be explicit.

Finishing. Anticipate bindery problems. Measure trim size to be sure it's what you specified. Check that folds are correct and relate to copy as planned.

Colors. Ensure that you know what copy prints in each color when proofing multicolor jobs on bluelines.

Questions. Ask about anything that seems wrong. Queries that seem stupid are wiser than printed mistakes.

Costs. Discuss the cost of changes and agree who will pay for what.

11-4 Inspecting proofs. When examining a proof, keep the above items in mind. Above all, take your time. Proofs are the last chance to correct mistakes before plates are made.

for mistakes and should pay for corrections. Visual 11-4 tells how to read a proof.

With quick printing, you can only get a photocopy or press proof. A photocopy of your mechanical lets you see every element in position and, when given to your printer, shows how the finished newsletter should look. A press proof means you are present when the first sheets come off the press, so you can approve copy, ink color, paper, and other aspects.

Make two photocopies of every mechanical—one for you and one for your printer, whether quick or commercial. Stick sheets together back to back and collate, bind, and trim pages to look as close as possible to the finished newsletter. Leave nothing to imagination.

Commercial printers offer an important kind of proof in addition to a photocopy or press proof. Negatives can be contact printed to make a blueline, sometimes called a Dylux. If your newsletter includes halftones, screens, or reverses that the printer stripped in, ask for a blueline.

Working with printers

You can ensure a good relationship with your printer by having reasonable expectations and understanding the printer's point of view.

Most printers will deliver more copies than you specified, but they have a loophole if spoilage resulted in delivering too few. Business practices in the graphic arts include tolerance for an overrun or underrun of 10%. If you absolutely must have a certain number of newsletters, tell your printer that number is the minimum acceptable quantity.

Printers can meet the tight deadlines, but they are not magicians. You must deliver mechanicals when you promise if you expect newsletters when they promise.

Whether you pay on delivery, invoice, or statement, check every aspect of the printing before authorizing payment. Compare your newsletter to its specifications to verify receiving what the printer wants you to pay for. Visual 11-5 presents points to consider before authorizing payment.

If you question an invoice, discuss the matter candidly with the printer. Try to show that you are correct. The evidence is obvious if the specifications and invoice both called for printing on Wonder Gloss, but the press operator used Wonder Dull.

"My boss was real happy with some posters we had printed, so asked me to have the same printer do our newsletter. The sales rep gave us great service and every issue looked flawless. I didn't pay the bills, so didn't worry about cost. Two years later, when my boss left and I got her job, I learned we had been paying almost a dollar a copy. The printer for the full-color poster was totally wrong for the black-only newsletter. Our new printer gives us the same quality and service at half the price."

Final costs are often different from quotes because customers make changes. If you were late with mechanicals, your printer may have paid overtime to meet your deadline. The extra charge is justified, but should be clearly identified on the invoice.

Quality is more subjective. You are responsible to match your expectations to a printer's ability to produce and to explain your needs clearly. If you feel unhappy with quality, tell your printer exactly what you think is wrong.

You should not have to pay for poor quality work, but might feel stuck if there is not time to reprint. If the errors or flaws don't make your newsletter useless, you can negotiate the price and distribute the poorly printed issue.

Negotiating requires that you assess how strongly you feel. Arguing with your printer may save some money, but it will also take time and energy and may detract from your smooth business relationship. Make sure the rewards are worth the effort.

Too often newsletter customers are in such a rush that they forget to say, "Thanks. Nice work." When you like your printing, say so.

Photocopy

Photocopy machines place electrostatic charges on a belt or drum in the images of type and graphics. Toner, a powder, sticks to the imaged areas. When the toner comes into contact with paper, it is transferred and fused with heat.

Photocopy machines that yield dense blacks can make copies suitable as camera-ready copy for quick printing. Machines that reduce and enlarge provide much of the flexibility of stat cameras. If you make camera-ready copy using photocopy, load the machine with matte or dull coated paper for best results.

Plain paper photocopiers handle any grade, surface, or weight of paper with the exception of gloss coated. If you want to use the technique of preprinting, you can load a photocopy machine with paper previously offset printed with color. Keep in mind, however, that photocopy machines do not register nearly as well as printing presses; avoid register closer than 1/8 inch.

Getting good quality photocopies requires

the same attention to detail necessary for offset printing. You need clean originals ready for lights and lens. The single light source characteristic of most photocopiers sometimes causes shadow lines. Make originals as flat as possible. If cutlines remain, try turning the original around on the glass or printing in light copy mode. If that doesn't work, clean up a first generation copy with correction fluid and use it as the original. And clean the glass.

Most photocopies are limited to paper 8½ inches wide. If your newsletter is four or eight pages, have it printed offset on 11 x 17 paper.

If you're on a very tight budget for a newsletter with a small audience, look for free photocopying. Most large institutions and agencies have equipment idle during noon hours, evenings, and weekends. Access to one of those machines is an easy form of donated support. Even if photocopying is not free to the owner of the machine, letting you reproduce a few hundred newsletters may be an easier way to express support than writing you a check. Put a printed "thank you" in your newsletter.

Laser copies

Laser printers use photocopy technology. Instead of copying an image photographically they create it digitally, but the image is still formed by toner.

Desktop laser printers are not appropriate for reproducing a newsletter unless you need just a few copies in a big hurry, but larger machines may be. If you need several hundred copies of an 8½ x 11 newsletter printed almost instantly after finishing computer composition, a large laser printer may be right for the job. Using a laser printer to reproduce, not just create, camera-ready copy also allows individualizing with mailmerge and other software.

Printing by laser photocopy has advantages for the newsletter publisher needing fast distribution to several locations distant from each other. Data can go via modem to computers elsewhere and be reproduced on laser printers at quality much better than FAX. Articles and even whole newsletters written this morning in Manzanita can print out this afternoon in Montreal, Minneapolis, and Miami.

Analyzing the delivered job

Contents. Examine one copy to verify colors, tints, photographs, and other features listed on specifications and invoice.

Quality. Study several copies to verify printing to the standard of quality you expected.

Paper. Certify that the job is on the correct paper.

Quantity. Confirm the right amount. Compare delivery records with your invoice and count the contents of a box or two.

Extra charges. Study charges for alterations to ensure they are for changes that you agreed to.

Schedule. Note whether delivery was on time and, if not, whether contract with printer included a late penalty clause.

Shipping. If charges seem out of line, ask for copies of postal receipts or bills of lading.

Taxes. If your bill includes a tax, verify that you are liable.

Arithmetic. Check that percentages and totals are correctly figured.

11-5 Analyzing the delivered job. Before authorizing payment, examine the invoice, random copies from the print run, and your specifications, keeping the above points in mind.

Paper

The cost of paper represents 20% to 40% of the cost of printing your newsletter. The exact percentage depends on the quality of paper, method of printing, number of copies, and several other factors.

Upgrading paper is an easy and relatively inexpensive way to improve an entire publication. The price difference between routine and outstanding paper is insignificant compared to the overall cost of producing your newsletter. Upgrading paper adds to the value of writing, design, and printing without adding any time to those tasks.

Although quality paper can improve your image with little effort, remember that paper is a variable cost. Dollars to raise quality might work much harder if spent instead on a fixed cost such as professional design, computer software, or training.

Grade	Common names	Common sizes	Appropriate weights	Appropriate finishes
Bond	bond, photocopy, cotton, sulphite	8½ × 11, 11 × 17, 17 × 22	20 or 24	linen, vellum, wove, laid
Uncoated book	offset, opaque, general printing	8½ × 11, 11 × 17, 19 × 25, 23 × 35	50, 60 or 70	antique, vellum, smooth, wove
Coated book	coated offset, enamel, gloss, dull, matte	19 × 25, 23 × 35	60, 70, or 80	gloss, dull, embossed, matte
Text	text	23 × 35, 25 × 38	60, 70, or 80	vellum, felt, linen, laid

11-6 Guide to newsletter papers. This chart is a broad guide to paper suitable for printing newsletters. Names for paper vary from mill to mill and in different parts of the country. Use this chart to stimulate ideas and inquiries, not as an exclusive guide to ordering paper.

Four grades of paper are suitable for newsletters: uncoated book, coated book, bond, and text.

Uncoated book. Often called offset paper, uncoated book is for general printing of all kinds. It's the paper used most frequently by commercial printers and is readily available for quick printing and photocopying.

Offset paper comes in several shades of white plus half a dozen light colors useful for newsletters. It's available in a variety of finishes and weights and five levels of quality. Quality #1 is smoothest and brightest; quality #3 is most commonly used. Avoid #4 and #5 paper altogether.

Halftones on #1 paper look satisfactory, whereas photos on #3 tend to look flat. Uncoated paper, especially less than #1 quality, absorbs ink quickly, resulting in fuzzy dots and halftones that don't look sharp.

Sheet for sheet, uncoated book paper costs about the same as bond of comparable quality, but is better for newsletters. Bond is designed for printing on one side; offset paper on both sides. If your newsletter is printed both sides, ask the printer to use uncoated book paper.

Coated book. Sometimes called enamel paper, coated book gives better ink holdout than uncoated book or bond.

Ink holdout refers to the extent to which ink dries on the surface of paper instead of soaking in. It is especially important when printing halftones because dots stay crisp at their edges. Holdout also enhances ink gloss, making colors look brighter.

Coated paper comes in several finishes such as matte, dull, and gloss, and a variety of shades of white such as cream and ivory. It costs about 20% more than comparable quality uncoated stock.

Quick print presses don't reproduce well using coated paper. Photocopy machines print well on matte or dull coat, but not on gloss coat.

Bond. Mills make bond for 1-page correspondence such as letters and forms, thus it lacks the opacity of book or text paper. Showthrough may be a problem, particularly when printing with ink instead of the toner of photocopy.

Bond comes in a wide variety of colors and finishes found in the inventory of quick and in-plant printers and retail paper outlets.

Text. A premium uncoated stock, text (short for textured) has patterns pressed into the surface that give added depth and a rich feel. This stock comes with surfaces such as laid, linen, and felt in a wide range of colors. Using it can bring combinations of color and finish to newsletters that must be especially impressive and have budgets to match.

Halftones may not reproduce as faithfully on text as you want because of its surface patterns. Study samples carefully.

Paper characteristics

Understanding traits that grades of paper have in common helps clarify differences among the grades and how they can affect your newsletter.

Weight. The weight of paper is expressed as the weight of 500 sheets cut to a standard size. With bond papers, the weight is known as substance weight (Sub); with book and text papers, as basis weight (BS). Often packages of paper identify both sub and basis weight of contents. Higher pound numbers (#'s) mean heavier paper, thus more opacity and cost.

Bond paper that is sub 20# is the same weight as 60# book; sub 24# bond is the same as 70# book. (I *know* it doesn't make any sense. Trust me!)

Understanding paper weight helps control costs. Paper that is 70# costs about 15% more than 60#. If you print 25,000 copies per year of an 8½ x 11, 8-page newsletter, the cost difference of the paper might be several hundred dollars.

If you mail first class, weight of paper can affect postage. Some postal scales show an 8-page newsletter on 70# paper weighing slightly more than one ounce, meaning it qualifies for the 2-ounce rate. The same publication on 60# paper dependably weighs about .9 ounce, so it goes for one stamp.

Weight of paper affects how bulky it feels, but is an imperfect guide. Paper that has been compressed to make it smooth may feel thinner, but weigh the same as paper with a rougher surface. A 70# coated sheet feels about the same thickness as a 60# uncoated one.

Opacity. Type on one side of the paper should not show through to interfere with type on the other. Opacity restricts show-through. It is affected by coatings, colors, chemicals, ink color and coverage, and impurities. Heavy papers are more opaque than lighter ones.

Bond paper is not as opaque as book or text. If you must print on bond, use 24#, not the 20# most commonly provided for photocopy machines and quick print jobs, and specify paper with a slight color.

Some uncoated book papers are made in regular and opaque versions. For best opacity when specifying uncoated book, make sure that the word "opaque" is part of the description.

Surface. As mills turn pulp into paper, its surface can be adjusted to affect look, feel, and printability. Paper can be very smooth or have a pattern such as laid or linen. It can be given various thicknesses of coatings which themselves can be relatively shiny or dull.

Paper with surface patterns or coating costs a little more, but not as much more as you may think. Don't hesitate to compare costs.

Color. Mills add dyes and pigments to pulp to make paper of virtually any color. Colors vary from mill to mill and there is no standard for naming them. What one mill calls ivory may be called buff, cream, or sand at another.

White is the least expensive paper because it's in greatest demand and is easiest to make. Light colors cost slightly more and prices go up as colors get darker.

Color in paper increases opacity but decreases legibility because of the loss of contrast between type and background.

Newsletters should be printed on white, on shades of white such as cream or ivory, or on a very light tone of grey, blue, or brown. Dark colors and tones of red are not appropriate, even for holiday issues. Neither is it necessary to print different issues on paper of different colors. Using a variety of colors increases costs for no benefits and may confuse readers.

If you must match the color of newsletter paper to the color of business stationery, use a sub 24# sheet of the brand and color of the bond paper used for the letterhead.

"The sales rep from our lettershop convinced me to send specifications to her when we got printing quotes. She said our newsletter would fit their small web press because of our large quantity and modest quality requirements. She showed me printed samples on light weight, coated paper. Her prices were a third lower than any other printer. As a bonus, we saved time with printing and addressing all under one roof."

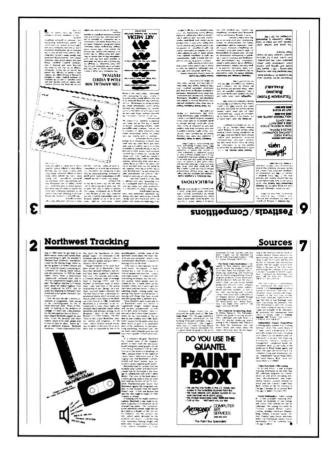

11-7 Four-up printing of an 8-page newsletter. If you need more that about 2,000 copies of one issue, printing on larger sheets may be more cost effective than printing on paper already cut to 11 x 17. If the large sheet is bond paper, it would be 17 x 22; if it's text or either grade of book, it would be 17½ x 23—half of the 23 x 35 commonly found as the house sheet. The imposition above assumes the parent sheet will be folded at least twice, then trimmed to yield the 8-page newsletter.

Size. The entire graphic arts industry in the United States, from making paper to using it, is coordinated to 8½ x 11 sheets and multiples of that size. Almost every small press, photocopy machine, computer printer, and typewriter is designed to use 8½ x 11 as the most common size. The same is true of binders, envelopes, file folders, and other products related to paper.

Because 8½ x 11 is so standard, it is the most economical page size for newsletters. Page size, however, should not be confused with sheet size.

Paper comes in a large variety of sheet sizes. Quick printers use 8½ x 11 or 11 x 17 sheets. Commercial printers have larger presses, so use 19 x 25 or 23 x 35 sheets. Visual 11-7 shows how a newsletter might be printed on a 17 x 22 sheet.

Most newsletters are printed on 11 X 17 sheets. If your publication is four or eight pages, try to have it printed on 11 x 17 stock that is folded once to 8½ x 11, not printed on 8½ x 11 sheets that must be stapled together.

Grain. During papermaking, fibers become aligned in one direction. When the paper is cut so that fibers run parallel to the longest edge of a sheet, the stock is grain long; when fibers run crosswise, the sheet is grain short.

Paper folds more cleanly with the grain than against it, especially when folds are on relatively thick sheets. If your newsletter folds only once, having it printed on grain short paper will make the fold easier; if it folds twice with the second creases at right angles to the first, then having it printed on grain long paper assures the best second folds.

Quantity. Paper comes in reams of 500 sheets. Cartons contain any number of sheets or reams; there are no standards. Paper distributors use cartons as units of sales. Ordering less than a full carton means increased packing and inventory costs, so the price per ream or pound goes up.

Buying paper

Paper for newsletters is best purchased as part of the cost of printing. Printers buy lots of paper, so get better prices than you can.

Printers have "house sheets," paper kept in inventory and suitable for a wide range of jobs. A 60# uncoated book and 70# coated book, each white, would be typical. Using the house sheet usually gives satisfactory quality at the best price.

If you don't want the house sheet, you may select a stock from swatch books or by matching another printed product. Your printer will help you decide by telling you how each possibility affects price. Do not, however, expect printers to suggest using Olde Antique Cream instead of Modern Mauve. Design is not their job.

You have several ways to cut paper costs. The easiest is to authorize your printer to use any stock available within a certain range of weights and colors. Printers always have small batches of paper they are happy to use up. If you are willing to have an issue appear on two, three, or even four different papers, ask how much you would save by using whatever stock is convenient at press time.

The second way to save money on paper is to buy from a distributor having a sale or close-out. If you buy paper yourself, work closely with your printer. Ask which distributors to investigate and how to interpret listings on sales

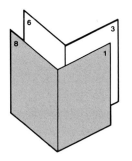
folded sheets (outside)

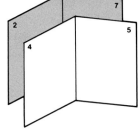
folded sheets (inside)

11-8 Imposition for an 8-page newsletter. Newsletters with four or eight pages may be reproduced on 11 x 17 paper that is folded to 8½ x 11, not on 8½ x 11 sheets stapled together. If you produce your publication by photocopy on 11 x 17 sheets or make 2-up mechanicals, you must impose pages as shown above so they are in the correct order after folding.

sheets. Your printer can also tell you how to specify cutting and packaging.

The third way to save on paper is to buy cooperatively with other printing customers. Unit costs drop as purchase quantities go up. Distributors have a price break at four cartons, but four cartons is more than most newsletters need in a year. By pooling your buying power, you can take advantage of the price break whether you buy directly from a distributor or through a printer.

Regardless of what paper you use and how you buy it, decide on an annual basis. Choosing for a year at a time means dealing with the most economically reasonable quantities.

To become more familiar with papers, examine sample books at a print shop, paper distributor, or retail outlet. A few moments of actually feeling and seeing various papers will tell you more than I could in several more pages of description. □

12 Distribution

How your newsletter gets to its audience affects decisions about schedule, content, and budget. It may also affect choice of paper.

Most newsletters reach readers by mail. Controlling costs of postage and speed of delivery requires thorough knowledge of both your mailing list and USPS regulations.

This chapter tells how to maintain your address list most efficiently and explains the major alternatives with regard to postal service. It describes lists and labels, classes of mail, presorting, and how to work with mailing services.

Postal regulations are too long, complicated, and changeable for presentation here. If you're starting a newsletter, get a copy of regulations before making final decisions about schedule and design. If you have experience, read the regulations to discover cost-saving opportunities you may be missing.

Although they seem very specific, postal regulations are subject to interpretation by local officials. Learn from the same people who check your mailings how they view regulations.

In addition to publications of the USPS itself, many private organizations produce guides that summarize and interpret regulations. The best handbooks come from the Direct Marketing Association and Pitney Bowes Corporation.

Local postal officials in larger cities offer frequent workshops. There is a USPS Mailer Education Center in New York City with a regular schedule of classes. And, of course, you can

Address lists

Address labels

Mail classifications

Non-profit status

Presorting

Mailing services

Other methods

read a newsletter. *Memo to Mailers* comes free from USPS, Springfield VA 22150-0999.

Address lists

The list of addresses used to send a newsletter offers potential savings of hundreds and perhaps thousands of dollars per year. You can achieve the savings by ensuring that your publication goes only to people who want it, that their addresses are correct, and that you presort each mailing.

Many copies of the typical newsletter go to people who don't want them. It's not unusual for 15% or even 25% of copies to be thrown away immediately on delivery. Considering what you pay to print, fold, and address those copies as well as mail them, you can cut costs substantially by never producing them in the first place.

Every year, without fail, study your address list one name at a time. Make sure that each name really belongs. Don't hesitate to spend money surveying readers to certify those who want to continue receiving your publication.

In addition to reducing your list to people whom you know want your newsletter, verify having correct addresses.

Postal officials estimate that 15% of mail is improperly addressed, so can't be delivered or arrives later than it should. The figure may be 25% for third class mail. The main problems come from people who have moved and from incorrect numbers for suites, apartments, street addresses, and zip codes.

After doing everything possible within your own system to ensure correct addresses, consult with local postal authorities about how they can help. The postal service has several ways to help customers maintain accurate address files. They include printing "Address Correction Requested" on the newsletter itself and the computerized National Change of Address system (NCOA).

To have addresses on your computer disk updated via the NCOA system, ask local postal authorities for a list of vendors. The Postal Service licenses vendors who keep their files current through the national Zip + 4 database.

Unless you mail just a handful of newslet-ters, your address list should be computerized. Names should be in a database or mailing program that can be sorted by zip code, not in an ordinary word processing file.

Most organizations have one database for names and addresses that can be used for a variety of purposes. The database should have fields, such as renewal dates, applicable to your publication. Ideally fields will include detailed information about readers so you can send special inserts to certain addresses or decide whether you need a second newsletter.

If you ever use someone else's mailing list, check very carefully how it's been maintained. Old names, sloppy keyboarding, and other errors can mean that half the addresses are undeliverable. Stick with lists of active subscribers to periodicals; avoid names of people who attended trade shows or appeared in a directory.

Address labels

Strong language in postal regulations prohibits from the mails pieces which do not conform to requirements about size, color, indicia, return address, and bar codes. Rules about the location and format of addresses affect how accurately and rapidly mail is delivered.

The post office can sort mail most efficiently when addresses can be read by optical character recognition (OCR). To be OCR readable, the last line of the address must be one inch from the bottom of the envelope or address panel. You need good contrast between ink and paper and the address should align with edges of the paper, not be skewed.

Optical character recognition requires a standard typeface and plenty of space between letters, words, and lines, but does not require punctuation. City, state, and zip code should be on the last line. Use standard 2-letter abbreviations for states.

"When we studied our mailing list, we found 158 households that no longer belong. We pay about half a dollar to print, label, and mail one newsletter. The bad addresses represented $79 per issue—$948 per year. That's almost $1,000 per year we were tossing into the wastebasket."

```
Marketing director          Marketing director          Marketing director          Marketing director
Providence Hosp             W Seattle Community          Northwest Hospital          Highline Community
17th & E Jefferson          2600 SW Holden St            1550 N 115 St               16250 Sylvester SW
Seattle WA 98122            Seattle WA 98126             Seattle WA 98133            Seattle WA 98166

Marketing director          Marketing director          Marketing director          Marketing director
Riverton Hospital           Univ Hospital               General Hospital eve         Providence Hospital
12844 Military Rd S         1959 NE Pacific St          14 and Colby 1147           Box 1067
Seattle WA 98168            Seattle WA 98195            Everett WA 98206            Everett WA 98206

Marketing director          Marketing director          Marketing director          Marketing director
St Joseph Hospital          St Lukes General Hos        Skagit Valley Hosp          Harrison Memorial Ho
3201 Ellis St               809 E Chestnut St           1415 Kincaid St 1376        2520 Cherry Ave
Bellingham WA 98225         Bellingham WA 98225         Mt Vernon WA 98273          Bremerton WA 98310

Marketing director          Marketing director          Marketing director          Marketing director
Olympic Memorial Hsp        Good Samaritan Hosp         St Joseph Hospital          Tacoma General
939 Caroline St             407 14 Ave SE #1247         1718 S I St bx 2197         315 K St 5277
Port Angeles WA 98362       Puyallup WA 98372           Tacoma WA 98401             Tacoma WA 98405

Marketing director          Marketing director          Marketing director          Marketing director
Humana Hospital             Puget Sound Hospital        Medigan Gen Hosp            Veterans Admin Hosp
PO Box 11414                PO Box 11412
Tacoma WA 98411             Tacoma WA 98411             Tacoma WA 98431             Tacoma WA 98493

Marketing director          Marketing director          Marketing director          Marketing director
Western State Hosp          Lakewood General            St Peter Hospital           St Joseph Hospital
                            5702 100 St SW              413 N Lilly Rd              1006 N H St
Ft Steilacoom WA 98494      Tacoma WA 98499             Olympia WA 98506            Aberdeen WA 98520
```

12-1 Cheshire labels. Standard label format for cutting and gluing by machine is 44 labels printed 4-up on wide computer paper. Side-to-side measurements are flexible, but vertical measurements should be one inch from the top of one address to the top of the next. Zip code order starts with lowest zip at upper left and goes across lines, not down columns. Most lettershops have Cheshire labeling machines.

If you maintain your mailing list with ZIP+4 codes in a computer database, you may be able to barcode each newsletter as it's addressed, thus saving on first or third class postage. Ask for details at a mailing service.

Mail classifications

Newsletters that are mailed get off to a good start. The mail brings the most personal written messages. Whether you use first, second, or third class depends on your budget and need for speedy delivery.

When considering what class of mail to use and how diligently to study the regulations, remember that postage is a variable cost. The percent of your budget it requires increases along with number of newsletters that you mail. If you send only a few hundred copies four times a year, postage amounts to very little when compared to the fixed costs of writing and preparation for printing. If you send several thousand copies twelve times a year, postage might be your largest single expense.

First class. When you need overnight delivery locally and 2- or 3-day service nationwide, mail first class. It's the fastest category—and, of course, the most expensive.

Commercial newsletter publishers use first class to convey the image of important news arriving in timely fashion. Many organizations with tiny budgets and memberships also use it to ensure that news of special events arrives quickly.

Because first class postage is by the ounce, weight of paper can affect what you pay. Weigh a dummy on a USPS scale to avoid an expensive surprise when your first issue goes into the mail. If you use an envelope, make sure it's on the scale along with your dummy.

By using first class that must be returned if undeliverable, you can clean up your mailing list. It's cheaper and less hassle than some of the other address correction options, but doesn't tell you a new address.

Second class. Periodicals published at regular intervals at least four times per year may be mailed second class. Publications must be presorted and go to people who pay to receive them. Payment can be via subscription or a membership fee that specifically includes the newsletter.

Second class pieces receive the same handling as first class pieces, but rates are much lower. Costs are based on complicated formulas that take into account percentages of adver-

Postage for one copy of a newsletter

		1988 rates in cents		19___ rates in cents	
		Regular	Nonprofit	Regular	Nonprofit
First class	Basic unsorted	25	—		
	ZIP + 4 unsorted	24.1	—		
	Five-digit presorted	21	—		
	ZIP + 4 presorted	20.5	—		
	ZIP + 4 barcoded presorted	20			
	Carrier route presorted	19.5	—		
Second class	Basic presorted	16	12.5		
In addition to piece rate, pay 12.4 per lb regular 8.6 per lb non profit 9.4 per lb in county for total mailing.	Five-digit presorted	12.4	8.9		
	Carrier route presorted	9.9	6.8		
	In-county basic	5.7	5.7		
	In-county carrier route	3.2	3.2		
	Intra SCF basic	15	11.5		
	Intra-SCF five digit	11.4	7.9		
	Intra-SCF carrier route	8.9	5.8		
Third class	Basic presorted	16.7	8.4		
	ZIP + 4 basic presorted	16.2	7.9		
	five-digit presorted	13.2	7.6		
	Five-digit ZIP + 4 presorted	12.7	7.1		
	ZIP + 4 barcoded presorted	12.2	6.6		
	Carrier route presorted	10.1	5.3		

12-2 Postal rates chart. As the number of copies per issue increases, postage becomes a larger percentage of overall costs. Discounted rates can lead to substantial savings.

The chart above shows single-piece rates applicable to the typical newsletter. The rates shown are only for postage and do not reflect costs of permits, applications, or other fees. Also keep in mind that each class of mail has additional regulations about number of items, size, weight, advertising, and other matters. Check carefully with officials at your post office before making final decisions.

tising and editorial content, weight, and other factors.

Most newsletters qualify for second class rates and service; few take advantage of them. If you want first class service at about half the cost, do what it takes to get classified for second class.

Third class. Also known as bulk rate, third class is the least expensive mail category. Per piece costs vary greatly depending on the level of presort and status (commercial or non-prof-

it) of the mailer. Generally speaking, third class rates are half of first class.

Each piece of third class mail must be identical except for its address and all pieces must be presorted. There's a 200 piece minimum. Most newsletters easily qualify.

Third class mail moves more slowly than first or second class. Postal officials claim local and regional delivery takes two to six days. Experienced mailers double those figures.

If you use third class, mail in the middle of the month to avoid competition with large first class mailings and in the middle of the week to avoid the Friday deluge of second class magazines and newspapers.

Non-profit status

Organizations that are not for profit may send second and third class mail for about half of what commercial mailers pay.

As you can guess, not every organization qualifies for non-profit status. You must apply to the USPS, whose publications and officials tell you the information to provide. As a minimun, you need documents such as by-laws, financial reports, and minutes of annual meetings. Already having non-profit status with the Internal Revenue Service helps, but does not guarantee that USPS will think you equally deserving.

Once you have non-profit status, protect it carefully. Don't let anyone else mail under your permit and diligently keep the records that postal officials may ask to examine.

The USPS delivers newsletters for free to people with a condition that prevents normal reading. The condition could be visual or muscular. Check with postal officials for details.

Presorting

The post office pays customers to sort their own outgoing mail. Payment takes the form of discounts from standard rates.

In the case of first class mail, presorting is optional and earns a 20% discount. You must send at least 500 newsletters and you get a slightly higher discount for using ZIP + 4 codes and/or barcodes. In the case of second and third class mail, presorting is required and earns discounts from 50% to 80%. You must send at least 200 newsletters.

"You only get what you inspect, but after inspecting all those words, photos, drawings, mechanicals, and proofs who has energy for anything else? I learned to find the energy when a third of my newsletters weren't delivered. The address list I rented was full of typos and poorly printed. No wonder postal employees complain about us as much as we do about them."

Mailers who presort must conform to strict and detailed regulations. Regulations govern how many pieces must be in categories such as 5-digit zip codes, and how bundles must be tied, sacked, and labeled. The rules are best learned from USPS publications and workshops.

Presort rules are worth learning. For example, if you send 4,000 copies of a monthly newsletter by first class, presorting saves $2,400 per year in postage.

If you lack just a few names to make the minimum for presort, calculate what you would save by sending a handful of newsletters to yourself.

When many copies of your newsletter go into just a few neighborhoods, consider carrier route sorting. Carrier route sorts require additional label codes, but can cut postage costs another 50%. You can get labels already sorted from most lettershops. Consult with people at your post office or lettershop for details.

Presorting does involve some costs. First, there is a small annual permit fee. Second, someone must do the work that otherwise would be done at the post office. With large organizations, that would ordinarily be a specialist at a lettershop. With smaller mailings, that someone might be you.

If your organization does not use a professional mailing service, someone should specialize in knowing postal rules and fees. There are huge savings and efficiencies for people who take the trouble to learn their way around USPS.

Mailing services

Correctly preparing several thousand newsletters for mailing is so tedious and complex that it often makes sense to have professionals do it.

Mailing services, also known as lettershops, specialize in handling large mailings. They have machines to put glue on labels and affix them automatically. They have staff trained to presort newsletters into the most cost-efficient bundles, then get them sacked and tagged according to post office standards.

Once you use a good lettershop, you'll wonder why you ever spent one minute twisting the arms of family, friends, or fellow work-

---

ers to help you peel and stick labels and sort newsletters. Lettershops charge by the service and the number of pieces handled. Their staff can explain postal regulations and help you get permits.

Most lettershops have computers and high-speed printers to help you maintain and print your list. They could keep your list up to date and print as you need it, or print only when you supply a disk. Their computer printer can probably produce labels faster and better than yours, and their ink jet printers may be able to apply barcodes to envelopes in addition to character addresses.

Look under "mailing services" in a classified directory to find lettershops in your area. As with any other business, ask for references to previous customers. Pay particular attention to how you might be treated as a small customer. You may think your six or eight thousand newsletters impressive, but they are peanuts compared to the mountains of monthly utility bills and offers from discount stores that the lettershop also handles.

Most communities have sheltered workshops run by organizations such as Goodwill and United Cerebral Palsy whose workers can label, sort, and bundle newsletters. They take a little longer, but charge a little less than a commercial lettershop.

Other methods

If you prefer not to use the mails, there are several other ways to handle distribution.

Handouts. Newsletters left in lunchrooms or on store counters meet uncertain fates. Some copies get read, but many get tossed when the one on top has coffee stains.

If you hand out newsletters door to door, don't leave them in mail boxes. The USPS thinks it owns mail boxes and may try to fine you. It's not worth the hassle.

| Bulk Rate U.S. Postage PAID Yourtown, State Permit # | Non-profit Org. U.S. Postage PAID Yourtown, State Permit # |

12-3 Postal indicia. You may use stamps, meters, or a printed indicia as postage for any class of mail. Indicia must include the information shown in the above examples.

Door-to-door delivery can be either uncertain (volunteers, scout troups) or expensive (professional services). It's better to use the mails.

Piggybacks. Your publication delivered in an envelope along with a paycheck or invoice must be relatively small and light. A single 8½ x 11 sheet is a popular format.

You can get lightweight papers that look and fold well, and snuggle up to a companion piece without raising postage. Ask your printer about 40# and 45# uncoated or coated book paper. Because the paper is mainly for catalogs and direct mail, it's more available on rolls for web presses than as sheets.

Modem mix. Newsletters distributed internally at several locations distant from one another may be sent computer-to-computer and printed at each location. Transmitting 20 minutes to the Atlanta facility is easier, cheaper, and faster than shipping 400 copies from Anaheim.

If you distribute by modem, consider a format that allows local editors to insert a story or two. Local news could take the form of a 1-sheet insert or fill some column inches deliberately left blank.

Regardless of how you distribute, the satisfaction of seeing your newsletter finally in the hands of readers is matched only by the contentment of finishing this book.

Appendices

Glossary

This glossary includes all the technical and business terms used in this book plus many others. Terms come from the fields of publishing, photography, computers, typesetting, graphic design, and printing.

Because the meaning of many terms is more fully understood in context, you may wish to examine a portion of text in which the term is used. The index identifies the page in text where a term occurs.

A

AA. Author Alteration. Any change or correction made by a customer. Also proofreader's mark showing such an alteration.

Acetate. Thin, flexible sheet of transparent plastic used to make overlays and provide base for high-contrast film and peel-off masking materials.

Against the grain. At right angles to the grain direction of paper.

Airbrush. Device held like a pen used to spray mist of ink to create illustrations and retouch photos.

Alley. Space between columns of type on a page.

Alteration. Any change in a typesetting or printing job once specifications have been agreed on.

Aperture. Opening behind lens of a camera whose size may be adjusted to control amount of light reaching film.

Artwork. Images prepared for printing. Some printers include type in "artwork," others don't.

ASA. American Standards Association. Measure of photographic film speed. Alternate term for *ISO*.

Ascender. Portion of a lower case letter rising above its x height.

ASCII. American Standard Code for Information Interchange. Standard code used to help interface computers and peripherals. Pronounced "asskey."

Available light. Artificial or natural light falling on scene to be photographed without addition of lighting controlled by photographer.

B

Back light. Light falling from behind subject to be photographed causing rim of light around or along edge of subject.

Backup copy. Duplicate of original data, software, or printout made in case original is lost or damaged.

Banner. Alternate term for *Nameplate*.

Baseline. Imaginary rule under each line of type touching bottoms of all characters with the exception of those having descenders.

Base negative. Negative made from copy pasted to mounting board, not overlays.

Basis weight. Weight in pounds of a ream of paper cut to the basic size for its grade.

Baud. Number of signalling elements, usually bits, transmitted per second from one digital device to another.

Bind. To put sheets in order and secure them in place.

Bindery. Print shop department or separate business that does trimming, folding, and binding.

Bit. Acronym for binary digit, the smallest unit of storage in a computer.

Bleed. Printing that extends to the edge of a sheet or page after trimming.

Blocked up. Characteristic of shadow areas in a photo or halftone that lack detail because of overexposure or poor printing.

Blueline. Prepress, photographic proof where all colors are represented by blue image on white paper.

Blue pencil. Pencil that writes in light blue that does not record on graphic arts film.

Blurb. Short quotation from an article repeated in large type as a graphic element within the column of text.

Body copy. Copy set in text type. Also the bulk of a story, not its headline or subheads.

Bond paper. Grade of paper commonly used for writing, photocopying, and printing.

Book paper. Grade of paper suitable for newsletters and general printing needs.

Bracket. To take several photos of the same subject at different exposures to ensure that one is acceptable.

Brightness. Characteristic of paper referring to how much light it reflects.

Bulk. Thickness of paper, expressed in thousandths of an inch or pages per inch (ppi).

Bulk mail. Alternate term for *Third class mail.*

Bullet. Bold dot used for typographic emphasis and often used in place of numerals in a list.

Burn. In photography, to give extra exposure to a specific area of a print. In printing, to expose a proof or plate to light.

Burnish. To smooth and seal by rubbing elements adhered to a mechanical.

Byte. Group of eight bits representing one letter, numeral, or other character in a computer memory. Pronounced "bite."

C

Cable release. Flexible device that attaches to a camera shutter button so exposure may be made with minimum vibrations.

Callout. Descriptive label as part of an illustration. Sometimes also used as alternate term for *Blurb.*

Camera-ready copy. Mechanicals, photographs, and art fully prepared for printing.

Camera service. Business using a process camera to make PMTs, halftone negatives, printing plates, and other elements for printing.

Cap height. Height of the capital letters of a typeface, expressed in points, usually about 2/3 of the type size.

Caption. Identifying or descriptive text accompanying a photograph or other visual element.

Center marks. Lines on a mechanical, negative, printing plate, or press sheet indicating the center of a page or press sheet.

Character. Any letter, numeral, symbol, punctuation mark, or space between words.

Character count. Number of letters, numerals, punctuation marks, and symbols plus word spaces in a pica, inch, line, column, or page.

Cheshire labels. Addresses printed on wide computer paper in a format that can be cut into labels and affixed to newsletters by machines built by the Cheshire Company.

Clip art. Copyright-free drawings printed on white, glossy paper or stored in computer memory that are camera-ready for printing.

Coated paper. Paper with a coating of minerals that improves reflectivity and ink holdout.

Cold type. Type from typewriters, computer printers, and photo type machines as distinguished from "hot type" which is metal.

Collate. To assemble sheets of paper into proper sequence.

Collateral. Ad agency term for newsletters and other printed pieces that are not directly related to advertising.

Color break. In multicolor printing, the point or line at which one ink color stops and another begins.

Color matching system. System of numbered ink swatches that helps communication about color.

Color process printing. Alternate term for *4-color process printing.*

Column inch. One inch measured vertically up or down a column.

Column rule. Thin vertical line that separates columns.

Commercial printer. Printer whose business emphasizes good quality, medium and large press size, and full service, and who normally uses metal plates.

Comp. Short for comprehensive dummy.

Composite negative or photo. Negative or photo made by combining two or more images.

Comprehensive dummy. Handmade, full-sized simulation of a newsletter complete with type, graphics, and colors.

Computer graphics. Charts, maps, and other pictorial representations generated by software.

Condensed type. Style of type in which characters are narrow in proportion to their height.

Contact print. Photographic image made by exposing paper held against negative, thus not enlarged.

Continuous-tone copy. All photographs and other art having a range of shades.

Contrast. Range of gradations in tones between lightest white and darkest black in continuous-tone copy or the abrupt change between light and dark in line copy.

Copy. In editing and typesetting, all written material. In graphic design and printing, everything to be printed: art, photographs, and graphics as well as type.

Copyedit. To check and correct a manuscript for spelling, grammar, punctuation, inconsistencies, inaccuracies, and conformity to style requirements.

Copyfit. To edit copy and adjust type specifications so that type fits space allotted by the layout.

Copy preparation. In typesetting, marking up a manuscript and specifying type. In pasteup and printing, making the mechanical and writing instructions that ensure proper placement, printing, and finishing.

Copyright. Ownership of creative work by the writer, photographer, or artist who made it.

Copywriter. Person who writes copy for advertising.

Corner marks. Lines on a mechanical, negative, plate, or press sheet showing the corners of a page or finished piece.

Crop. To eliminate portions of an image so the remainder is more clear, interesting, or correctly sized to fit the layout.

Crop marks. Lines near the edges of an image showing portions to be eliminated.

Crossover. Type or art that continues from one page across the gutter to the opposite page.

Cursor. Marker such as small block or line displayed on a computer screen designating which character or location will be affected by the next keystroke.

Cutline. Alternate term for *Caption*.

D

Daisy wheel. Circular print element consisting of spokes containing letter quality type that will print when struck against carbon ribbon in contact with paper.

Data base. Collection of information organized according to fields and records and stored on a computer disk or tape.

Data conversion. To change digital information from its original code so that it can be recorded by a disk or other electronic memory using a different code.

Default. Action that computer program automatically performs unless instructed otherwise by operator.

Densitometer. Instrument to measure light reflecting from or transmitted through copy. Used by printers to ensure proper exposure for halftones and measure density of ink on paper.

Density. Relative darkness of copy, ink on paper, or emulsion on film, as measured by a densitometer.

Density range. Difference between darkest and lightest areas of copy.

Depth of field. Term for relative sharpness of features in a photograph regardless of their distance from the camera in the original scene.

Descender. Portion of a lower case letter falling below its baseline.

Desktop publishing. Process of writing, drawing, manipulating, and laying out type, graphics, and other visual elements using a personal computer, then using a laser printer or typesetting machine to print out the assembled pages.

Digital. Characteristic of information in binary code.

Digitize. To transform information from any non-digital form to digital form.

Dingbat. Typographic symbol, such as a bullet, used for emphasis or decoration.

Display type. Type of 14 points or larger.

Dodge. To block light from selected areas while making a photographic print.

DOS. Disk operating system. Used often to refer specifically to operating system for IBM and compatible computers. Pronounced "doss."

Dot matrix printer. Computer printer that forms characters from dots made when points of pins strike a carbon ribbon.

Double burn. To expose a printing plate to two negatives, creating a composite image.

Drop out. To lose halftone dots or fine lines due to overexposure during camera work or platemaking. The lost copy is said to have dropped out.

Dropout halftone. Halftone in which contrast has been increased by eliminating dots from highlights.

Dropout type. Alternate term for *Reverse type.*

Dry transfer lettering. Type and clip art that can be rubbed off its backing sheet onto another surface.

Dummy. Drawing showing layout of type and graphics, ideally presented on paper specified for the newsletter.

Duotone. Photograph reproduced from two halftone negatives and usually printed in black and one other ink color.

Duplicator. Sometimes used to refer to press for quick printing. Not to be confused with spirit duplicator or photocopier.

Dylux. DuPont trade name for photographic paper used to make bluelines.

E

Editor. Person who selects words and visual elements such as photographs so they accomplish their communication goals within the space and budget allotted them.

Electronic memory. Disk, chip, tape, or other device that holds information in digital form.

Electronic page assembly. Assembly and manipulation on a computer screen of type, graphics, and other visual elements stored in memory.

Elite type. Smaller of the two standard typewriter typefaces, being ten point and usually set in 12 pitch.

Em. In typography, measure of width equal to the point size of the type being used and best represented by width of the lowercase "m."

Emulsion. Chemical coating on papers, films, and printing plates that records an image when exposed to light.

En. Half an em.

Enlarger. Device used to project image from photographic negative onto paper that will be developed to become the print.

Equal spacing. Typographic system of allocating the same amount of space to each character regardless of its width: "i" gets the same space as "p" and "w" or a punctuation mark.

Estimate. Statement of what a newsletter will cost to print based on initial specifications from customer.

Exposure time. Time required for light to record an image while striking photosensitive emulsion.

Extended type. Style of type in which characters are wide in proportion to their height.

F

Fair use. Concept in copyright law allowing, without permission from copyright holder, short quotations for purposes of reviewing or teaching.

Fast film. Film that requires relatively little light (short exposure or small f stop) to record an image.

Fast lens. Lens capable of being opened to relatively large aperture such as f1.9.

FAX. Short for "facsimile." Process and output of type and graphics by digital transmission via telephone system. Pronounced "facs."

Field. One line of information, such as a name or zip code, that is part of a record in a data base.

Field of view. Amount of scene as seen through viewfinder of a camera.

Fill-in flash. Flash used to supplement available light, usually in shadow areas of scenes.

Fill pattern. Alternate term for *Screen tint* used with reference to software for graphics and desktop publishing.

Film speed. Measure of sensitivity of emulsion on photographic film to light. Fast film is highly sensitive, slow film less sensitive.

Filter. Colored glass or gelatin used to reduce or eliminate specific colors from light before it strikes film or paper.

Final count. Number of newsletters delivered and charged for by the printer.

Finish. With regard to paper, its surface characteristics. With regard to printing, any process taking place in the bindery.

Flag. Alternate term for *Nameplate.*

Flat. In photography, characteristic of an image that lacks contrast. In printing, an assembly of negatives taped to masking material ready for platemaking.

Floating rule. Rule, usually between columns, whose ends do not touch other rules.

Flop. To reproduce a photograph or illustration by printing its negative upside down so that its image faces opposite from the original.

Flush left or right. Type aligning vertically along the left or right side of the column.

Fold marks. Lines on a mechanical, negative, printing plate, or press sheet indicating where the newsletter is to be folded.

Folio. Page number. Low, even-numbered folio is the left hand page; high, odd-numbered folio the right.

Font. Complete assortment of characters of one typeface.

Footer. Information, such as its name, that appears at bottom of every page of a newsletter.

Format. Size, shape, and style of a layout or printed piece.

Formula pricing. Printing prices based on standard papers, formats, ink colors, and quantities.

4-color process. Technique of printing that uses process colors—black, red, blue, and yellow—to simulate color photographs.

f stop. Measure of aperture setting on a camera. Large-numbered f stops (f16 and f22) signify small apertures and are referred to as small f stops; small-numbered f stops (f3.5 and f1.9) indicate wide aperture openings, thus are called large f stops. Changing from one f stop to another doubles or halves the amount of light that will reach the film.

G

Galley proof. Proof of typeset copy.

Gang print. To reproduce two or more printed pieces or multiple copies of the same piece simultaneously on one sheet of paper.

Gang shoot. To halftone or separate more than one image in only one exposure.

Gloss. Characteristic of paper, ink, or varnish that reflects relatively large amounts of light.

Gothic type. Type without serifs.

Grade. Classification of paper according to use. Four grades are appropriate for newsletters: bond, uncoated book, coated book, and text.

Grain. In paper, the direction in which fibers are aligned. In photography, crystals that make up emulsion on film.

Grain long or grain short. Paper whose fibers run parallel to the long or short dimension of the sheet.

Graphic arts. The crafts, industries, and professions related to designing and printing messages.

Graphic arts film. Film whose emulsion responds to light on an all-or-nothing principle to yield high contrast images.

Graphic arts magnifier. Lens built into a small stand and used to inspect copy, negatives, plates, and printing.

Graphic designer. Professional who conceives the design for, plans how to produce, and may coordinate production of a printed piece.

Graphics. Rules, screens, charts, tables, photos, drawings, and other visual elements used to make printed messages more clear.

Grid. Pattern of non-printing guidelines on pasteup board or computer screen used to help align copy.

Gutter. White space between columns of type where facing pages meet at the binding.

H

Hairline. Line or gap about the width of a hair: 1/100th inch.

Halftone. To photograph continuous-tone copy through a screen to convert the image into dots. The result is also called a halftone. A halftone on paper is a halftone positive; a halftone on film is a halftone negative.

Halftone dots. Thousands of dots that together create the illusion of shading or a continuous-tone image.

Halftone screen. Piece of film containing a grid of lines that breaks light into dots as it passes through.

Hard copy. Copy on paper, thus permanent.

Hardware. Keyboard, CRT, chips, and other physical units of a computer system.

Header. Information, such as its name, that appears at top of every page of a newsletter.

Headliner. Machine made exclusively to set display type, often on a transparent tape ready for pasting up.

Headline type. Alternate term for *Display type*.

Hickey. Donut-shaped spot or imperfection in printing, most visible in areas of heavy ink coverage.

High contrast. Few or no tonal gradations between dark and light areas.

Highlights. Lightest areas in a photograph or halftone.

Holdout. Alternate term for *Ink holdout*.

Hot type. Type made from metal characters and used for letterpress printing.

House list. List of customers, subscribers, or other names developed within an organization, not acquired from an outside supplier.

House sheet. General-use paper kept in inventory by a printer.

I

Icon. Symbol for a file or command displayed on a computer screen.

Image. Type, illustration, or other original scene as it has been reproduced on computer screen, film, printing plate, or paper.

Image area. Portion of a mechanical, negative, or plate corresponding to inking on paper. Portion of paper on which ink appears.

Imposition. Arrangement of pages on mechanicals or flats so they will appear in proper sequence after press sheets are folded and bound.

Imprint. To print new copy on a previously printed sheet.

Indicia. Postal permit information printed on objects to be mailed and accepted by USPS in lieu of stamps.

Ink holdout. Characteristic of paper allowing ink to dry on its surface rather than by absorption.

In-plant printer. Department of an agency, business, school, or association that does printing for the parent organization.

Input/output. Information entering or leaving an electronic system such as a typesetter or computer. Also refers to hardware: keyboards are input devices and printers are for output.

Interface. To link two or more electronic devices so they can function as one unit.

ISO. International Standards Organization. Measure of photographic film speed. Alternate term for *ASA*.

ISSN. International Standard Serial Number. Number assigned by the Library of Congress to newsletters and other serials requesting it.

Issue. The end result of one production sequence, such as the September issue or the fall issue.

Italics. Letterforms that slant to the right.

J

Jump. Point at which newsletter story moves from one page to another, indicated with "continued p. _ _ ."

Justified. Characteristic of type set so that lines begin and end evenly (flush) both left and right.

K

K. Letter representing the numeral 1024 (one kilobyte). The number of bytes in a computer memory might be expressed as 64K, meaning 65,536 bytes.

Kern. To reduce space between letters so that more characters fit on a line or so that certain letters appear better fitted together.

Key. To relate photographs or loose pieces of copy to their positions on a layout or mechanical using a system of numbers or letters.

Keyline. Alternate term for *Mechanical*.

Keylines. Lines on a mechanical or negative showing the exact size, shape, and location of photographs or other graphic elements.

Kicker. Small, secondary headline placed above an article's primary headline to supplement it.

L

Landscape mode. Horizontal format on a computer screen or printout that can resemble two newsletter pages side by side.

Laser. Acronym for "light amplification by stimulated emission of radiation."

Laser printer. Device using laser beam to create a pattern of dots on paper that, when they attract toner, reproduce type and graphics as they appear on a computer screen.

Layout. Plan for a newsletter showing position and size of text and graphics.

Leaders. Rows of dots or dashes that lead the eye across a page from one piece of information to another.

Leading. Amount of space between lines of type, expressed in points or hundredths of an inch. Pronounced "ledding."

Legible. Characteristic of typography that can be easily read because it is well designed.

Letter quality. Type of the quality produced by typewriter keys, type element, or daisy wheel.

Lettershop. Alternate term for *Mailing service*.

Letter spacing. Amount of space between letters. Adjustable using computer or typesetting software, but only adjustable on most typewriters by changing pitches.

Light meter. Instrument on a camera that measures intensity of light and may indicate or control aperture and shutter speed.

Light table. Translucent glass surface illuminated from below and used by production artists and strippers.

Line copy. Type, rules, clip art, and other images that are high contrast.

Line measure. The width of a line of type.

Line negative. High contrast negative usually made from line copy.

Line spacing. Alternate term for *Leading*.

Lines per inch. Measure of screen ruling expressing how many lines or rows of dots there are per inch in a screen tint or halftone.

Lithography. Method of printing using a chemically coated plate whose non-image areas repel ink and image areas attract ink.

Logo. Artistic assembly of type and art into a distinctive symbol unique to an organization, business, or product.

Long lens. Alternate term for *Telephoto lens*.

Lower case. Letters that are not capitals.

M

Macro. Frequently used phrase, paragraph, or other keyboarding that can be brought to the screen with a command determined by the software user.

Macro lens. Camera lens capable of focusing from six inches to two feet. Often referred to as "close-up lens."

Mailing service. Business specializing in addressing and mailing large quantities of printed pieces.

Makeready. All activities required to set up a printing press before production run begins. Also refers to paper consumed by the process.

Manuscript. Typed or handwritten copy that editors check and from which, when corrected, the typesetter may set type.

Margin. Space forming border of a page or sheet.

Mark up. To write instructions on copy or proofs using standard symbols and proofreader marks telling how type should be prepared or corrected.

Masking material. Opaque paper or plastic used to prevent light from reaching selected areas of film or printing plate.

Mask out. To cover selected copy or art so it will not appear on a photocopy, negative, or printing plate.

Masthead. Block of information in a newsletter that identifies publisher and editor, tells how to contact them, and may give subscription and other business information.

Matte finish. Slightly dull finish on coated paper.

Mechanical. Camera-ready assembly of type and graphics complete with instructions to the printer. Often called "pasteup" or "keyline"; sometimes called "artwork."

Mechanical artist. Alternate term for *Production artist*.

Media conversion. Alternate term for *Data conversion*.

Megabyte. One million bytes or 1,000 K.

Menu. List of possible computer functions displayed on a computer screen.

Merge/purge. To combine two or more mailing lists (merge), then eliminate duplicated addresses (purge), usually with the help of a computer.

Middle tones. Tones in a photograph or illustration about half as dark as its shadow areas and represented in halftones by dots between 30% and 70% of full size.

Mimeograph. Method of printing using a plastic stencil mounted on a rotating drum containing ink.

Mockup. Alternate term for *Dummy*.

Model release. Contract authorizing commercial use of a photograph that includes image of a recognizable person or, under some circumstances, of private property.

Modem. Acronym for "modulator/demodulator." Device that converts digital signals to analog tones and vice versa so electronic systems can interface over telephone lines.

Moire. Undesirable pattern in halftones and screen tints made with improperly aligned screens. Pronounced "moray."

Mottle. Spotty, uneven ink coverage especially noticeable in large solids.

Mounting board. Any thick, smooth piece of paper used to paste up copy or mount photographs.

Mouse. Device connected to a computer which, when rolled over a hard surface, moves a cursor.

Multicolor printing. Printing in more than one ink color (but not 4-color process).

N

Nameplate. Portion of front page of newsletter that graphically presents its name and subtitle and may include logo, date line, and other information.

Near-letter-quality. Characteristic of dot matrix computer printer doing its best work at about 360 dots per inch.

Negative. Characteristic of an image on film or paper in which blacks in the original subject are white or clear and whites in the original are black or opaque. Also piece of film on which negative image appears.

Negative space. Alternate term for *White space*.

Newsletter. Short, usually informal publication presenting specialized information to limited audiences on a regular basis.

Non-repro blue. Light blue color that does not record on graphic arts film, therefore may be used to write instructions on mechanicals.

O

OCR. Optical Character Recognition. Process of using a scanner to digitize type from paper and read it into computer memory.

Offset paper. Alternate term for *Uncoated paper*.

Offset printing. Method of lithographic printing that transfers ink from a plate to a blanket, then from the blanket to paper.

Opacity. Characteristic of paper that helps prevent printing on one side from showing through to the other.

Opaque. Not transparent. Also a verb meaning to cover flaws in negatives with paint or tape.

Orphan. Single line of type appearing as first line of a column or page.

Outline halftone. Halftone in which background has been removed to isolate or silhouette the main image.

Output. See *Input/output*.

Overexposure. Photograph that appears washed out or too contrasty because too much light reached the film or print.

Overlay. Sheet of tissue or acetate taped to a mechanical to cover it.

Overprint. To print one image over a previously printed image, such as printing type over a screen tint.

Overrun. Number of pieces that were printed in excess of the quantity specified.

Overs. Printed pieces in an overrun.

P

Page proof. Type output in page format complete with headings, rules, and numbers.

Paper dummy. Unprinted sample of a proposed printed piece trimmed, folded, and, if necessary, bound using paper specified for the job.

Parent sheet. Paper distributor term for sheet 17 x 22 or larger.

Paste up. To adhere copy to mounting boards and, if necessary, overlays so it is assembled into a camera-ready mechanical. The mechanical produced is often called a "pasteup."

Percentage wheel. Alternate term for *Proportional scale*.

Perfecting press. Press capable of printing both sides of the paper during a single pass.

Peripherals. Hardware connected to a computer system for additional or alternate input, output, or memory.

Photocopy. Printing using xerography.

Photostat. Process used to make positive paper prints of line copy and halftones. Often used as alternate term for *PMT*.

Photo type. Type set by projecting light onto photosensitive paper.

Pica. Unit of measure equaling 1/6th of an inch or 12 points and often used to express line measure or column width.

Pica type. Larger of the two standard typewriter typefaces, being 12 point and usually set in ten pitch.

Pi font. Font with math symbols, dingbats, and other characters for special needs.

Pitch. Number of equally spaced characters per inch that a typewriter or computer printer will produce. Standard pitches are 10, 12, and 15.

Pixel. Acronym for "picture element." Dot made by a computer, scanner, or other digital device.

Platemaker. In quick printing, process camera that makes plate automatically after photographing mechanical. In commercial printing, machine used to make plates from negatives.

Plugged up. Undesirable characteristic of printing when halftone dots have run into each other, causing loss of shadow detail.

PMS. PANTONE MATCHING SYSTEM. Commonly used initials of Pantone, Inc., trade names for ink colors in that company's color matching system.

PMT. Photo Mechanical Transfer. Kodak trade name for process used to make positive paper prints of line copy and halftones.

Point. In paper industry, unit of thickness of paper equaling 1/1000 inch. In typesetting, unit of measure equaling 1/12 of a pica and 1/72 of an inch, used to express size (height) of type.

Pointer. Arrow on a computer screen that can be moved by dragging the mouse and that gives commands by pointing at icons.

Portfolio. Collection of best work by an artist, photographer, or designer for showing during meetings with prospective clients.

Portrait mode. Vertical format on a computer screen or printout that resembles one newsletter page.

Position stat. Photocopy or PMT made to size and pasted to a mechanical showing how to crop, scale, and position loose art or photos.

Positive. Characteristic of an image on film or paper in which blacks in the original subject are black or opaque and whites in the original are white or clear.

Preparation. Camera work, stripping, platemaking, and other activities by the printer before press work begins.

Prepress. Alternate term for *Preparation*.

Preprint. To print work in advance to be ready for inserting or imprinting.

Pre-sort. To sort newsletters by zip codes before mailing.

Press check. Event at which test sheets from the press are examined before authorizing production run to begin.

Press-on type. Alternate term for *Dry transfer type*.

Press proof. Proof made on press using the plates, paper, and ink specified for the job.

Press run. The number of pieces printed.

Press sheet. One sheet of paper, regardless of size, delivered from a specific printing press, but not yet folded or trimmed.

Price break. Quantity level at which unit cost of paper or printing drops.

Printing. Any process that repeatedly transfers to paper or other material an image from an original such as a mechanical, negative, electronic memory, or printing plate.

Printing plate. Surface that carries the image.

Printing trade customs. Business terms and policies codified by the Printing Industries of America and selectively followed by printers.

Print wheel. Alternate term for *Daisy wheel*.

Process camera. Graphic arts camera used to photograph mechanicals and other camera-ready copy.

Production artist. Person who does pasteup.

Production manager. Person who coordinates designers, printers, and others who work together to produce printing.

Proof. Test sheet made to reveal errors or flaws, predict results, and record how a newsletter is intended to appear.

Proof OK. Signature from customer approving a proof and authorizing the job to advance to the next stage.

Proofread. To examine a manuscript or proof for errors in keyboarding.

Proofreader marks. Standard symbols and abbreviations used to mark up manuscripts and proofs.

Proof sheet. In photography, term for sheet of images made by contact printing negatives.

Proportional scale. Device used to calculate percent that an original image must be reduced or enlarged to yield a specific reproduction size.

Proportional spacing. Typographic system of allocating spaces to characters according to their width: "i" gets less space than "p," "w" more space than "a."

Publish. To pay for producing and distributing or marketing a newsletter or other message such as a book, tape, or software disk.

Push. To develop film longer than normal to compensate for underexposure.

Q

Quick printer. Printer whose business emphasizes basic quality, small presses, and fast service and who normally uses paper or plastic plates.

Quotation. Printer's offer to print a job for a price calculated from specifications provided by customer.

R

Ragged. Characteristic of type not justified.

RAM. Random Access Memory. Computer memory used

to perform functions on files in immediate use. Pronounced "ram."

RC. Resin Coated. Paper for typesetting and PMTs that, when properly processed, does not yellow with age.

Readable. Characteristic of messages that are written and edited to make them easy to understand.

Ream. Five hundred sheets of paper.

Record. Unit of logically related information such as names and addresses in a data base.

Register. To place printing properly with regard to edges of paper and other printing on the same sheet. Such printing is said to be in register.

Register marks. Cross-hair lines on mechanicals and negatives that guide strippers and printers.

Repro. Type with corrections made and elements in position ready to reproduce by printing.

Retouch. To enhance a photographic print or correct its flaws using techniques such as spotting and airbrushing.

Reverse. Type or graphic reproduced by printing ink around its outline, thus allowing underlying color or paper to show through and form the image.

River. Distracting pattern of white space running down through text type.

ROM. Read Only Memory. Computer memory used to store instructions needed for immediate use. Pronounced as in "bomb."

Roman type. Style of type with serifs. Also type that is upright (not italic). Sometimes called "plain type."

Rough layout. Sketch giving general idea of size and placement of text and graphics.

Rub-on lettering. Alternate term for *Dry transfer lettering*.

Rubylith. Ulano trade name for red masking film.

Ruby window. Window on mechanical made with piece of Rubylith.

Rule. Line used as graphic.

Ruling. See *Screen ruling*.

Run. Total number of copies ordered or printed.

Runaround. Type set to conform to part or all of the outline of a photograph or illustration.

Running head or foot. Information appearing at the top or bottom of every page of a publication.

S

Saddle stitch. To bind by stapling sheets together where they fold at the spine.

Sans serif. Type without serifs.

SASE. Self Addressed, Stamped Envelope. Not pronounced as a word, but spoken as four letters.

Scale. To identify the percent by which artwork should be enlarged or reduced. The process is called "scaling."

Scaling wheel. Alternate term for *Proportional scale*.

Scallop. Page layout in which columns of unequal length are aligned at the top so their bottoms vary.

Scanner. Device used to digitize type, illustrations, and photographs.

Screen. Piece of film containing halftone dots of uniform density and used to make plates that will print screen tints or halftones.

Screen density. Amount of ink, expressed as percent of coverage, that a specific screen allows to print.

Screen ruling. The number of rows or lines of dots per inch in a screen for tint or halftone.

Screen tint. Area of paper printed with dots so ink coverage is less than 100% and simulates shading or a lighter color.

Scum. Undesirable thin film of ink on non-image area of printed sheet.

Self-mailer. Newsletter designed to be mailed without an envelope.

Self-publisher. Publisher who is also the writer of newsletter being published.

Serif. Short line crossing the ends of main strokes of characters in some type families.

Serif type. Type with serifs.

Setoff. Undesirable transfer of wet ink from the top of one sheet to the underside of another as they lie in the delivery stack of a press.

Set solid. Type set with no leading between lines.

Shading. Alternate term for *Screen tint*.

Shadows. Darkest areas in a photograph or halftone.

Sharp. Characteristic of an image at optimum focus.

Short lens. Alternate term for *Wide angle lens*.

Show-through. Printing on one side of paper that can been seen on the other side.

Shutter. Device on a camera that, when opened, allows light to reach the film.

Sidebar. Block of information related to and placed near an article.

Sizing. Alternate term for *Scaling*.

Slow film. Film that requires a relatively large amount of light (long exposure or large f stop) to record an image.

SLR. Single Lens Reflex. Camera using system of mirrors to allow viewing of subject through same lens that focuses image on film.

Slur. Undesirable phenomenon that may occur during printing when halftone dots become slightly elongated.

Small caps. Capital letters approximately the height of lower case letters used for subheads and leads into first paragraphs.

Soft copy. Copy in a computer memory, not on paper.

Software. Digitized instructions controlling a computer.

Solid. Any area of the sheet receiving 100% ink coverage.

Specifications. In printing, complete and precise descriptions of paper, ink, binding, quantity, and other features of a printing job. For type, instructions about typeface and size, line measure, indentations, headlines, etc.

Spec sheet. Short for sheet on which specifications are written.

Spread. Two pages that face each other. Also the layout, especially of photos, on such pages.

Standing headline. Headline whose words and position stay the same issue after issue.

Stat. General term for inexpensive photographic print of line copy or halftone.

Stat camera. Small process camera.

Stet. Proofreader mark for "let it stand" instructing a typesetter to ignore an indicated change and stick with the original version.

Stock photo. Photograph in a commercial collection.

Straight copy. Copy that contains no charts, tables, formulas, or other elements that complicate typesetting.

Strip. To assemble negatives in preparation for making printing plates.

Style. In copyediting, the rules for treatment of such matters as modes of address, titles, and numerals.

Substance weight. Alternate term for *Basis weight* used when referring to bond papers.

Subtitle. Phrase that is part of nameplate and tells why newsletter is published, for whom, and how often.

Surprint. Alternate term for both *Overprint* and *Imprint*.

Swash. Flourish on selected characters of a typeface.

Swatch book. Book with samples of papers or ink colors.

T

TA. Typesetter Alteration. Any change made because of typesetter error. Also proofreader mark showing such a change.

Telephoto lens. Camera lens with focal length greater than 105mm that significantly magnifies objects.

Text paper. Grade of paper characterized by textured surfaces.

Text type. Type of less than 14 points.

Thumbnail sketch. Alternate term for *Rough layout*.

Tick marks. Alternate term for *Corner marks*.

Tint. Alternate term for *Screen tint*.

Tissue. Thin, translucent paper used for overlays.

Tombstone. Two headlines placed next to each other so they seem at first glance to be only one.

Tonal range. Photographic term for density range.

Toner. Powder forming the image in photocopy and laser printing.

Transfer type. Alternate term for *Dry transfer type*.

Trim marks. Lines on a mechanical, negative, printing plate, or press sheet showing where to cut edges off paper or cut paper apart after printing.

Trim size. Size of the finished product after last trim is made.

Turnaround time. Amount of time needed to complete a job or one stage of it.

Type. Letters, numerals, punctuation marks, and other symbols produced by a machine and that will be reproduced by printing.

Typeface. Set of characters with design features making them similar to each other.

Type family. Group of type styles with similar letterforms and a unique name.

Typesetter. Machine that creates photo type or hot type. Also person who operates such a machine.

Type shop. Typesetting business.

Type size. The height of a typeface measured from the top of its ascenders to the bottom of its descenders and expressed in points.

Type specimen book. Book showing examples of all typefaces available from one type shop.

Type style. Italic, condensed, bold, and other variations of a typeface that form a type family.

Typo. Short for "typographical error."

Typography. The art and science of setting type. Also the style and arrangement of type on a printed piece.

U

Uncoated paper. Paper that has not been clay coated.

Underexposure. Photograph that appears too dark or lacks shadow detail because too little light reached the film or print.

Underrun. Production run of fewer copies than the amount specified.

Unjustified. Alternate term for *Ragged*.

Up. Printing two up or three up means printing the identical piece twice or three times in one impression on one sheet of paper.

Upper case. Capital letters.

V

Varnish. Clear liquid applied like ink to paper on press to protect and enhance underlying printing.

Vellum finish. Relatively rough finish on sheet of uncoated paper.

Velox. Kodak trade name for high-contrast photo paper. Often used to refer to any halftone positive.

W

Weight. For paper, see *Basis weight*. In typography, char-acteristic of type determined by how light or dark it appears when set.

White space. Designer term referring to non-image area that frames or sets off copy.

Wide angle lens. Camera lens with focal length less than 40mm whose field of view is wider than the eye normally sees.

Widow. Partial or objectionably short whole word appearing as final line in a paragraph.

Window. On a mechanical, block of masking material that shows position of a photograph or other visual element. On a computer screen, rectangular portion of the screen within which information appears.

With the grain. Parallel to the grain direction of paper.

Word spacing. Amount of space between words. Manually adjustable with a typewriter, automatically adjusted by most computer and typesetting software when operating in justify mode.

Wraparound. Alternate term for *Runaround*.

WYSIWYG. What You See Is What You Get. The ability of a computer system to represent on its screen type and graphics precisely as they will output on paper. Pronounced "wizzywig."

X

Xerography. Method of printing that transfers images electrostatically and creates them with powder (toner) bonded to paper by heat. Photocopy machines and laser printers use xerography.

x-height. Height of lower case letters without their ascenders or descenders.

Z

Zoom lens. Camera lens that can be adjusted to various focal lengths along a continuum.

Resources

The following list of resources is divided into the categories awards, books, directories, instruction, organizations, periodicals, and software. Titles are listed alphabetically by name of author, organization, or periodical.

This list was updated in May 1989 so is slightly different from the list in previous printings of this book.

Awards

Many organizations and periodicals give awards for newsletters as part of annual contests for publications. Fees, entry dates, categories, and criteria for evaluation vary greatly. Write for details.

American Society of Association Executives
1575 Eye Street NW
Washington DC 20005

American Society for Hospital Marketing
and Public Relations
840 North Lake Shore Drive
Chicago IL 60611

Communications Concepts
2100 National Press Building
Washington DC 20045

The Editor's Forum
PO Box 411806
Kansas City MO 64141

International Assoc. of Business Communicators
870 Market Street #940
San Francisco CA 94102

National Composition Association
1730 North Lynn Street
Arlington VA 22209

National Press Club
National Press Building
Washington DC 20045

Newsletter Association
1401 Wilson Blvd #403
Arlington VA 22209

Newsletter Clearinghouse
44 West Market Street
Rhinebeck NY 12572

Printing Industries of America
1730 North Lynn Street
Arlington VA 22209

Publishing Technology Magazine
401 North Broad Street
Philadelphia PA 19108

Society of Illustrators
128 East 63 Street
New York NY 10021

Society of Natl Association Publishers
1010 Wisconsin Avenue NW #630
Washington DC 20007

Society for Technical Communication
815 15th Street NW
Washington DC 20005

Society of Typographic Arts
233 East Ontario Avenue #301
Chicago IL 60611

Women in Communications
PO Box 9561
Austin TX 78766

Many other trade and professional associations have competitions that include newsletters. Some are for overall efforts in marketing or public relations that have newsletters as only one part. Consult leaders of organizations in your field for details.

Books

Most of the following volumes were recommended in the appropriate chapter of the book you are reading. They are among the best of thousands an editor could consult.

Space does not permit listing the publisher's address for each of the following books. Addresses are listed at the end of the reference guide *Books In Print*, available in almost every public and school library and in many bookstores.

Books about computers and software tend to be written for specific machines and programs, thus go out-of-date quickly. None are listed here unless they are about newsletters.

ASMP. *Professional Business Practices in Photography*. 4th edition. American Society of Magazine Photographers, 1986.

Associated Press Stylebook and Libel Manual: The Journalist's Bible. Addison-Wesley, 1987.

Beach, Mark, Steve Shepro and Ken Russon. *Getting It Printed*. Coast to Coast Books, 1986.

Beach, Mark, and Ken Russon. *Papers For Printing*. Coast to Coast Books, 1989.

Berkman, Robert. *Find It Fast: How to Uncover Expert Information on Any Subject*. Harper and Row, 1987.

Bove, Tony, and Cheryl Rhodes. *Desktop Publishing with Pagemaker*. John Wiley, 1987. (Comes in either IBM or Macintosh version.)

Cheney, Theodore. *Getting the Words Right: How to Revise, Edit, and Rewrite*. Writer's Digest Books, 1983.

Davis, Frederic, and John Barry. *Newsletter Publishing with Pagemaker*. Dow Jones-Irwin, 1988.

Goss, Frederick. *Success In Newsletter Publishing: A Practical Guide*. Newsletter Association, 1985.

Graham, Walter. *Complete Guide to Pasteup*. 3rd edition. Dot Pasteup Supply, 1987.

Graphic Artists Guild. *Handbook of Pricing and Ethical Guidelines*. Graphic Artists Guild, 1989.

Holmes, Nigel. *Designer's Guide to Creating Charts and Graphs*. Watson-Guptill, 1984.

Hudson, Howard. *Publishing Newsletters*. 2nd edition. Scribners, 1988.

Judd, Karen. *Copyediting: A Practical Guide*. 2nd edition. Crisp Inc., 1989.

Lem, Dean. *Graphics Master 4*. Dean Lem Associates, 1988.

Lem, Dean. *Type Processing*. Dean Lem Associates, 1988.

Lichty, Tom. *Design Principles for Desktop Publishers*. Scott-Foresman, 1989.

London, Barbara. *A Short Course in Photography: An Introduction to Black and White Photographic Technique*. Scott Foresman/Little, Brown, 1987.

Lubow, Martha, and Jesse Burst. *Publishing Power and Ventura*. New Riders Publishing, 1988.

Lubow, Martha, and Polly Pattison. *Style Sheets for Newsletters: A Guide to Advanced Designs for Xerox Ventura Publisher*. New Riders Publishing, 1988. (See listing in Software section at end of this appendix.)

Makower, Joel, and Alan Green. *Instant Information*. Prentice-Hall, 1987.

McGraw-Hill Book Company. *Guidelines for Bias-Free Publishing*. McGraw-Hill, 1983.

Parker, Roger. *Desktop Publishing with WordPerfect*. Ventana Press, 1989.

Parker, Roger. *Looking Good in Print: Basic Design for Desktop Publishing*. Ventana Press, 1988.

Sitarz, Daniel. *Desktop Publisher's Legal Handbook*. Nova Publishing, 1989.

Skillin, Marjorie. *Words Into Type*. Prentice-Hall, 1974.

Smith, Peggy. *Mark My Words: Instruction and Practice in Proofreading*. Editorial Experts, 1987.

Strong, William. *The Copyright Book*. Massachusetts Institute of Technology Press, 1986.

University of Chicago. *Chicago Guide to Preparing Electronic Manuscripts*. University of Chicago Press, 1986.

Weil, Ben. *Modern Copyright Fundamentals*. Van Nostrand Reinhold, 1985.

White, Alex. *How to Spec Type*. Watson-Guptill, 1987.

White, Jan. *Using Charts and Graphs*. R R Bowker, 1984.

Volumes about graphic design, production, and business management are less likely to be stocked by bookstores than titles about writing and editing. Furthermore, few art supply stores have book departments.

To get catalogs of books about the graphic arts, write to one of the following:

APA Graphics Store
307 North Compton Avenue
St Louis MO 63103

Dover Publications
31 East Second Street
Mineola NY 11501

Dynamic Graphics
PO Box 1901
Peoria IL 61656

Graphic Artist's Book Club
PO Box 12526
Cincinnati OH 45212

Graphic Books International
PO Box 349, rue de Goddards
Castel, Guernsey
Channel Islands ENGLAND

Print Graphic Design Bookstore
6400 Goldsboro Road
Bethesda MD 20817

Writer's Digest Book Club
1507 Dana Avenue
Cincinnati OH 45207

In addition to books, you can benefit from using the video training tapes about desktop publishing produced by Computer Training Resources, 219 Ilihau Street, Kailua HI 96734. Write for details about their *VideoTutor* series.

Directories

The four directories below list among them almost 50,000 newsletters, a small fraction of the total published. The directories are revised periodically. Most public libraries own at least one of them, although it may not be the most recent edition.

Newsletters In Print
Gale Research Company
Book Tower
Detroit MI 48226

Newsletter Yearbook Directory
44 West Market Street
Rhinebeck NY 12572

Oxbridge Directory of Newsletters
150 Fifth Ave
New York NY 10011

Working Press of the Nation, vol. 5
National Research Bureau
424 North Third Street
Burlington IA 52601

Because most organizations produce a newsletter, almost any directory of organizations is also a directory of newsletter publishers. Use the directory in your field as a guide to further ideas about names or about newsletters you might want to read.

Instruction

The organizations listed below offer newsletter workshops in cities nationwide. Workshops vary greatly in emphasis on topics such as design, writing, and marketing. Read advertising materials carefully and don't hesitate to call for details.

People who teach workshops sponsored by these organizations often consult as well and may live in your city or region.

Cassell Communications
PO Box 9844
Ft Lauderdale FL 33310

Dynamic Graphics Educational Foundation
6000 North Forrest Park Drive
Peoria IL 61614

Editorial Experts
85 South Bragg Street
Alexandria VA 22312

Newsletter Clearinghouse
44 West Market Street
Rhinebeck NY 12572

Pattison Workshops
5092 Kingscross Road
Westminster CA 92683

Performance Seminar Group
325 Myrtle Avenue
Bridgeport CT 06604

Promotional Perspectives
1955 Pauline Blvd #100-A
Ann Arbor MI 48103

Ragan Communications
407 South Dearborn Street
Chicago IL 60605

In addition to those sponsored by the organizations above, newsletter workshops are commonly offered during conventions and locally by a wide range of groups. If you want to find a local instructor or consultant, start by calling the continuing education department of a college or university.

Many colleges and universities teach about newsletters as part of degree programs, usually in public relations, business communications, or technical writing courses. Get information from an academic advisor in a department of journalism or communications.

Organizations

The most important part of your newsletter is content, so the most important organizations are those within your own field of interest. Ensure your membership and involvement with them before you join groups for editors or publishers.

If you want to join an association for editors, ask for ideas from more experienced editors in your local area. Call the director of public relations at a large hospital, bank headquarters, or university for suggestions.

The local health of an organization is more important than its national stature. Go to a few meetings to learn if the organization is worth your time.

Periodicals

There are several hundred magazines and newsletters about editing, design, and production that you could subscribe to. Many are published by organizations whose addresses appear in these pages under other categories. Following are several of the most useful.

Communication Briefings
140 South Broadway
Pitman NJ 08071

Communications Concepts
2100 National Press Building
Washington DC 20045

The Desktop
4550 Montgomery Avenue
Bethesda MD 20814

Desktop Publishing Buyer's Guide
150 Fifth Avenue
New York NY 10011

Editorial Eye
85 South Bragg St #402
Alexandria VA 22312

Editor's Forum
PO Box 411806
Kansas City MO 64141

In House Graphics
4550 Montgomery Ave #700N
Bethesda MD 20814

ITC Desktop
2 Hammarskjold Plaza
New York NY 10017

Newsletter Design
44 West Market Street
Rhinebeck NY 12572

Newsletter on Newsletters
44 West Market Street
Rhinebeck NY 12572

Personal Publishing
191 South Gary Avenue
Carol Stream IL 60188

Publish!
501 Second Street #600
San Francisco CA 94107

Ragan Report
407 South Dearborn Street
Chicago IL 60605

For more newsletters, look in the directories listed earlier in this appendix. For magazines, look in *The Standard Periodical Directory* found in many libraries.

Directories of newsletters and magazines have subject indexes, so are good resources for information about your own field of interest. Use them for leads to more interesting content.

Software

The annual directory issue of *Personal Publishing* lists names and addresses for almost 200 computers and peripherals and almost 400 programs. Listings include software for charts and graphs, clip art, page makeup, type fonts, and word processing—all relevant to producing newsletters.

Some publishers of desktop publishing software have newsletter designs either built in or as optional programs. Get details about specific programs from the following publishers.

PageMaker and
Pagemaker Portfolio: Designs for Newsletters
Aldus Corporation
411 First Avenue
Seattle WA 98104

Publishing Pack, Newsletters
Adobe Systems
PO Box 7900
Mountain View CA 94039

Ready Set Go
LetraSet USA
40 Eisenhower Drive
Paramus NJ 07653

Quark Express and
Quark Style
Quark, Inc.
300 So Jackson #100
Denver CO 80209

Style Sheets for Newsletters:
Advanced Designs for Xerox Ventura Publisher
New Riders Publishing
PO Box 4846
Thousand Oaks CA 91360

Ventura Publisher
Xerox Corporation
101 Continental Blvd
El Segundo CA 90245

For up-to-date information about software, consult with a sales representative at a full-service computer store. Look for a sales rep who has helped customers with needs similar to yours, then talk with some of those customers. Ask to examine samples of the newsletters produced with the software in question. After deciding on a program, pay retail price for it to ensure you get the complete information, training, and support that you need.

Copy-ready forms

Request for Quotation

Newsletter name_____ Date_____

Contact person_____ Phone_____/_____

Business/organization_____

Address_____

Format # of pages___ page size___x___inches folded size___x___inches

Quantity per issue _____copies   Issues per year_____

Date(s) mechanicals to printer_____

_____

Date(s) newsletters needed_____

_____

Mechanicals each issue ___line copy camera-ready

   screen tints ___printer adds ___on mechanicals

   halftones ___printer adds ___on mechanicals

Paper weight___ color_____ finish_____ brand name_____

Ink colors cover side_____ other sides_____

Proofs ___galley ___page ___photocopy ___blueline ___overlay color

   ___press check ___dummy included with these specifications

Miscellaneous instructions_____

_____

_____

Copyright 1988 Coast to Coast Books

Editor's job organizer

Newsletter name _____ Editor _____

Function	Person responsible	Supplier
Decide purpose/goals		
Establish objectives		
Identify audience		
Set schedule		
Develop budget		
Select name/subtitle		
Choose distribution method		
Design format/nameplate		
Specify typography		
Select type/production services		
Specify paper/printing		
Select printer		
Verify work done per specifications		
Approve/pay invoices		
Gather information		
Select content		
Write headlines/articles/captions		
Create/select photographs/drawings		
Create/select charts/graphs/maps		

Editor's job organizer (continued)

Function	Person responsible	Supplier
Copyedit copy/visuals		
Proofread copy/visuals		
Approve copy/visuals		
Keyboard copy		
Produce type		
Copyfit type		
Do layout/make dummy		
Do miscellaneous camera work		
Create mechanicals		
Approve mechanicals		
Approve proofs		
Work with printer		
Print/trim/fold		
Maintain address files		
Prepare for mailing		
Work with lettershop/post office		
Evaluate production process		
Evaluate achieving objectives		
Evaluate address list		
Evaluate costs to produce/distribute		

Index